Suburban Differences
and
Metropolitan Policies

A Philadelphia Story

Suburban Differences
and
Metropolitan Policies

A Philadelphia Story

by

Oliver P. Williams
Harold Herman
Charles S. Liebman
Thomas R. Dye

Philadelphia
University of Pennsylvania Press

7458
Printed in the United States of America

To
Ruth, Jessica
Melissa, Andrew
Rachael, Aaron
Tommy, Cheryl

Preface

This is a one-sided book on governing metropolitan areas. It presumes the reader has read the other side of the story. Most books on government in metropolitan areas stress the interdependence of local units of government and the resulting need for integrative governments to formulate and execute area-wide policies. This is a study of the forces for independence, the values that impel local units to cherish and protect their separate identities. It seeks to describe these values not as sentiments, but as actual public policies realized through the actions of local governments.

We are not immediately concerned with devising "solutions to the metropolitan problem." No position on metropolitan government is advocated. The authors frankly disagree among themselves on this subject. Our one-sidedness is, therefore, based not on a normative position, but on the empirical focus of the investigation. To the social scientist, such an approach needs no justification. To the layman or public official, it may be looked upon as a background for strategic decisions.

One of the most difficult choices faced in reporting the results of empirical investigations is the choice of style of presentation. It involves decisions as whom to bore, whom to confuse, whom to disappoint, and whom to please and satisfy. When the choice is made by four authors, all not necessarily in full agreement, the process becomes even more complicated. We hope that this book will at least interest both the researcher and the layman who is concerned with urban affairs. We know that all passages will not satisfy both. However, we feel there is no lengthy portion of the book that can be skipped by either, if the central points of the volume are to be followed.

We have made several assumpions in our presentation. One of these is that some readers who are interested in our subject are less than fully informed in the use of statistics and statistical mehods. Since our material demands some statistical demonstrations, we have explained the techniques used in lay terms. We beg the indulgence of those who are familiar with them.

We also assume that this volume will be of interest to persons schooled in various disciplines. Our documentation of related works may be obvious to the expert, but more useful to the student who is at an earlier stage in the exploration of one or more of the several disciplines contributing to an understanding of urban affairs.

In assuming that the study will be of interest to both a national and local audience, we have confined most specific place references to a lengthy statistical appendix. But, in order to make the study more meaningful to Philadelphians, local place names are, on occasion, included in the text. We hope that, in thus trying to report a study to many, we have not failed to communicate its essentials to any.

This study was initially encouraged by Penjerdel, and throughout the project Penjerdel has assisted the study in various ways as part of its program of stimulating research into the metropolitan problems of the eleven-county region extending from Trenton to Wilmington. The staff and financial support for this study were contributed, at Penjerdel's request, by the Fels Institute of Local and State Government, which has been pleased in this way to assist in Penjerdel's work. During the major part of the reasearch, the authors were all members of the Institute faculty. For the full support he gave us throughout the life of this research effort, we wish to thank Stephen B. Sweeney, Director of the Fels Institute.

Charles E. Gilbert, H. W. Bruck, Barbara Terrett, John W. Bodine, David H. Kurtzman, Morton Lustig, William G.

Grigsby and others have read all or parts of the manuscript, and have given us many useful suggestions for its improvement. Since there are four of us to share the blame—or to pass it— we are not at all reluctant to absolve them from any responsibility for errors that remain.

James G. Coke, Thomas J. Davy, and Thomas J. Anton all participated in the early discussions from which this study subsequently developed. Karl Deutsch and James Toscano were most helpful in working out the technique for measuring inter municipal cooperation patterns used in Chapter IX. Among those who labored long and hard in data gathering and processing were David Livingston, Jaipaul and David McGonigle. To each of them, our thanks. Portions of the data were processed at the Computer Center of the University of Pennsylvania.

The gathering of data was simplified by the cooperation of the Penn Jersey Transportation Study which made available to us its compilation of school and municipal financial data. Where, as was often necessary, original data sources had to be probed, we were more than adequately assisted by public officials and agencies of all levels of government in Pennsylvania. In particular we would like to express our appreciation to the staffs of the Bureau of Municipal Affairs, Pennsylvania State Department of Internal Affairs, the Pennsylvania State Tax Equalization Board, the Bureau of School Business Affairs, Department of Public Instruction, the Planning Commissions of Bucks, Delaware, and Montgomery Counties, and the school superintendents' offices of Chester, Delaware, and Montgomery Counties.

To these, and others too numerous to mention, our thanks and our hope that this volume is worthy of their efforts in our behalf.

O.P.W.
H.H.
C.S.L.
T.R.D.

Contents

Preface

I. Urban Differentiation and the Governing of Metropolitan
   Areas   17

II. Specialization and Differentiation in the Metropolitan Area 35

III. Fiscal Responses: Method of Analysis   75

IV. Fiscal Responses: Municipal Programs   91

V. Fiscal Responses: School Revenues   139

VI. Fiscal Responses: Tax Policy   163

VII. Land-use Policy   187

VIII. Attitudes, Opinions and Local Policies   211

IX. Inter-local Cooperation   239

X. Functional Transfers: Two Cases   268

XI. Urban Differentiation and the Future of Metropolitan
    Government   289

   Appendices   313

   Index   361

List of Illustrations

Map I — Suburbs, Towns, Townships   40-41

Map II — Age Distribution Percentage Adults   46-47

Map III — Social Rank   50-51

Fig. I — Distribution of Social Rank   54

Map IV — Market Value Property Per Capita, 1960 64-65

Map V — Municipal Expenditures Per Capita, 1960 100-101

Map VI — Suburbs   104-105

Fig. II — Towns   127

Map VII — Cooperative School Arrangements, 1960 142-143

Map VIII—Percent of School Revenue From State
                Aid   156-157

Fig. III — Range of Prices for Homes Built Between
                1950 and 1960   200

Suburban Differences
and
Metropolitan Policies

A Philadelphia Story

I

Urban Differentiation and the Governing of Metropolitan Areas

The central proposition of this study is that differentiation and specialization in metropolitan areas result not only in interdependence among local units of government, and consequently in pressures for governmental integration, but also in divergent local interests and policies that perpetuate demands for autonomy. If, especially in the light of continued rejections of proposals for metropolitan reform, this statement appears to be no more than axiomatic, a review of the literature of political science will show it to have been largely ignored.

Political science has given little heed to a commonplace of sociology—that the concepts urbanism and specialization are virtually synonomous. To the sociologist, the study of the city has been that of a center wherein numerous specialized functions and roles are performed. Indeed, to the layman as well as to the sociologist, the city's major attraction has often been its diversity. Within it are to be found a multitude of products and enterprises supplied by peoples of widely differing background. Moreover, as the cities have grown, specializations have become spatially distributed. Whole sections of cities are identified with

17

particular industrial and commercial activities and entire neighborhoods are given over to one racial, ethnic, or otherwise socially differentiated group.

Transportation technology has been the key to the character of urban and especially metropolitan growth. Older urban centers, the center cities of today's metropolises, were developed at high densities; for without the accessibility provided by modern transportation, the territorial expansion of specialized urban activities was severely limited. Modern transportation has permitted the city to grow far beyond its geographic boundaries, distributing its specialized functions and roles over increasingly larger areas. While the dormitory suburb has been a part of urban life since the development of commuter railroads, the term "suburbia" is of recent origin. Suburbia is the extension and acceleration of the process of spatial specialization made possible by the automobile and a number of post-war phenomena including increases in personal wealth and changes in national housing policies.

Roderick McKenzie, one of the first to perceive the impact of the automobile, characterized the pre-auto metropolis as one dominated by mass participation in centrally located facilities and institutions.[1] Dependence on rail transportation had riveted major economic and social institutions to the central city. All social classes utilized these centrally located facilities and the location possibilities of their residences were also circumscribed by transportation technology. While neighborhoods with distinct social compositions were common the city as a whole was composed of heterogeneous economic activities and social groups which competed for space and place. The automobile emancipated both persons and activities from competition for favorable locations in relation to the central facilities.

The characteristic that has given currency to the metropolitan area as a political problem is the fact that the economically and socially specialized sub-areas of the metropolis are now separate governmental entities, each with its own legal apparatus, through which it exercises its preferences in responding to its unique environment. Whereas, in the past, the particular claims of neighborhoods and districts were pressed upon a city government presiding over the bulk of the urban complex, there is now no general government to process such claims.

The major purpose of this study is to determine whether or not this new political milieu has led to the formulation of distinct sets of local policies reflecting the economic and social specialization of these subareas and to weigh the divisiveness inherent in such differences against the integrative pressures in a metropolitan area. More specifically, inquiry is directed first toward understanding the effects of differentiation upon the policy choices of individual governments within a metropolitan area, and secondly toward evaluating the impact of differentiation upon patterns of intergovernmental relations in the metropolitan area. These two research objectives are intimately related; for if differentiation produces separate and conflicting community interests, and these diverse interests are reflected in policy choices, it will certainly have a profound influence on the prospects for metropolitan political integration.

The Myopia of Political Science

Political science has approached the study of metropolitan areas with its long-time concern for questions of area and power. No other question has come so near to dominating political science and American history. The writings of Thomas Jefferson reveal an early and intense concern with bringing government close to the people and at the same time avoiding friction between multiple units of government. James Madison felt that in the proper areal division of power lay the key to controlling factions. Controversy over the division of sover-eignty in American government has become a political tradition, renewed in ever changing policy contexts. Early preoccupations were with the division of power between the federal and state governments. Late in the nineteenth century, area and power issues exended to state and local questions during the "home rule movement." Now metropolitan areas raise questions about area-wide and municipal interests.

The area and power tradition in political science remains a most instructive approach to the study of politics. But its appli-cation to metropolian areas has been affected by the reform myopia that has long infected the state and local specialists. Recommendations for altering distributions of power necessi-tate taking sides on burning substantive issues. But the advocacy of metropolitan reorganization has often been embraced with what appears to be no other motivation than a penchant for organizational neatness, and with little examination or recogni-tion of the wide range of values affected by such proposals. Too often, the mere recitation of figures showing the number of governmental units in metropolitan areas has been accepted as conclusive evidence of the need to consolidate and enlarge po-litical jurisdictions in order to make them coterminous with the boundaries of the metropolitan community.

That the reformers could ignore the social and political val-ues threatened by their proposals is testament to their own overwhelming commitment to the values of governmental and administrative efficiency. And since study after study concluded that the administrative considerations of delegation, decentrali-zation, and specialization were outweighted by the administra-tive considerations of coordination, centralization, and economy of large scale organization, it appeared that efficiency mandated the consolidation of metropolitan governments to fit service re-quirements. As Robert Wood explains:

Technical specialist after technical specialist moved from one city to another, engaging in painstaking examinations of the current conditions in his own narrow proficiency, and solemnly proclaiming that no public health department could work properly unless it had a clientele of at least 50,000 people; or that no zoning regulations made sense without reference to a master plan of land use for a region as an entity; or that no police force could support a qualified crime laboratory until X number of precinct stations were in being. . . .[2]

Sufficient disenchantment with metropolitan reform has now been experienced to merit a re-examination of the divisive forces in metropolitan politics, employing the insights of other disciplines.[3] This would appear to be a necessary step in the discovery of the political preconditions for metropolitan integration.

Metropolitan Areas and the Study of Human Ecology

It is possible to view the research reported in this volume as an exercise in political ecology. Ecology, strictly speaking, is the study of the adjustment of an organism to its environment. In recent years, the meaning of ecology has been extended to include the adjustment of men and even institutions to their social as well as physical environment. We have chosen to examine the types of policy adjustments that separate urban governments make in response to variations in the social and economic conditions of their environment.

The ecological approach to the metropolitan area is particularly concerned with the spatial distribution of persons and activities. Its focus is the uniqueness of each site in the metropolitan area. Sites (lots, blocks, sections, suburbs) are unique because each is located at a different distance from every other site, and consequently each bears a different time-distance relationship to all other parts of the metropolitan area. As an urban area is settled, lands acquire urban uses. As additional uses develop, each activity seeks a location close to, or removed from, particular existing uses. Any single site will be evaluated according to its relationship to all others. A site's efficiency for a specific use is measured in terms of characteristics valuable for that use. The central value of spatial economics is accessibility, measured by the time and energy consumed in traversing distance to other sites. But economic values have no monopoly on human motivations—sites are also evaluated according to their social and aesthetic qualities.

Sites in close physical proximity to one another will bear similar relationships to other sites in the metropolitan area. Consequently, activities which stand to reap the greatest advantage from a particular set of relationships will tend to cluster. Of course, even in the traditional small town one finds clustering and certain locations differentiated according to social and functional criteria, e.g. "the other side of the tracks," "the main drag." However, areal specialization in the metropolis refers to a scale of differentiation, dependency, and interaction which is unique. As a modern industrial city increases in size, complexity, and heterogeneity, the degree of areal specialization increases.[4] Increasing differentiation and increasing scale involve interaction over greater distances. The metropolitan area's dependence on transportation facilities is evidence of the distinguishing scale of contemporary urban living.

Early urban ecology relied heavily on biology for its descriptive concepts and economics for its value base. The concentration on economic values may be termed the ecologists' myopia. The economic determination of land uses can be forcefully supported, but the dangers of oversimplification are not reduced thereby. Although McKenzie was one of the first to appreciate the automobile's impact on urban society, his view of the metro-

polis was still largely economic. Bogue, who gave his propositions their most explicit formulation, as well as Duncan and
Riess continued to stress the economic patterns of differentiation and dominance in metropolitan areas.[5] The social and
political correlates and consequences of economic specialization
were left undeveloped. Indeed, far greater effort was expended
in refining the techniques of urban ecology than in thinking
through the implications of differentiation.[6]

In Hawley's authoritative 1950 summary of the progress of
human ecology, one finds the first suggestion that areal specialization may have implications for the social and political structure of the metropolitan system. Hawley's analysis is replete
with obvious political connotations:

A hierarchy of power relations emerges among differentiated units.
Two consequences of differentiation contribute to that result. In the
first place, inequality is an inevitable accompaniment of functional
differentiation. Certain functions are more influential than others;
they are strategically placed in the division of labor and thus impinge directly upon a larger number of other functions . . . Secondly
mutual supplementation through functional differentiation necessitates a centralization of control. . . . Dominance attaches to that
unit that controls the conditions necessary to the functioning of
other units.[7]

Kish, a student of Hawley's, set about to measure the correlation between economic function and a variety of socio-economic
and demographic characteristics. He found that differentiation
increased with proximity to a dominant central city, and noted
that for reasons of 'choice," "influence" (influence of residents
in close proximity to each other), and "propensity" (propensity
of people with similar income, occupation, etc. to have similar
social and political tastes and behaviors), that "the attitudes and
behaviors of persons in each suburb tend to homogeneity,"
and consequently, behaviors reinforce each other.[8]

Despite early suggestions regarding the importance of social and political variables in the urban environment, ecology continued to approach the city with concepts and hypotheses devised from classical economics, particularly the classical theory of land value and rent.[9] Not that this work was unimpressive; in fact, important concepts of urban structure emerged from these efforts as well as sophisticated applications of equilibrium, gravity, and potential models.[10]

Later, however, urban analysis began to express some dissatisfaction with the exclusive economic preoccupation in urban ecology and regional science. A series of articles by sociologists voiced misgivings about the adequacy of economic ecologists' explanations of urban spatial structure and dynamics.[11] These works suggested that space has not only an impeditive quality, but an additional property, that of being a symbol of certain cultural values that have been associated with specific areas. Economic theory alone appears unable to explain land-use choices and locational decisions of individuals and groups, factors which must be accounted for in any theory of urban structure. It seems quite clear, for example, that land use and population density decisions are influenced by a variety of social and political values which manifest themselves in struggles over zoning regulations.[12]

Increasingly, sociologists were becoming aware of spatial patterns in social relations.[13] Some, for example, pointed to important spatial aspects of social status in urban society. Persons with equivalent status are known to behave in similar ways, including their choices of residential location. Certain areas tend to acquire value as a symbol of the status groups who choose to reside there. Consequently, persons who aspire to, or identify with a given status level choose, wherever possible, to locate in an area that possesses an identification with that status level.[14] As a result of the consistent spatial distribution of status groups, a consistent spatial distribution of life-styles could be identified. In short, urban ecology was being urged to turn its attention from the physical and economic environment of the metropolitan area to the social environment and to its impact upon individuals and institutions.

Concurrent with these developments in social theory, an important methodological tool, termed by its designers social area analysis, was introduced into the field of metropolitan analysis.[15] Eshref Shevky and Wendell Bell selected several measures of social rank, urbanization, and segregation from census-tract data and combined them in a general technique for the classification of population aggregates. The result is a three-dimensional matrix in which measures of other social or political phenomena can be allocated. But Shevky and Bell attribute to their device something more than a mere classification scheme. They hypothesize that the attributes they use in the construction of their three-dimensional framework constitute the basic factors of urban differentiation and stratification.[16]

A number of subsequent studies have tried to measure the influence of social environment on behavior through the use of social area analysis.[17] For example, using the social area analysis tool, center city residents were found to be functionally rather than spatially organized, mobile, autonomous, and lacking in identification with local areas. Suburban residents were found to be quite the opposite. Social participation in terms of formal group membership, attendance, and office holding was found to be not only a function of individual status characteristics but also, independently, a function of the social area. Thus, by comparing individual with aggregate characteristics, it was observed that the aggregate social characteristics of the community are important indicators of the dominant reference groups for persons living there, and that they define general expectations with regard to social behavior.

An adaptation of social area analysis is the major methodological tool employed in this study. However, we use only one of Shevky and Bell's three measures, social rank. Pretests of indices of familism and ethnicity showed little relationship between these traits and municipal policy variations. Our emphasis on municipal policies represents an elaboration on the use of social area analysis. We seek to relate a number of distinguishing urban characteristics not to the behavior of individuals or groups, but to the political behavior of the institutions that represent social areas. When specialization, reflecting as it does differences in values, is institutionalized within suburban corporate entities, a portion of those differences is expressed through differing public policies. By making the relationship between local policy and urban differentiation explicit, this study may contribute to both ecology and political science. To the former it may suggest additional variables that influence patterns of urban differentiation; to the latter it may give a clear picture of some of the values and problems that must be confronted in dealing with the question of area and power in metropolitan areas.

Specialization and the Need for Integrating Mechanisms

One of the reasons for the emphasis on economics in metropolitan analysis has been the difficulty of defining the metropolitan area in any but economic terms. One may recognize the political and social implications of metropolitanism and yet be hard put to find a framework around which to organize the concept of a metropolitan area other than economics and the economic dominance of the center city. Our concern is primarily with the political consequences of urbanization and consequently with social as well as with economic specialization. While this concern leads to virtual neglect of the center city in some of our investigations, we accept a definition of the metropolitan area that is largely economic. Bogue's description, despite its many subsequent elaborations, is still more than adequate. A metropolitan area is "an organization of many subdominant and subinfluent communities, distributed in a definite pattern about a dominant city and bound together in a territorial division of labor through dependence upon the activities of a dominant city."[18]

Economics organizes the components of the metropolitan area in much the same way that the market mechanism organizes the specialized elements of a free economy. But the market mechanism is often viewed as imperfect and government is called upon to supply alternative organizing influences. Dissatisfaction with the market mechanism may grow out of the operation of the economic system itself. We have long since abandoned private roads for economic as well as other reasons. In shifting transportation policies from the market to a governmental decision-making arena, the impact of highway locations upon the economy is in no way lessened. Governmental highway decisions have a most profound effect upon the way in which the metropolis is organized. Streets provide the primary mode of access between specialized places. (Rails cannot be neglected, but indicative of the greater importance of highways is the rather halfhearted way in which government has been involved in mass transit decision-making.) Their availability influences private locational and development decisions. Thus the market is influenced by government, while, at the same time, government is continually adjusting itself to the composite of forces generated in the market.

Although public streets are the most obvious examples of government organizing specializations within metropolitan areas, a variety of other policies also have contributory effects. The provision or absence of governmental services—fire and police protection, water supply, waste disposal, etc.—all influence the economic and social efficiencies of sites. Government often attempts to organize the use of space directly through zoning, subdivision regulation and redevelopment.

The interplay of private and governmental decisions results in various distributions of advantages at any one time. Every adjustment in the mechanisms organizing the entire system effects its parts and at times effects them severely. A new freeway may transform a suburb from a quiet upper middle class villa to a bustling commercial center. The building of a regional sewerage facility may enable a denser development pattern, precipitating the construction of lower priced homes and the influx of a "new element" into a suburb.

The need for some integrating mechanisms within the metropolitan area is apparent. Whether provided by the market or government, these mechanisms undergo and stimulate change, and change in turn affects the values of specialization. However, the manner or suddenness with which change takes place may well depend on whether government or the market is the organizing agent. And the nature of the changes induced by government may well depend on *which* government is acting. Thus, to understand the politics of metropolitan integration, we must recognize the stakes involved in the struggle for integration and we must understand the discreet values of individual local units.

Metropolitan Adjustment to Differentiation and Specialization

Our general hypothesis is that there are clear and consistent relationships between the policy choices of local communities in the metropolitan area and the pattern of spatial differentiation which characterizes the urban environment. As communities strive to adapt themselves to the social and economic forces in their environment, they will select characteristic policy alternatives designed to cope with these forces. Our objective is to determine what these policy alternatives are, and to what attributes of the suburban community they are related. Policies considered are revenues, expenditures, land-use decisions, and responses to certain recurring issues in metropolitan affairs.

As interesting as these findings may prove to be in themselves, it is our hope that they will also contribute to a better understanding of the forces operating to preserve our existing "fragmented" structure of local government in suburbia and to inhibit metropolitan integration. For when one begins to understand that the "crazy quilt" governmental pattern of the metropolitan area is superimposed upon a mosaic of socially and economically differentiated communities, it is not surprising that the local governmental system remains decentralized and does not produce common policies for the metropolitan area as a whole. Governmental decisions for the metropolitan area are made at hundreds of decision centers, each set in a separate social and economic environment, each responding to different types of values and interests, and each struggling to maintain its autonomy. Each of these governmental constituencies experiences metropolitan problems in separate fashions and with varying degrees of urgency; each experiences different proportions of the cost of metropolitan growth. It is true that there are pressures generated by urbanization which impinge upon all metropolitan communities with little regard for municipal boundaries, but these pressures impinge upon, and are interpreted by, separate constituencies in different ways because of their different locations and different social and economic characteristics.

In short, we are contending that urban differentiation is fundamental to the entire question of government in metropolitan areas; that community specialization with respect to class or status, life-style and economic function results in divergent interests and policies that operate to maintain a decentralized governmental structure and to inhibit the growth of inter-governmental cooperation. In this context, the strategies, insularities and parochialism of local governments can hardly be said to be born of ignorance or caprice. They represent an intuitive grasp of the realities of urbanization as they affect particular localities and are adjusted to by their residents.

Social-area Analysis — A Methodological Note

Throughout this study, our unit of analysis will be the municipality. We are interested in measuring the responses (policies) of municipalities grouped according to certain characteristics they share. While responses often lend themselves to precise measurement, especially if money is to be spent, community characteristics pose certain problems of measurement. This study employs an adaptation of the social-area analysis technique designed by Eshref Shevky and Wendell Bell for this purpose.

Although social-area analysis has been widely employed in recent years, use of this research technique has vexing conceptual difficulties. First of all, sociology, traditionally, and political science, recently, have been concerned with the structure of human interaction. Yet ecological observations of spatial clustering of similar types of people are not in themselves evidence of social structure.[19] These observations do not directly describe patterns of social interaction. Since areal data is seldom collected by recognized structures or other units of structured interaction, one cannot claim that such data even describes the properties of any social system. The term "structure," as it was used by the early urban ecologists, referred not so much to social patterns as to the physical layout of the metropolis.

Fortunately for the student of urban government, the very nature of local government relieves him of the necessity of coming squarely to grips with this problem. Local governments are by nature areally defined. The area encompassed by a government jurisdiction is politically structured whether it is otherwise socially structured or not. A formal political institution imposed upon an area insures structured political interaction. If areal observations are grouped by local government jurisdictions as they are in this study, such observations by definition describe the environment of specific political structures. Subsequent statements about the response or adjustment these political institutions make to their environment are conceptually justified.

A second problem that concerns urban ecologists has been termed "Robinson's dilemma." [20] It was W.S. Robinson who demonstrated conclusively that observations about the behavior of social aggregates did not constitute a basis for valid inferences about the behavior of individuals.[21] For example, the fact that the Republican percent of the total vote in a number of municipalities correlates to a certain degree with the percent of work force engaged in white-collar employment in these municipalities does not justify the inference that individual Republican voting is influenced by white-collar employment. However, if the unit of analysis remains the aggregate, Robinson's dilemma is avoided.[22] Observations of correlations in aggregated data can be the basis of valid inferences about the behavior of aggregates. The focus of this book is upon the behavior of political communities, not upon individuals. Thus if we observe a correlation between the Republican percent of the total vote in a number of communities and the percent of their work force in white-collar jobs, we are justified in making inferences about the political effect on these communities of having a certain proportion of their work force so employed.

A final problem that confronts all who deal in social analysis is that of change, or dynamics. The chapters that follow describe and analyze a metropolitan area as it appeared in 1960.

Throughout, the reader's attention is directed toward selected changes in society, economics, and technology that appear to have affected the present state of the metropolis, but no systematic treatment of change over time has been undertaken. Certain variables measuring change were programmed into the analyses, but, for the most part, proved unfruitful. While we can therefore say little about how it got that way, and even less about what may become of it, we will be more than satisfied if the remainder of this volume can present a clear and adequate picture of the metropolitan area at one point in time.

NOTES

1. Roderick D. McKenzie, *The Metropolitan Community* (New York: McGraw Hill, 1933). See passage on page 71.

2. Robert C. Wood, "A Division of Powers in Metropolitan Areas," in Athur Maass (ed.), *Area and Power* (Glencoe: Free Press, 1959), p. 59.

3. Luther Gulick, one of the earliest advocates of metropolitan reform, recently delivered this confession: "Our aproach, our theory, was wrong . . . We lectured business leaders, minority groups, professional politicians, and class conscious subordinates on their duty to be 'rational' and to support 'efficiency', without understanding that these groups each have solid selfish reasons for keeping the present structures. . . . We prayed for 'metropolitan leadership' to guide us into the promised land, forgetting that political leadership is firmly tied to a political constituency in being . . . Finally, it must be admitted, we thought that the metropolitan problem was much simpler than it is and that it could be 'solved' by getting up one nice new piece of local government machinery." Luther Gulick, *The Metropolitan Problem and American Ideas* (New York: Knopf, 1962), pp. 125–127.

4. Leslie Kish, "Differentiation in Metropolitan Areas," *American Sociological Review*, Vol. 19 (August, 1954), pp. 388–398.

5. See Donald J. Bogue, *The Structure of the Metropolitan Community* (Ann Arbor: University of Michigan Press, 1949).

6. See Richard D. Andrews, "Mechanics of the Urban Base: Historical Development of the Base Concept," *Land Economics*, Vol. 29 (March, 1953), pp. 161–167.

7. Amos A. Hawley, *Human Ecology: A Theory of Community Structure* (New York: Ronald Press, 1950), p. 229.

8. Leslie Kish, *On the Differentiation of Ecological Units* (Ann Arbor: University of Michigan Press, 1952), p. 108.

9. J. Douglass Carroll, "Some Aspects of Home Work Relations of Industrial Workers," *Land Economics*, Vol. 25 (September, 1949), pp. 414–422; and "The Relation of Homes to Work Places and Spatial Patterns of Cities," *Social Forces*, Vol. 30 (March, 1952), pp. 271–282; Leo F. Schnore, "Separation of Home and Work: A Problem in Human Ecology," *Social Forces*, Vol. 33 (May, 1954) pp. 336–344, and The Functions of Metropolitan Suburbs," *American Journal of Sociology*, Vol. 21 (March, 1956) pp. 453–458.

10. B. H. Stevens and R. E. Coughlin, "A Note on Inter-Areal Linear Programming for a Metropolitan Region," *Journal of Regional Science*, Vol. 1 (Spring, 1959), pp. 75–83; I. D. Herbert and B. H. Stevens, "A Model for the Distribution of Residential Activity in Urban Areas," *Journal of Regional Science*, Vol. 2 (Fall, 1960), pp. 21–36.

11. Walter Firey, "Sentiment and Symbolism as Ecological Variables," *American Sociological Review*, Vol. 10, (April, 1945), pp. 140–148; William H. Form, "The Place of Social Structure in the Determination of Land Use: Some Implications for a Theory of Urban Ecology," *Social Forces*, Vol. 32 (May, 1954), pp. 317–323.

12. James G. Coke and Charles Liebman, "Political Values and Population Density Control," *Land Economics*, Vol. 37 (November, 1961), pp. 347–361.

13. See Otis and Beverly Duncan, "Residential Distribution and Occupational Stratification," *American Journal of Sociology*, Vol. 60 (March, 1955), pp. 493–503.

14. William H. Form and Gregory P. Stone, "Urbanism, Anonymity, and Status Symbolism," *American Journal of Sociology*, Vol. 62 (March, 1957), pp. 504–514.

15. Eshref Shevky and Wendell Bell, *Social Area Analysis* (Stanford: Stanford University Press, 1955).

16. Shevsky and Bell describe the reasoning which led to their development of indices of social rank, familism, and ethnicity in the second chapter of their study. However, their essay is rather difficult. For a much more readable essay on this same topic see Scott Greer, *Governing the Metropolis* (New York: John Wiley, 1962), pp. 23–41.

17. Wendell Bell and Maryanne T. Force, "Urban Neighborhood

Types and Participation in Formal Associations," *American Sociological Review,* Vol. 21 (February, 1956), pp. 25–34; Walter Kaufman and Scott Greer, "Voting in a Metropolitan Community: An Application of Social Area Analysis," *Social Forces,* Vol. 38 (March, 1960), pp. 196–204; Duncan MacRae, "Occupations and the Congressional Vote, 1940–1950," *American Sociological Review,* Vol. 20, (June, 1955), pp. 332–340.

18. Bogue, *op. cit.,* p. 61.

19. See Amos A. Hawley and Otis D. Duncan, "Social Area Analysis: A Critical Appraisal," *Land Economics,* Vol. 33 (November, 1957), pp. 337–345; and James M. Beshers, "Statistical Analysis from Small Area Data," *Social Forces,* Vol. 38 (May, 1960), pp. 341–348.

20. W. S. Robinson, "Ecological Correlations and the Behavior of Individuals," *American Sociological Review,* Vol. 15 (June, 1950), pp. 351–357; Leo A. Goodman, "Ecological Regression and the Behavior of Individuals," *American Sociological Review,* Vol. 18 (December, 1953), pp. 663–664.

21. Only if the average intra-areal individual correlation is not less than the total individual correlation, will an ecological correlation provide a basis for inferences to individual behavior. And all available evidence suggests that this is not usually the case.

22. Herbert Menzel, "Comment on Robinson's Paper," *American Sociological Review,* Vol. 15 (December, 1950), p. 674; Otis D. Duncan and Beverly Davis, "An Alternative to Ecological Correlation," *American Sociological Review,* Vol. 19 (December, 1953), pp. 665–666; and James M. Beshers, *op. cit.*

II

Specialization and Differentiation
in the Metropolitan Area

This chapter serves several purposes. It is primarily a description of the metropolitan area, hopefully sufficiently quantitative to permit comparisons with other metropolitan areas and sufficiently graphic to impart a sense of the area to readers. The characteristics employed for descriptive purposes were chosen not only for their ability to distinguish between municipalities, but also because of their possible relationship to differences in municipal behavior. These descriptive and analytic characteristics are also used to determine whether the more densely populated portions of the metropolitan area are really more differentiated and specialized than the less densely populated. If urbanism and specialization are synonomous, this procedure will permit us to test whether density is an acceptable measure of urbanism.

The study area is a five-county sector in southeastern Pennsylvania which comprises the Pennsylvania portion of the Philadelphia Standard Metropolitan Statistical Area. The five counties are Philadelphia, Bucks, Chester, Delaware and Montgomery. This sector is only a portion of an urban region that stretches along the Delaware River Valley for approximately seventy miles and includes such old urban centers as Trenton and Camden in New Jersey, Philadelphia and Chester in Pennsylvania, and Wilmington in Delaware. The five-county sector includes about two-thirds of the region's 5,000,000 residents and over half of the total units of local government. The sector extends from a major metropolitan core city on the east to rural fringe areas north and west. It contains old industrial centers along its two major rivers, the Delaware and the Schuylkill, residential suburbs developed early in this century and many more recently-developed communities. In brief, the five-county sector contains the range of types of political subareas commonly found in a major metropolitan area.

The population of the five-county area is approximately three and one-half million, two million of which reside in Philadelphia. Within the five counties, there are 238 local governments, classified under Pennsylvania law into cities of the first and third classes, boroughs, and townships of the first and second classes. The only city of the first class is Philadelphia, which operates under a home-rule charter. All of the other units under study are similar to one another in their powers to provide services. Though there are minor variations, these legal powers may be dismissed as having little influence on prevailing municipal policies. Philadelphia, because of its size, deviant characteristics and differing legal powers, will be treated as *sui generis*.

Under Pennsylvania law, all areas of the state are under the jurisdiction of some local governmental unit capable of supplying urban services. Pennsylvania, today, has no equivalent of the unincorporated area as it exists in some states, where counties or special districts provide local urban services outside of incorporated municipalities. At one time, townships had few powers and the need for specialized services stimulated urban populations to separate from townships and incorporate into boroughs and cities. Early in this century, townships began to receive increasingly broader grants of power and the incorporation movement subsided. Consequently, older urbanized portions of the metropolitan area tend to be divided into many boroughs of relatively small land area. Areas suburbanized since the 1920's have remained as townships.

Because the distinctions in governmental form are relatively unrelated to their authority to provide services, this study will refer to all local governments as *municipalities*. Occasionally, for the sake of variety, they will be called communities, political subareas, local governments, or simply "units." It is hoped that avoiding legal nomenclature will spare non-Pennsylvania readers some confusion.

Municipal Classifications for Study Purposes

Many of the sector's subareas are far from urban. In some, population densities are less than 50 persons per square mile. The distribution of municipalities by density is shown in Table II–1. As indicated, 101 units have densities under 500 persons per square mile. Units in this population density-range are entirely or predominantly rural. The exact point in the density continuum at which a unit becomes urban is difficult to establish and is certainly dependent upon the purpose of classification. In this case, classification must relate to municipal policies. Any municipality with 300 or more persons per square mile has at least some scattered subdivision activity. The typical services of the rural municipalities under 300 per square mile are restricted to road mainteance and perhaps police or fire. By the time densities reach 500, other services such as subdivision or planning controls, parks, health, waste disposal, and street lights are provided and, without exception, all have police and fire services. Thus depending on the pattern of development, some municipalities under 500 per square mile may initiate urban services, but all of those over 500 are responding to urban conditions. Since municipal policy is a primary concern of this study, the 500 level is used to define "urban."

Table II-1

Distribution of Municipalities by Population Density, 1960

Density Range Persons/sq. mi.	No. of Municipalities
Under 100	29
100–200	39
200–300	17
300–400	12
400–500	4
Sub Total Under 500	101
500–1000	26
1000–1500	16
1500–2000	14
2000–2500	7
Sub Total 500–2,500	63
2500–5000	34
5000–7500	15
7500–10,000	12
10,000–15,000	8
15,000–20,000	4
Over 20,000	1
Sub Total over 2500	74
TOTAL	238

Around Philadelphia there is a band of 94 contiguous municipalities that meet our urban density standard. These will hereafter be referred to as *Suburbs*. In the remaining semi-urban portions of the counties there is a mixture of municipalities, some rural and others with densities above 500 persons

per square mile. Most of the latter are cities or boroughs which
have been in existence for half to a full century or more. Their
origins were not primarily related to the emergence of metropolitan Philadelphia. They are farm commercial service centers
and, in a few cases, industrial complexes that developed around
a labor force which was distinct from that of Philadelphia and
its suburbs.

These centers have population densities sufficiently high to
be urban by our definition, but represent a different type of
urban form from the contiguous urban area. They differ from
the Suburbs in their political responses and in their social and
economic characteristics. While their governments usually offer
urban services, their populations exhibit the kind of overall
homogeneity typical of more rural areas. Thus for many purposes of analysis they must be treated separately, and they will
henceforth be referred to as *Towns*. The rural areas are designated *Townships*.

The above description suggests the following classification
of political subareas in the Pennsylvania sector (see Map I) of
the Philadelphia Metropolitan region:

Table II–2

Classification of Study Units

Classification	Total No. of Units	No. of Units in Study
The Core City (Philadelphia)	1	1
Suburbs	94	90
Semi-Urban Area	143	135
Townships	101	94
Towns	42	41
TOTAL	238	226

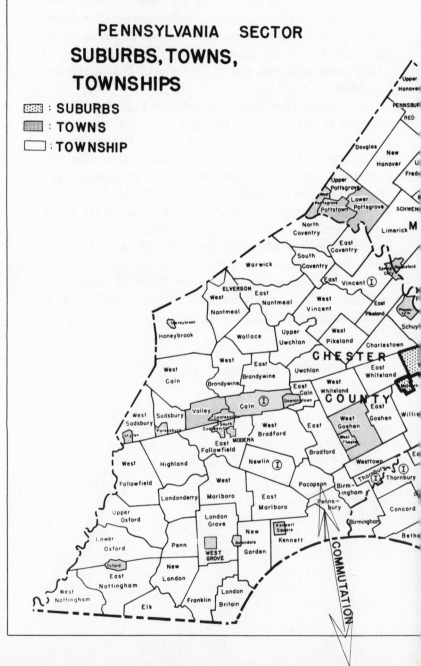

MAP I

PENNSYLVANIA SECTOR
SUBURBS, TOWNS,
TOWNSHIPS

▦ : SUBURBS
▤ : TOWNS
☐ : TOWNSHIP

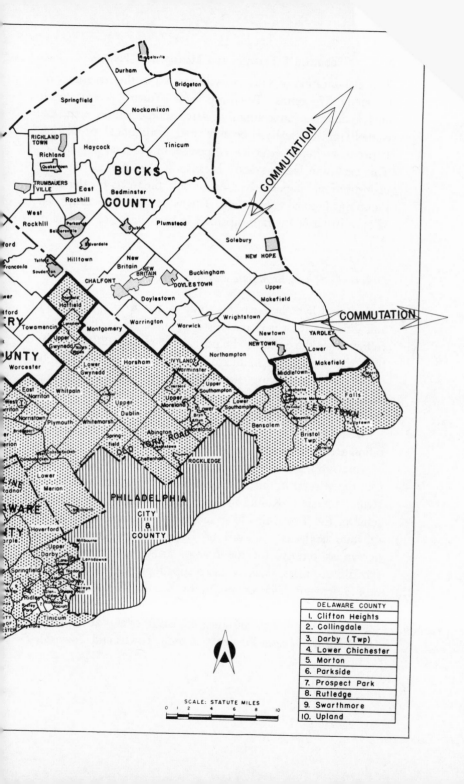

DELAWARE COUNTY
1. Clifton Heights
2. Collingdale
3. Darby (Twp)
4. Lower Chichester
5. Morton
6. Parkside
7. Prospect Park
8. Rutledge
9. Swarthmore
10. Upland

SCALE: STATUTE MILES
0 1 2 4 6 8 10

classification of subareas will be used in the remainder of
study. The terms "Township" and "Town" have no legal,
y a density, connotation.[1] Twelve municipalities were excluded from the analysis because their institutional population
(prisons, asylums) exceeded 10 percent of the total population.
This exclusion was necessary because of the atypical character
of institutional populations.[2] As a result, the totals for the three
groupings become Suburbs 90, Towns 41, and Townships 94.
(For a listing of the municipalities in each class, see Appendix
A.)

Differentiation in Economic and Social Characteristics

A central hypothesis of this study is that areal specialization
and differentiation is characteristic of urban areas. It therefore
follows that the Suburbs should exhibit greater differentiation
than the semi-urban municipalities. This hypothesis will be
tested for the following characteristics: age, education, occupation, social rank, race, religion, wealth property-composition,
and size of total population.

As the term "semi-urban" implies, the units in this classification are not a control group designed to portray the sharpness
of rural and urban contrasts. Even the Townships, although
considered rural in this study, are probably atypically rural as a
result of their proximity to large urban centers. For example,
some of the Townships have substantial populations of an ex-
urbanite character. Sections of Bucks County are nationally
known as retreats for the *literati,* artists and other highly-
specialized professionals whose occupations, while urban-based,
do not demand daily commuting to the city. The "Little Switz-
erland" area in Chester County is fox-hunt country and the
home of a number of millionaires. Large estates and "hobby"
farms dot the region. Elements of some Towns and Townships

are related to the urban economies of other metropolitan areas by easy access via rail and expressway. Thus the units in the semi-urban group, to a certain extent, exhibit considerable differentiation by virtue of metropolitan influence. Despite these factors, it can be demonstrated that specialization is greater within the Suburbs than within the semi-urban area, or in the Town and Township components of the latter. The Suburb-Town comparison is particularly interesting, for it demonstrates that urbanism as defined by density assumes a different form in the contiguous urban area than it does in the noncontiguous.

In describing the differences among the three study groups, several measures of central tendency will be employed, primarily the *mean,* the *standard deviation,* and the *coefficient of variability.* Extreme values are given as ranges. A standard deviation is essentially a measure of the dispersion of a group of values around their mean. If the hypothesis about differentiation and urbanism is correct, the standard deviations for the Suburbs should be larger than those for the semi-urban Towns and Townships.

Size. The most obvious variation in population characteristics of the municipalities is in the total number of inhabitants Here the differences are so marked that employment of standard deviations is not necessary. Table II–3 shows the distribution of municipalities by size. Most of the units are quite small, 65 percent having populations of 5,000 or less. Practically all of the semi-urban units are under 10,000, and most of the Suburbs fall within this range, as well. The largest of the Suburbs is Upper Darby, population 93,158, and the smallest is Ivyland, 425. Ivyland is an example of an old rural commercial center that is being engulfed by the widening band of urbanization. There are about a dozen similar places in the urban mosaic, small centers whose boundaries were drawn decades ago to set them off from then rural surroundings, but whose surrounding

44   Suburban Differences and Metropolitan Policies

municipalities have now reached urban densities. (For a complete list of population figures see Appendix A).

Table II–3

Distribution of Municipalities by Population, 1960

Population	Suburbs	Towns	Townships
0– 5,000	31	32	93
5,000–10,000	28	6	8
10,000–15,000	15	2	0
15,000–20,000	4	1	0
20,000–25,000	4	0	0
25,000–30,000	3	1	0
30,000–35,000	0	0	0
35,000–40,000	3	0	0
40,000–45,000	0	0	0
45,000–50,000	0	0	0
50,000–55,000	1	0	0
55,000–60,000	3	0	0
Over 60,000	2	0	0
Total	94	42	101
Range	425–93,158	489–26,144	453–6,492
Philadelphia:	2,002,512		

Age of Population. The measure of age used is the percentage of persons 21 and over in the age bracket 25–34 (frequently referred to as the young adult variable). This age group was chosen to approximate the principal household-forming years. It is hypothesized that persons within this age range share certain circumstances which may shape their views on local policies. The economic duress of large personal outlays associated with establishing a home, a common concern for the education of children and, perhaps, at the same time, aspirations for economic achievements which make the initial homesite a temporary place of residence may color the outlook of the young adults toward local-government expenditures.

A close examination of Map II will show some of the geographical concentration of age groups in the metropolitan area. Actually, two patterns can be discerned, one in the suburban and one in the semi-urban area. There are many fewer Suburbs in the middle quartiles of age distribution relative to the total number of Suburbs, than there are Towns or Townships. In other words, the Suburbs are more likely to specialize in either older or younger adult populations.

The Suburbs with the largest concentrations of older populations are of two types, the earlier established residential Suburbs on the Main Line (Lower Merion, Haverford, Radnor), or on Old York Road (Cheltenham and Jenkintown), and some of the old industrial river communities (Tinicum, Eddystone, Norristown, Conshohocken). The Suburbs with younger populations are, without exception, the new rapidly growing municipalities. They constitute an irregular perimeter around the Suburban rim, from Upper Chichester and Ashton in Delaware County, through Upper Merion and mid-Montgomery County, to the Levittown complex of Lower Bucks.

The semi-urban portion of the metropolitan area shows the comparatively youthful character of rural populations. The Townships, if not in the middle quartiles of the distribution are more than likely in the highest quartile in terms of their percentages of young adult populations. Most of the few that do cater to older populations are located at the points of the commutation arrows. Here are municipalities that are oriented to other urban centers, Wilmington, Trenton and even New York City. They are populated not by rural workers, but by high-income space-seekers, whose age characteristics will be reflected, as we shall see in subsequent maps, in social status as well.

The pattern of age distribution throughout the metropolitan area bears a marked relationship to distributions of wealth and status. A close comparison of Maps II and III will show, however, that this relationship is not always in the same direction.

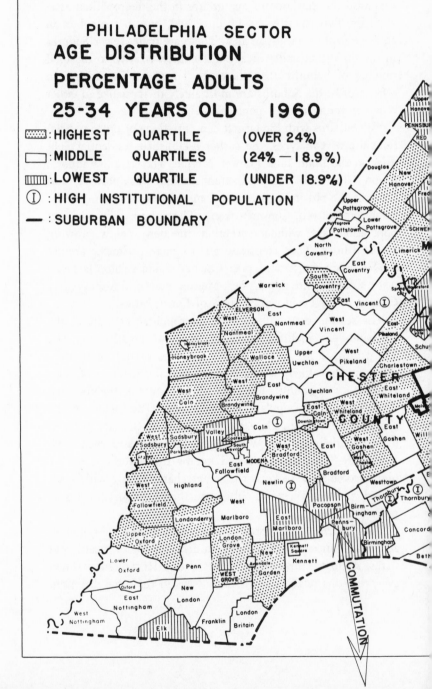

MAP II

PHILADELPHIA SECTOR
AGE DISTRIBUTION
PERCENTAGE ADULTS
25-34 YEARS OLD   1960

▦ : HIGHEST   QUARTILE   (OVER 24%)
▢ : MIDDLE   QUARTILES   (24% — 18.9%)
▥ : LOWEST   QUARTILE   (UNDER 18.9%)
Ⓘ : HIGH INSTITUTIONAL POPULATION
— : SUBURBAN BOUNDARY

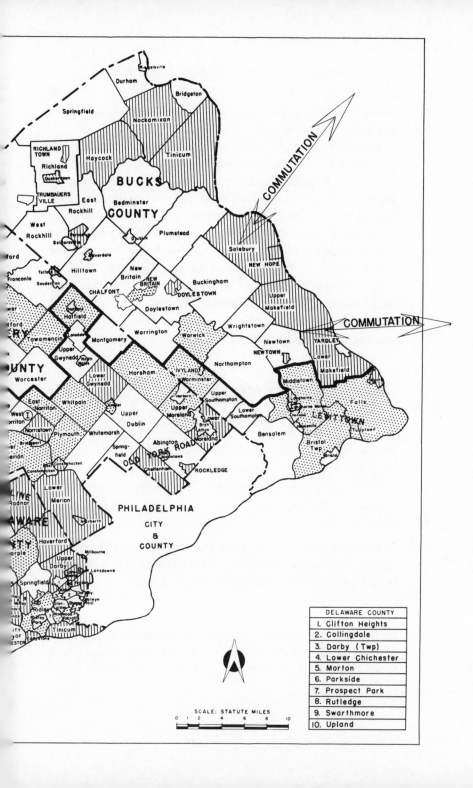

DELAWARE COUNTY
1. Clifton Heights
2. Collingdale
3. Darby (Twp)
4. Lower Chichester
5. Morton
6. Parkside
7. Prospect Park
8. Rutledge
9. Swarthmore
10. Upland

SCALE: STATUTE MILES
0 1 2   4   6   8   10

Some places specialize in young high-status, and others in young low-status populations, and so forth through the various age-status combinations.

Although specialization by age of population occurs throughout the area, the more extreme forms of specialization are among the Suburbs, as can be seen in Table 11–4, where the range of the percentages of adult populations in the 25–34 bracket are presented. These extremes are also reflected in the difference between the Suburban and semi-urban measures of central tendency. Note, however, that while the mean percentage of young adults declined in all areas between 1950 and 1960, as a result of the low birth rate of the depression years, the standard deviations increased between 1950 and 1960, suggesting that specialization by age of population is an increasing urban phenomenon.

Table II–4

Percentage of Adults 25 to 34 Years of Age,
Central Tendency by Study Area, 1950 and 1960

Area	1950				1960			
	Mean	S	V	Range	Mean	S	V	Range
Suburban	25.1%	4.7%	.187	14.7-44.4%	22.0%	6.7%	.034	9.2-41.0%
Semi-urban	24.4	3.6	.147	18.2-37.9	21.6	4.2	.194	11.0-31.9
Towns	24.5	3.6	.147	18.6-37.9	22.6	3.6	.167	11.0-28.1
Townships	24.4	3.1	.127	18.6-37.7	22.4	4.0	.178	12.7-31.9

Philadelphia: 19.3

The lower means raise a question regarding the interpretation of the standard deviations. This statistical measure shows central tendencies in relationship to a mean; thus as the mean changes, different standard deviation scores could describe the same central tendencies (i.e., the shape of the curve implied by the standard deviation value could be the same). The *coefficient of variability* can aid in making comparisons where means differ. It is derived from dividing the standard deviation by the mean. The results are the V values in Table II–4 and in others that follow. The larger the V value, the greater the dispersion.[3]

A final caution needs to be interjected here regarding the means in Table II–4. These means (and all others in subsequent tables, unless otherwise noted) are means of the values for each municipality. The actual percentage of adults who are 25 to 34 in each of the study areas cannot be deduced from the table because both large and small municipalities are given equal weight. The actual percentages for 1960 are: Philadelphia 19.3, Suburbs 16.5, Towns 21.0 and Townships 28.7 The adult population is generally older, as the area is more urban, a fact obscured by Table II–4.

Social Rank. The status of a community finds expression in styles of life which may be reflected in numerous public policies. A high status community is likely to state its service preferences in ways ranging from numerous auxiliary programs in the schools to backdoor, instead of street garbage pickups. But what is high status; how is it measured? Possible indices include education, occupation and wealth. While all three of these population attributes are correlated, the decision was made to include only the first two in scoring social rank, with wealth being given separate treatment, for reasons explained below.

The means of earning a living are the most visible manifestation of status in our society. Census occupational classifications suggest a basis for a dichotomous status scaling of occupations by the separation of managerial, technical, professional, and sales occupations from clerical, craftsmen, laborers and household workers. This dual classification is only approximate since occupational titles are deceptive and the census groups are broad. Since a college education is generally the prerequisite for the higher status white collar positions, the combination of education and occupation is calculated to offset some of the disadvantages of using occupation alone.

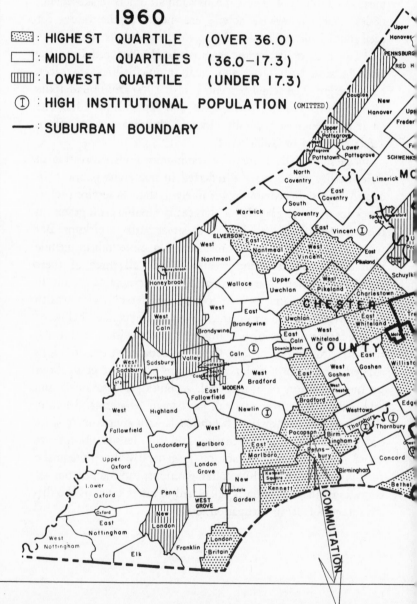

MAP III

PENNSYLVANIA SECTOR

SOCIAL RANK

1960

▨ : HIGHEST QUARTILE (OVER 36.0)

▢ : MIDDLE QUARTILES (36.0-17.3)

▥ : LOWEST QUARTILE (UNDER 17.3)

Ⓘ : HIGH INSTITUTIONAL POPULATION (OMITTED)

— : SUBURBAN BOUNDARY

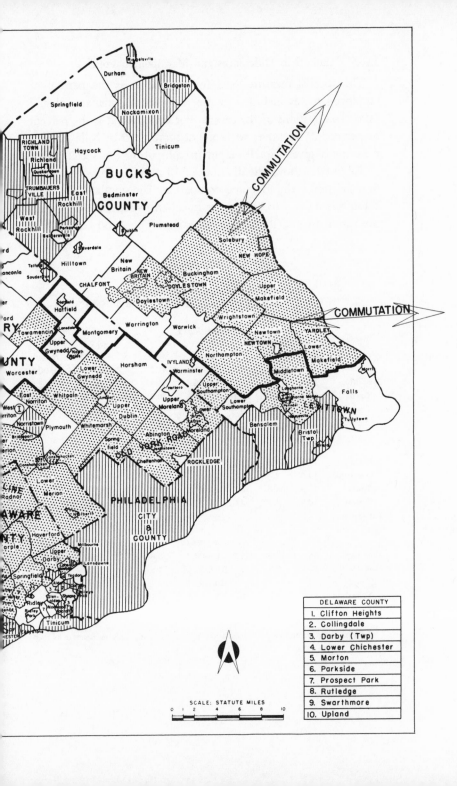

SCALE: STATUTE MILES
0 2   4   6   8   10

DELAWARE COUNTY
1. Clifton Heights
2. Collingdale
3. Darby (Twp)
4. Lower Chichester
5. Morton
6. Parkside
7. Prospect Park
8. Rutledge
9. Swarthmore
10. Upland

The specific measure used for occupation is the percent of employed males included in the professional, managerial and sales classifications of the census. For education it is the percent of persons 25 and over with one or more years of college. Each measure is given equal weight in computing the social rank.[4]

Table II–5 shows the distribution of municipalities according to social rank, education and occupation. The standard deviation column is the key to differences in subarea specialization within the suburban and the semi-urban areas. The 1960 central ten-

Table II–5

Social Rank, Education and Occupation,
Central Tendency by Study Area, 1950 and 1960*

Social Rank

		1950				1960		
Area	Mean	S	V	Range	Mean	S	V	Range
Suburban	27.6	16.9	.612	3.0-88.5	31.2	20.9	.670	1.0-90.6
Semi-urban	24.3	19.9	.407	3.9-56.4	25.9	11.2	.432	3.2-63.6
Towns	19.0	8.9	.468	3.9-38.3	20.7	9.4	.454	3.2-41.2
Townships	26.6	9.4	.353	7.4-56.4	28.2	11.8	.418	13.3-63.6
Philadelphia:	15.9				17.2			

Education

Suburban	16.7	11.6	.695	2.3-63.5	19.6	12.5	.638	2.5-70.8
Semi-urban	14.0	7.8	.557	1.0-32.0	17.1	8.8	.515	1.5-43.9
Towns	11.8	16.6	.559	1.0-27.5	13.9	7.1	.511	1.5-27.0
Townships	14.9	8.1	.544	1.0-32.0	18.5	9.2	.497	5.5-43.9
Philadelphia:	8.7				10.2			

Occupation

Suburban	33.5	15.3	.457	8.4-89.2	35.8	17.7	.494	6.3-84.0
Semi-urban	31.1	9.4	.302	10.9-63.1	30.5	9.5	.311	9.3-63.7
Towns	24.9	7.8	.313	10.9-93.4	25.4	7.5	.295	9.3-47.8
Townships	33.7	8.8	.261	15.3-63.1	32.8	9.5	.290	11.8-63.7
Philadelphia:	26.0				24.4			

* Social Rank expressed as standardized scores, education and occupation as percentages.

dency measures for the suburban area ($S=20.9$, $V=.670$) are greater than for the semi-urban ($S=11.2$, $V=.432$). The differences underlying these two figures are shown graphically in Figure 1. The factor which contributes greatly to the suburban dispersion is the existence of a number of high-social-rank suburbs, the highest in the entire metropolitan area. In the Suburbs, place of work is frequently separated from place of residence; the concentration of high-status citizens in particular municipalities is a peculiarly urban trait. The fact that the curve peaks to the left of the scale simply reflects the fact that there are many more low-status than high-status communities. As the large number of 1–10 scores in Figure I indicate, there are many very low-social-ranking municipalities within each group.

Comparison of the 1950 and 1960 social ranks will identify several ecological trends in the metropolitan sector. Scores are standardized for the two years, so all changes indicate a shift along a common scale. All the means increase from 1950 to 1960 reflecting the national rise in educational and occupational levels. The standard deviations also increase. However, the coefficients of variability suggest that differentiation is increasing among the Suburbs and Townships.

The two components of social rank, education and occupation, pattern somewhat differently than the composite. Between 1950 and 1960, there was a general lessening of the educational differences among municipalities in all the study areas (note declining V values). On the other hand, there was slightly increased differentiation and specialization according to the occupational index. (The Towns are again an exception). Perhaps as post-high-school education is becoming more general, college attendance no longer identifies a discriminating social characteristic. If education is to be used as a measure of social differentiation in the future, perhaps we will need to ask the question what college, or at least what kind of college?

FIGURE I

DISTRIBUTION OF SOCIAL RANK

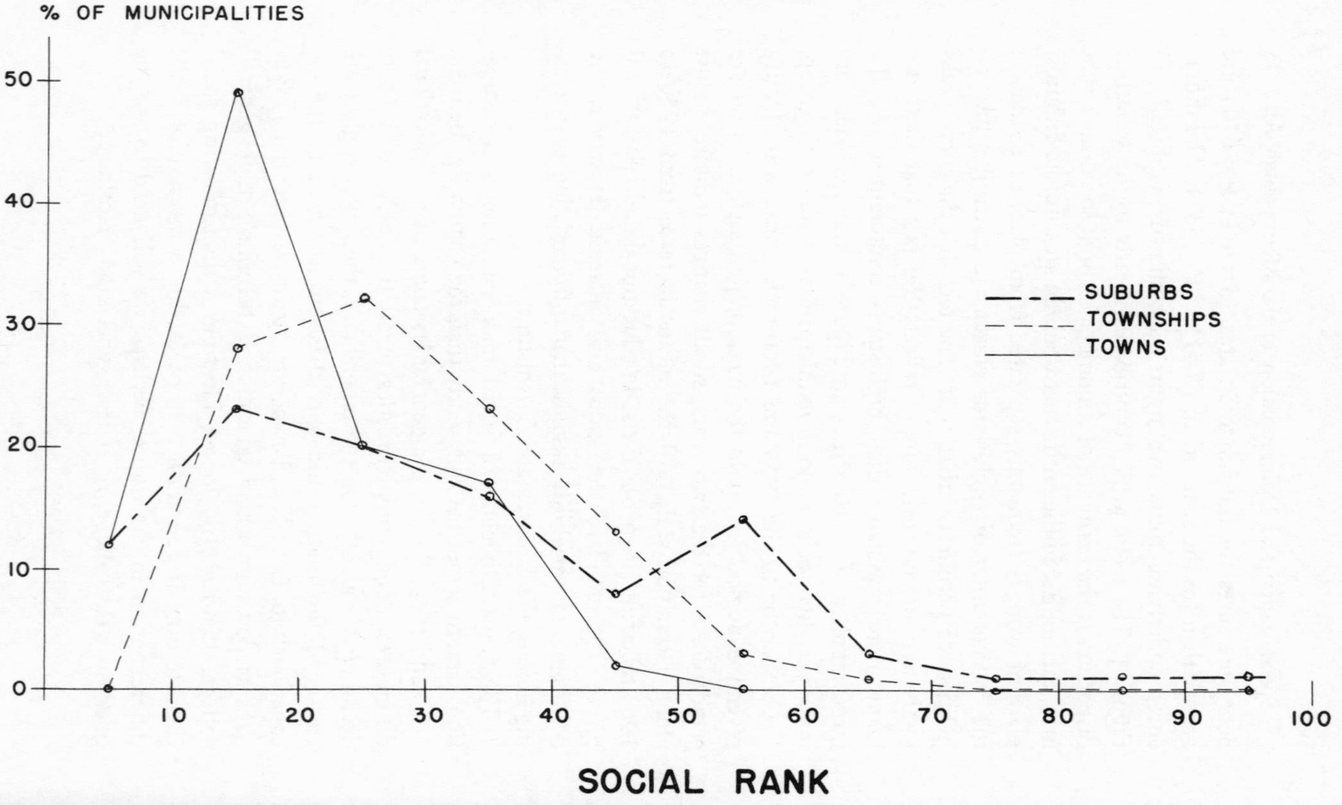

SOCIAL RANK

% OF MUNICIPALITIES

SUBURBS
TOWNSHIPS
TOWNS

The geographic distribution of status is portrayed in Map III. There are roughly four high-status sections in the Pennsylvania sector of the metropolitan area. The oldest and the biggest is the Main Line, anchored next to Philadelphia by Lower Merion and extending outward into the hunt country of Charlestown, West Pikeland and West Vincent. The second major Suburban high-status area is north of the city, fanning out from Old York Road across much of lower Montgomery County. The two additional high-status areas are at the points of the commutation arrows, where persons employed outside the area concentrate and where a number of large estates are to be found.

The major low-status areas follow the rivers—solidly along the Delaware River at the map's lower edge and intermittently along the Schuylkill, where they include the older industrial boroughs of Conshohocken and West Conshohocken, and extending up along the Montgomery-Chester County line, Pottstown. Other low-status communities include poor farm sections and some of the old industrial Towns.

Wealth. The assets that constitute a man's wealth include both his income and his possessions. A citizen's outlook toward taxation and local services is undoubtedly influenced by his wealth. It may well be that the form in which wealth is held has an additional effect (i.e., cash income as opposed to wealth in the form of property holdings may influence attitudes toward real property taxes, which are still the mainstay of most local governments).

For research in local areas, data limitations place strictures on the refinements possible in exploring such questions. One of the most closely-guarded secrets in social statistics is personal income data. Income, as reported to the United States Internal Revenue Service, is not recorded by municipality of residence. The census does report income by medians and levels. The

medians are reported by census tract, but since medians are
not additive, they cannot be combined for municipalities. Income by levels is reported in $1000 steps up to $10,000, after
which larger steps are used until all incomes over $25,000
are grouped together. In 1950, the steps ended with $10,000
the uppermost categorical limit. For both censal years, inspection of the highest income categories revealed that municipalities of the highest social rank and with reputations of being
exclusive residential communities frequently showed no higher
incidence of incomes in these brackets than some low social
rank units. This may indicate reluctance on the part of many
people to report income accurately to an official government
agency. Or distortions in the "uppermost" category may be accounted for by the fact that the "income not reported" class
very frequently ran as high as ten or fifteen percent of the
total persons reporting income.

The measure devised for an approximate indicator of differences in wealth was the market value of residential property
per household. This measure assumes that the value of a man's
home, whether owned or rented, reflects his wealth. The measure was obtained by multiplying the total assessed value of
residential property in a municipality by the assessment ratio
for residential property computed by the State Tax Equalization
Board. This yielded the total market value of residential property, which in turn was divided by the number of households
recorded by the census.

While this measure has certain shortcomings as a measure of
actual wealth, it also has advantages for work with municipal
fiscal policies. By calculating wealth based on residential property, a measure is created which has utility in assessing tax efforts and burdens in relationship to the householder. The central tendencies for this variable are shown in Table II–6.

The standard deviations for both 1960 and 1950 indicate
greater dispersion of average household values in the suburban

than in the semi-urban area, or in either of the components of the latter. Because of differences in the size of the means, again the coefficient of variability is utilized. The V values indicate greater differentiation in the Suburbs (.315) than in the semi-urban area (.295). However, the Suburbs appear to have become less differentiated during the last decade.

Table II–6

Residential Market Value Per Household,
Central Tendency by Study Area, 1950 and 1960*

Area	1950				1960			
	Mean	S	V	Range	Mean	S	V	Range
Suburban	$7195	$2895	.402	$2023-17,346	$10,421	$3281	.315	$5686-24,311
Semi-urban					8,235	2430	.295	4200-15,205
Towns	5255	1080	.206	3026-7515	7,420	1607	.217	4200-12,200
Townships	†	†	†	†	9,004	2676	.297	5605-15,205
Philadelphia:	5005				5,397			

* All Philadelphia State Tax Equalization figures are deflated approximately 15% from true market value.

† In 1950 farm households were classified as agricultural property, consequently no computations were possible in rural areas for that year. The same was true for Chester County in 1960, hence the Township figures were based on Bucks, Delaware and Montgomery Counties only.

The values reported in Table II–6 are not to be taken literally. They are derived from Tax Equalization Board calculations based on a fifteen percent deflation of what is probably a most conservative estimate of market value. Moreover, and in addition to other shortcomings in the measure, differences in home values between urban and less urban areas are not a reliable indication of differences in the wealth of their residents, since persons of similar wealth may have to pay more for an urban than a rural location. However, the measure is more reliable for intra-study area comparisons.

Religion. The importance of religion in a study of policies, is primarily related to school matters. There is no official census of religious affiliations in the United States. The membership figures released by some denominations are not useful for this study because the religious reporting units (parish or congregation) do not coincide with municipal boundaries. However, local schools do make estimates of religious ties which are more helpful. Each year a survey is made of school age children, and parents are asked to indicate which schools their children will attend the following year. The intentions are classified according to public, sectarian, and non-sectarian private. If we can assume that most children who attend sectarian schools are members of the sponsoring religious groups, it is possible to calculate an approximate ratio of parochial to public school enrollment.

While not a religious census, the sectarian-public school enrollment ratio does suggest where some religious groups locate, and is a sound measure for testing hypotheses about religion and school policies. It at least indicates the extent to which the parents in a municipality have a stake in public and parochial schools. While sectarian in the vast majority of the cases means Roman Catholic, this is not always true. There are a number of Protestant schools, but these generally have widely scattered pupils.[5] It is possible that sectarian schools in areas of poor public schools draw children away from public schools regardless of the faith of the parents, and, in areas where sectarian schools are relatively inaccessible, it is likely that nearly all children attend public school. However, the school surveys are the only approximation of the distribution of Roman Catholics in the metropolitan area that could be fitted to the political sub-areas of the study. The specific measure for each municipality is the number of intentions to attend sectarian schools as a percent of the total intentions for school attendance. Assuming a relationship between intention and actual attendance, and for the sake of simplicity, we will henceforth speak of public and parochial school enrollment when referring to these data which are summarized in Table II–7.

Given the great disparity in the religious composition of the suburban and semi-urban areas, the measures of central tend-

Table II–7

Parochial School Enrollment, Central Tendency by Study Area, 1960*

Area	Mean	S	V	Range
Suburban	33.4%	15.6%	.467	1 – 96%
Semi-urban	10.5	7.8	.752	0 – 49
Towns	11.9	9.8	.823	0 – 28
Townships	9.4	6.7	.787	0 – 49

Philadelphia actual enrollment percentage – 28.1
* Parochial school as a percent of total school enrollment.

ency are difficult to interpret. The *coefficient of variability* indicates greater differentiation in the Towns and Townships. It states that the rather small percentage of Catholics in the semi-urban area is indeed distributed unevenly. But as shown in the following distribution, very few semi-urban units contain large Catholic concentrations.

Table II–8

Percent Parochial Enrollment of Total	No. of Municipalities Suburban	Semi-urban
60+	4	0
50 – 60	6	0
40 – 50	11	1
30 – 40	25	1
20 – 30	29	10
10 – 20	12	38
0 – 10	3	85
Total	90	135

Race. Although there is some differentiation in the distribution of non-whites among Suburban municipalities, the most striking contrast is between the core city, Philadelphia, and the rest of the metropolitan area. Non-whites are essentially core city residents, both in number (535,033 in Philadelphia to

82,113 in the other four counties) and in percent (26.7 to 5.2).
Table II–9 summarizes the totals and percentages by area. The
most striking finding is that the disparity in racial composition
between the core city and outlying areas is increasing. In 1950
non-whites comprised 5.9 percent of the total Suburban population and 4.5 and 6.8 percent of the Townships and Towns
respectively. The over-all four-county percentage was 5.8. By
1960 the four-county percentage had declined to 5.2 percent,
while Philadelphia had increased from 18.2 to 26.7 percent
non-white. Outside of Philadelphia, only the Towns show an
increase in the percentage of non-whites between 1950 and
1960. Only in Philadelphia and the Towns, did the non-white
population increase at a rate faster than the white.

Stated differently, while the white population in the Suburbs
was increasing 55 percent, the non-white population was lagg-
ing at a 34 percent increase in the 1950–60 decade. The actual
numerical increase in non-whites was 15,368 persons. Two-
thirds of this increase took place in three old industrial centers
where over-all populations declined. In brief, non-whites are
not moving into the residential suburbs in any significant
numbers. In fact, their percentages and actual number declined
in several residential suburbs over the decade. Of three largely
residential suburbs which were over 50 percent non-white in
1950, all experienced a decline in the percentage of non-whites
during the decade. In 1950, their percentages non-white were
78, 70 and 56, and in 1960, 29, 67 and 34 respectively, with
the latter two showing absolute declines in non-white populations.[6] Only one residential municipality with above-median
social rank had an increased percentage of non-white residents,
in this case the increase was from 5.9 percent to 12.3, representing an influx of 780 non-whites.[7]

The social differentiation we have described depicts the
Suburbs as a kind of social cafeteria, from which choices con-
genial to an individual's style of life may be made. While all

Table II-9

Non-White Population, Distribution
by Study Area, 1950 and 1960*

Area	1950 Total Popu.	1950 White	1950 Non-White	1950 Per-Cent Non-White	1960 Total Popu.	1960 White	1960 Non-White	1960 Per-Cent Non-White	Percent Increase 1950-1960 Total	White	Non-White
Suburbs	762,577	717,570	45,007	5.9%	1,186,004	1,125,629	60,375	5.1%	55.5%	56.9%	34.1%
Towns	151,230	140,990	10,240	6.8	169,405	156,138	13,267	7.8	12.0	10.7	29.5
Townships	157,256	150,215	7,041	4.5	233,602	225,031	8,471	3.6	48.5	49.8	20.3
Total Outside Philadelphia	1,971,063	1,008,775	62,288	5.8	1,589,011	1,506,898	82,113	5.2	48.4	49.4	31.8
Philadelphia	2,071,605	1,692,637	378,968	18.3	2,002,512	1,467,479	535,033	26.7	-3.3	-13.3	41.2

* Includes populations of the 12 municipalities excluded from remainder of study because of their large institutional populations.

evidence indicates that this choice is a real one, at this point the caveat "a choice for whites only" must be added.

Despite the foregoing, there is significant variation in the percentage of nonwhites in the suburban and semi-urban areas. The places of non-white concentration are, however, of two kinds: old industrial complexes or rural areas. With a few exceptions, non-whites established themselves in these places generations ago, and their numbers in the last decade have declined or remained quite stable. Table II–10 summarizes this distribution.

Table II–10

Percentage Non-white, Distribution of Municipalities by Study Area, 1960

% Non-white	Suburbs	Towns	Townships
Under 5	72	30	77
5–10	7	4	10
10–20	7	4	5
Over 20	4	3	2

Property Value. There are obvious relations between the character of a municipality's population and the value and uses to which its property is put. One might well expect municipalities populated by wealthy, high-social-status residents to contain expensive homes, and therefore to enjoy high per capita market values of property. However, high per capita market value often reflects divergent tendencies in social composition. While it may reflect the existence of expensive homes, it may also result from a high ratio of industrial and commercial property to population. The former type of community is likely to have a population of high social rank, the latter one of low social rank. But industrial and commercial property is so distributed in the metropolitan area that cheap homes are not always accompanied by tax-base enriching, non-residential uses.

The market value of residential property was described earlier as an indicator of personal wealth. While residential property constitutes the major portion of most municipalities' tax bases, a more adequate measure of tax resources and municipal wealth is the per capita market of all property. A comparison of the study areas according to their tax resources again reveals greatest diversity in the Suburbs. The Towns are generally poorest and least specialized, most being industrial and trading centers mixed with modest housing.

Table II–11

Per Capita Market Value of Real Property,
Central Tendency by Study Area, 1950 and 1960

Area	1950				1960			
	Mean	S	V	Range	Mean	S	V	Range
Suburban	$3280	$1487	.453	$789-9722	$4130	$1760	.426	$1662-12,226
Semi-urban	2680	906	.338	1378-6360	3640	1250	.343	1711- 6922
Towns	2500	787	.315	1378-4906	3360	1100	.327	1920- 6922
Townships	2760	922	.334	1458-6360	3770	1270	.337	1711- 6799
Philadelphia:	2569				2871			

The Suburbs had the poorest and richest communities in the entire sector in both 1950 and 1960. Municipalities at the lower end of the range are working-class suburbs with little or no non-residential property. These islands of comparative poverty are distinctive problem areas within the metropolis. Densely populated and in need of all urban services, they are faced with the problem of extensive needs and few resources. Paradoxically, many of the richest communities are also working-class residential areas. In these cases, small populations are mixed with large industrial complexes. Thus the tax-base lottery of the metropolitan area does not always find the poor on the losing side. On the other hand the rich rarely lose, for where the wealthy congregate, their expensive homes and low-density living result in high per capita market values of property (Compare Map IV and Map III).

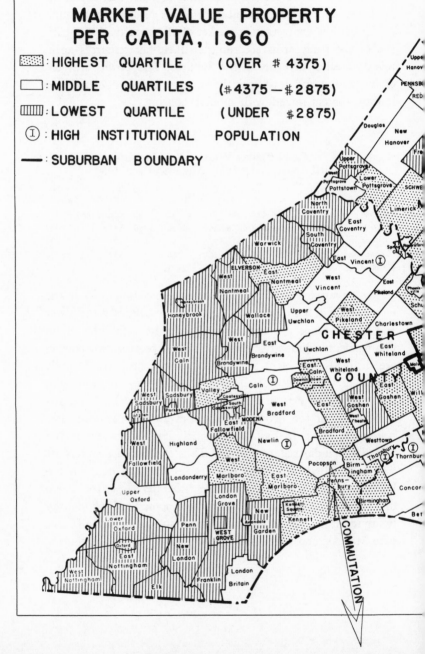

MAP IV

PHILADELPHIA SECTOR
MARKET VALUE PROPERTY
PER CAPITA, 1960

▨ : HIGHEST QUARTILE   (OVER $4375)

☐ : MIDDLE QUARTILES   ($4375 – $2875)

▥ : LOWEST QUARTILE   (UNDER $2875)

Ⓘ : HIGH INSTITUTIONAL POPULATION

▬ : SUBURBAN BOUNDARY

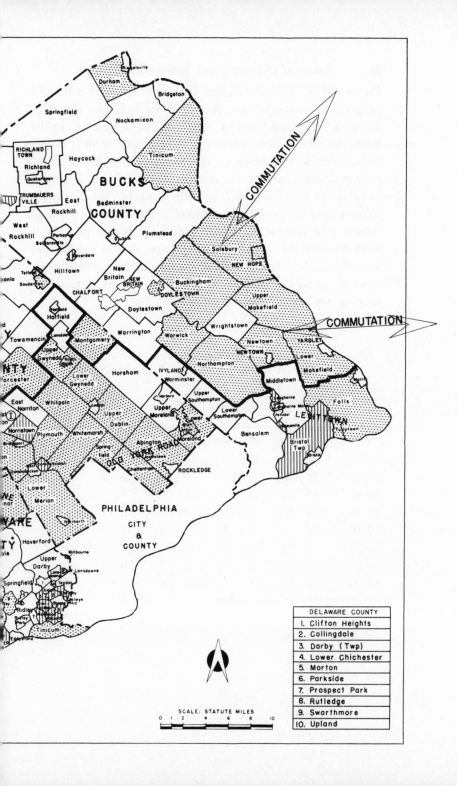

DELAWARE COUNTY
1. Clifton Heights
2. Collingdale
3. Darby (Twp)
4. Lower Chichester
5. Morton
6. Parkside
7. Prospect Park
8. Rutledge
9. Swarthmore
10. Upland

SCALE: STATUTE MILES
0 1 2   4   6   8   10

Property Use. The distribution of industrial and commercial property by municipality is shown in Table II–12. The wide range of functional types of municipalities is apparent in the Suburban column. The separation of home and work is clearly shown; nearly two-thirds of the Suburbs have less than 20 percent assessed valuation in commerce and industry. Less than one-third of the Towns fall into this category. The Township column must be interpreted differently, for in the Towns and Suburbs, the obverse of industrial and commercial property is residential. In the case of the Townships, it is residential and agricultural. In a few Townships, however, industrial installations are located at strategic transportation points in rural settings or are just outside old established Towns.

Table II–12

Percentage Assessed Valuation in Industrial and Commercial Uses, Distribution of Municipalities by Study Area, 1960

Percent Ind. and Com.	Total		Suburbs		Semi-urban		Towns		Townships	
	No.	%	No.	%	No.	%	No.	%	No.	%
0–10%	94	42%	25	28%	69	51%	2	5%	67	71%
10–20	62	28	32	36	30	22	11	27	19	22
20–30	24	10	9	10	15	11	12	30	3	3
30–40	19	9	11	12	8	6	7	17	1	1
40–50	14	6	5	6	9	7	6	15	3	3
50–60	3	1	2	2	1	1	1	2	0	0
60–70	6	2	3	3	3	2	2	5	1	1
70–80	2	1	2	2	0	0	0	0	0	0
80–90	1	*	1	1	0	0	0	0	0	0
Total	225		90		135		41		94	

Philadelphia 42.4%
* Less than 1%.

Because of the absence of the agricultural category, a different functional division is employed in Table II–13, based upon the percent of total assessed value in residential property. This measure shows the comparison of the degree of residential specialization by study area more clearly than Table II–12. Where municipalities within a study area all have similar ratios of residential to non-residential properties, the standard deviation should be low. Residential, commercial, or industrial specialization should raise the standard deviation. Perhaps the most significant finding here is that the difference in Suburban and semi-urban standard deviations is as small as it is (Suburban 17.7 and semi-urban 14.3). Increasing diversification of functions in some of the larger Suburbs undoubtedly holds this difference down.

Table II–13

Percentage Assessed Valuation in Residential Property,
Central Tendency by Study Area, 1960

Area	Mean	S	V	Range
Suburban	74.4%	17.7%	.238	13–100%
Semi-urban	65.3	14.3	.219	26–88
Towns	68.8	14.1	.205	26–88
Townships	62.1	13.3	.214	32–88
Philadelphia:	57.6			

Party Allegiance. No description of a metropolitan area would be complete without mention of its party politics. But, in this study, how are party allegiances to be treated; as independent or as dependent variables? Since this is a study of political responses, and voting can clearly be considered just that, it would seem at first glance to be a dependent variable. But is voting behavior truly influenced by urban specialization and differentiation; or is it more a product of social and economic factors conditioned by national and state events? One might well argue that party allegiance and voting participation are not dependent variables, but are (as are religion, age, social rank, and wealth) attributes of a community—independent variables—that influence other forms of political response.

The correlation matrix used as our major analytic tool did not distinguish between independent and dependent variables. Thus it was possible to view voting participation and the division of the two-party vote as both outcomes of urban differeniation, and aspects of differentiation that might affect other outcomes. From either perspective, party affiliations added little to our understanding of policy responses in the metropolitan area.

Voting behavior did correlate with certain kinds of policy responses, but reflection and further statistical analysis led to the conclusion that these relationships were a function of intervening variables. Thus a high correlation between expenditures for planning and Republicanism at either local, state or national elections was felt to suggest little about the policy preferences of Republicans or Democrats, but rather to verify the interrelationship between social rank and Republicanism and social rank and planned urban areas.

Not only did party allegiance fail to explain policy differences, it did not itself appear to be influenced by the metropolitan environment. To be sure, there are communities that attract Republicans and others that seem to invite Democrats as residents, but this specialization is a subsidiary funcion of urban social and economic specialization. As could have been expected, most high-social-ranking communities were Republican and most low-social-ranking industrial and commercial centers were Democratic.

In dismissing party allegiance as a factor influencing policy responses, we do not mean to minimize the role of political parties in organizing and providing leadership for municipal policy-making. Indeed, in Chapter X, a political party is viewed as a most important actor in one metropolitan decision. But in this case, partisan affiliation, as such, did not explain the behavior in question, rather it was the party as an organization of political power which took concerted action on a community issue.

Differentiation and a Decade of Change

Analysis to this point has shown the Suburbs to be more differentiated than the Towns or Townships. Furthermore, it has been suggested that specialization with regard to social rank and the location of residents of a particular age increased for the 90 Suburbs between 1950 and 1960, while differences in their tax resources and the wealth of their residents diminished. However, Suburban comparisons for 1950 and 1960 point to a methodological problem of possible significance.

A number of the 90 municipalities classified as Suburbs by virtue of their 1960 density and contiguity, were not Suburban according to our definition in 1950. Comparisons between 1950 and 1960 may have been distorted by the inclusion of then semi-urban units in the 1950 Suburban calculations. To control for this possibility, Table II–14 contrasts the measures of central tendency of selected characteristics for the 65 units that were Suburban in 1950 with the 90 that were so defined in 1960. In addition, Table II–14 shows the changes in the 25 municipalities that were in transition between 1950 and 1960 and in the 65 older Suburbs.

The necessity for distinguishing between the 1950 Suburbs and those in transition is immediately apparent. In every characteristic measured, the 25 Suburbs in transition were more like one another than were the already suburbanized units.

Moreover, in 1950, the variability of the Suburbs in transition was less than that of the semi-urban municipalities. The beginnings of suburbanization are evident in their high social rank and market value per capita. Their function within the metropolitan area is already indicated. On the suburban periphery, they will attract younger, high-social-ranking residents who will pay more for newer homes.

By 1960, the transitional Suburbs begin to display more differentiation. They continue to attract a generally younger, higher-social-ranking population than the older Suburbs. They enjoy more tax resources as land values increase faster than population, but relative differences between them are increasing.

Certain national trends affected the entire area. Educational levels are generally higher, white-collar jobs have increasingly replaced blue-collar occupations, inflation has caused property values to increase, and low birth rates in the thirties have altered the age distribution of populations. Each of these factors is reflected in the contrast of 1960 mean values to those of 1950. But the older Suburbs, on the average, have lost more young adults, have not gained in occupational and educational levels as much as the newer Suburbs, and have not shared equally in the area's increase in property value. Nevertheless, while differences in their individual and community wealth have decreased, in social characteristics, the 65 older Suburbs are more differentiated in 1960 than they were in 1950. This is entirely consistent with the expectation that the enlargement of the Suburban area would attract newer populations and functions to newer areas, accentuating the patterns of specialization already developed in older municipalities.

The extension of the Suburbs to include 25 newer municipalities lessened total Suburban differentiation between 1950 and 1960 with respect to each variable except young adults. However, what is true of the Suburbs as a whole does not re-

Specialization and Differentiation in the Metropolitan Area 71

flect the changes occurring within the older and newer Suburbs. Once again no clear pattern is visible.

One occurrence is obvious, and it, too, reflects national characteristics. Differences in municipal wealth are decreasing. It has often been asserted that intermunicipal differences in tax bases impede intermunicipal cooperation. We shall subsequently suggest that social-rank differences may provide as great, if not a greater motive for maintaining municipal independence. The tendencies in the past ten years have reduced the differences underpinning Suburban independence for the area as a whole. For Suburbs in different stages of development, however, specialization may even be increasing.

Table II–14

Measures of Central Tendency of Selected
Variables for Municipalities Classified
As Suburbs in 1950 and 1960

		1950 25 Suburbs in Transition	1950 65 Suburbs	1960 90 Suburbs	1960 65 Older Suburbs	1960 25 New Suburbs
Percentage	Mean	25.4%	25.0%	22.0%	21.4%	23.7%
Young Adults	S	2.2%	6.0%	6.7%	6.8%	5.8%
	V	.115	.238	.304	.318	.245
Social Rank	Mean	30.3	26.6	31.2	28.3	39.1
	S	8.6	19.0	20.9	21.8	15.9
	V	.286	.714	.670	.771	.407
Education	Mean	18.7	16.0	19.6	17.7	24.9
	S	9.7	12.1	12.5	15.3	12.0
	V	.519	.756	.638	.864	.482
Occupation	Mean	34.9	33.0	35.8	33.6	41.8
	S	5.6	17.5	17.7	18.6	13.1
	V	.160	.530	.494	.554	.313
Residential	Mean	$7,011	$7,263	$10,421	$10,030	$11,480
Value per	S	$2,031	$3,152	$ 3,281	$ 3,304	$ 2,970
Household	V	.290	.434	.315	.329	.259
Market Value	Mean	$3,511	$3,195	$4,130	$3,943	$4,636
per Capita	S	$ .646	$1,688	$1,760	$1,831	$1,436
	V	.183	.528	.426	.464	.310

Summary

Measured by each of the foregoing characteristics, municipalities in the more urbanized portion of the metropolitan area (Suburbs) are more specialized and differentiated from one another than the semi-urban municipalities (Towns and Townships). Suburbia, far from being a uniform social landscape, is really distinguished by its highly variegated character. Suburbs furnish examples of extreme specialization. There are communities for old persons and others for young adults. Some specialize in residential housing, even further sub-specializing in single family dwellings or multiple family units, while others serve for the location of industrial and commercial activities. The pattern of variation is one of extreme complexity. Few of the variables that contribute to the pattern of differentiation vary from community to community in a consistent fashion. Most community characteristics appear to be independent of one another. Although social rank, wealth, and some of the property characteristics are correlated, the intermunicipal variation among them is far from congruent.

The complexity of the differentiation pattern indicates that no simple typology of municipalities can be constructed. The size of a municipality, its density, its age; the age, wealth, educational, and occupational levels of its residents; the amount and nature of its tax base—all may affect political choices. Unfortunately for the researcher (but perhaps fortunately for the resident choosing a place to live), old municipalities may be rich or poor in tax base, and tax bases combine in a variety of ways with land-use and population characteristics. There are poor-rich and rich-poor communities, as personal wealth and municipal resources are combined in differing mixtures. There are poor and rich industrial places and poor and rich residential communities. High-status populations are to be found in municipalities with greater and lesser amounts of tax resources. Some high-status communities specialize in homes for young adults; others are apparently more attractive to older persons. Similar combinations can be found in low and middle status municipalities.

What is the political relevance of this amazing variety of economic and social characteristics? Is it translated into the political behavior of individuals and municipalities? If all municipalities were so specialized that each was *sui generis,* generalizations about municipal characteristics and political responses could not be attempted. However, there are certain regularities among municipalities, which, through classification and analysis, can be related to the manner in which they define their policies and react to their environment. These are explored in the remainder of this book.

NOTES

1. While the terms "Suburb," "Town" and "Township" as used in this study do not refer to a legal classification system, some confusion is invited by using the term "township," since legally designated Townships of the first and second class are to be found in all three study areas. However, we have found no synonym that will satisfactorily connote the character of Townships as a form of rural government. Accordingly, we use Township, with a capital T, to refer to a municipality below 500 in population density, regardless of the municipality's legal name. By the same token, townships of the first and second class with densities above 500 will be referred to as Suburbs or Towns, depending upon whether they are in the contiguity band. One additional use of the term will occur. That is where, as is often the case, two municipalities have the same name, but one is a borough and the other a first or second-class township. In such a case, "Twp." will be used to distinguish names, but not to designate a density classification. For example, Hatfield Twp. and Hatfield Boro. are both Suburbs. Where identical place names are used in more than one county, an additional suffix in parenthesis will be used: (B) (C) (D) (M) for Bucks, Chester, Delaware, and Montgomery Counties respectively.

2. The 12 municipalities excluded because of their institutional populations are, in Bucks County: Langhorne Manor; in Chester County: Easttown, East Vincent, Thornbury, Newlin, and Caln; in Delaware County: Middletown, Edgemont, Thornbury, and Chester Heights; and in Montgomery County: West Norriton and Skippack. (See Appendix B.)

3. The coefficient of variability is, however, a fragile measure, particularly when used with values expressed in percentages and where differences in means are great. For example, suppose that we were comparing the central tendency of variable X in sample areas A and B. The mean value of X for A is 30 percent and for B 2 percent. The variable is thus scarcely present in B, but substantial in A. In relationship to the miniscule 2 percent mean there may be great variation in area B and the coefficient of variability would be greater than for A. But this is hardly greater specialization and differentiation by subarea as that concept of variability is employed here.

4. Because the raw percentages are not additive, they were first standardized on the range 0 – 100. The formula used was: $S = x(r - o)$, where S = standard score, x = 100/range of the measure, r = value for the particular municipality, and o = lower limit of the measure. After standardization, the scores for education and occupation were averaged for each unit. Shevky and Bell, *op. cit.*

5. One exception should be noted. The highest sectarian school attendance percentage in the metropolitan area is in Bryn Athyn, a small borough in which many residents are of the Swedenborgian faith.

6. Darby Twp., Chester Twp., and Morton.

7. Yeadon.

III

Fiscal Responses: Method of Analysis

Municipal policy is as difficult to define as it is to measure. A community's commitment to specific goals and objectives may be stated formally in resolutions, ordinances, and local laws, or informally in reputation and understanding. Eventually, the attainment of most objectives necessitates decisions regarding tax rates and disbursements. Indeed, the municipal budget is tantamount to a political constitution, amended occasionally as new functions are added, and constantly reinterpreted through annual allocations of resources among alternative programs. This feature common to all municipalities, their tax and expenditure activities, is our major measure of their operative commitment to specific goals and objectives—in short, their policy choices.

To be sure, financial analysis does not reveal the full extent of municipal activity. One community's commitment to the protection of property values and neighborhood identity through rigid and unyielding land-use controls may be matched by another's equal concern, but relatively inexpensive employment of gentlemen's agreements and social sanctions. Thus, the first limitation of financial analysis is its concentration on measurable and formal municipal activity. For our purposes, however, the mere fact that a community chooses to utilize government for the attainment of some objecives and possibly not for others is significant.

A second consideration that has long plagued inter-municipal financial comparisons is the question of governmental efficiency. Differences in the level of municipal expenditures may be the result of many factors including the range of services, their quality, and the efficiency of municipal administration. Increases in the quality and range of services usually result in higher expenditures. Efficiency acts in a countering direction. However, a study of expenditures in metropolitan St. Louis found that increases in expenditures were likely to indicate increases in service quality, with efficiency having only a secondary effect.[1] This study assumes that when one municipality spends more than another, it has chosen to seek more or higher quality services. Whether the search is indeed rewarded with better services is irrelevant to our research purposes.

Our concern is less with the effectiveness or efficiency of municipalities than with their decisions to undertake activities and with the alternative purposes for which municipal resources will be put to use. Even if one community receives more services per dollar than another, the fact that one or the other chooses to spend more for the service is a reflection of the value it places on the service rendered. Looked at another way, if a municipality spends a great deal for its public schools it may be because: (1) It views education of its children of sufficient importance to warrant maximum or even over-extended use of its resources. (2). It has sufficient resources to be relatively unconcerned with the cost of devoting large amounts to public education. (Implicit also in this reasoning is an assignment of high value to education, for the rich community might just as well have chosen not to spend.)

Conversely, if a municipality spends little for education, it may be because it attributes little value to education or because it is so lacking in resources that it has not the money to spend. (As long as the municipality has not reached its statutory tax limit, there is also implicit in the latter reasoning an assignment of little value to education, for the poor community might conceivably increase expenditures through extraordinary tax effort.)

Obviously, the alternatives suggested for either high-or low-spending communities are the extremes of a continuum of value-judgements ranging from considering solely the importance of education to giving overriding attention to tax rates and economic circumstances. In between lie various combinations of judgements of costs weighted against benefits—in short, judgments of utility. For our purposes, the range represents stages of commitment to the quest for education, and, more specifically, to the expenditure of municipal resources for education. *We hypothesize that levels of expenditure and their distribution among alternative functions of government represent policy choices reflective of community values and that these values are structured by, and correlate with, certain measurable social, economic, and political attributes of a community.*

The phrase "policy choice" does not imply that all decisions reflect a conscious assignment of values to alternative courses of action. If school-age children and the resources to support school programs were uniformly distributed throughout the metropolitan area, differences in educational expenditures might be exclusively attributed to the value assigned education in various municipalities. But needs and resources are not so distributed, and they act almost independently of value structure to limit political choice.

Given the competitive nature of tax rates within a metropolitan area, a poor municipality may find itself unable to increase its school program despite valuing education highly. Raising tax rates may succeed only in reducing the amount of resources currently available. One may contend that concern for competitive position is itself a value-preference. Obviously, values are perceived and measured only in a relative sense. However, one may argue that some policies are more a product of differences in people and others are more a product of differences in physical circumstances. Accordingly, the three chapters that follow view policy as affected by three major sources of influence: *needs, resources* and *preferences.*

Needs are defined as the existence of conditions within a subarea which generate by themselves certain community responses. These conditions are essentially of an objective nature —the composition of the municipality in terms of function, physical make-up, intensity of the uses of space and the size and distribution of its service-demanding population. To a large extent, present policies rest on the course of past community development, a course that cannot be altered for the mature municipality. Needs tend to set upper and lower limits on policies. They supply the "must" and "can't" ingredients of policy decisions.

Resources are viewed as the endowments possessed by a municipality affecting the ease with which it can cope with its problems. Material wealth and the supply of leadership are its prime ingredients. Because of the difficulty of measuring the latter, the real property wealth of municipalities and home owners is used as the measure of resources available to communities.

Preferences are the expression of values concerning a consciously perceived image of how citizens wish to live. Within the limits of its needs and resources, each community has an additional leeway in choosing the emphases to be placed on various governmental services. Such choices are generally a reflection of the values associated with differing life-styles. No demographic variable can measure life-style with any precision.

We shall subsequently contend that social rank and the age of population may be used in specific contexts.

The above classification is introduced as an aid to visualizing the distinct types of characteristics that influence policy choice, "all other things being equal." Although their policy effects will be examined individually, it is their combined influence which is of most interest; for their interaction contributes to community value-structures by stimulating increased municipal differentiation and specialization. Subarea specialization within a metropolitan area fosters differing governmental responses to problems of environmental adaptation. In turn differences in municipal policy encourage further specialization by influencing the locational choices of persons and functions.

Measures of Policy Choice

The fiscal expression of political choice is examined in the following three chapters. Chapter IV deals with the over-all volume of activity in municipal services and the emphases bestowed on various types of services provided by municipal governments. School policy is treated separately in Chapter V. In Chapter VI school and municipal programs are compared and both are viewed in terms of the tax effort and distribution of tax burden expended in their support.

Fiscal data for municipalities and schools were chosen to coincide with the decennial census of 1950 and 1960. The municipal data are for 1950 and 1959, the closest year available when research commenced. School data are for the 1951–52 and 1959–60 school years.[2] Data for the earlier years are used only for the purposes of computing change. In all analysis comparing levels of fiscal activity with other characteristics 1959 or 1960 data were used.

Measures of Municipal Activity. The principal measures of

municipal activity are total revenue, total operating expenditures, revenue per capita and operating expenditures per capita. For the analysis of alternative emphases, operating expenditures are sub-classified into eight functional categories on the basis of dollars spent per capita. Virtually all analysis is confined to operating expenditures per capita and these functional subclassifications.

The use of operating expenditures is intended to avoid distortions in comparisons due to the "lumpy" character of capital expenditures. While it includes payment of interest on debt, it does not record payment on principal, nor does it take into account capital expenditures made from the proceeds of bonds. Thus it represents what may be considered the basic level of services provided annually.

Differences among municipal expenditures of communities are sometimes solely a function of the range of services performed. While a description of variations in services is a primary aim of this study, the inclusion of some services introduces distortion into the analysis. Certain utilities may be either privately or publicly owned. The question of public ownership is interesting and important, but was deemed outside the scope of the study. The magnitude of the expenditures and revenues of the handful of municipally operated electric companies and the several municipal water companies in the area are so large that their inclusion in total municipal fiscal comparisons obliterates all other differences. To discount their effect, revenues and expenditures for these two functions were simply subtracted from the municipality's account.[3]

The procedure for handling utilities was reversed for sewage disposal, a publicly provided service. Some municipalities operate their sewage disposal systems through authorities whose finances are independent of the municipality. Authority expenditures and revenues were assigned to the municipality served. Where authorities served more than one municipality their finances were distributed among them on the basis of estimates supplied by the joint-authority officials.

The total measures, that is, total revenues and total expenditures, are so influenced by community size that little analytical use is made of them. They do indicate the absolute level of financial activity for a year. Total revenue takes account of past capital expenditures by inclusion of funds raised to reduce principal on past debt. Thus the companion measure, revenue per capita, indicates not only present preferences but also responses of the past in the form of debt obligations. This measure was dropped in the course of analysis.

Measures of School Policy. The measures of school policy are: total school revenue, school revenue per pupil, percentage of school revenue from state aid, local school revenue, and local school revenue per pupil. The difference between *total* school revenue and *local* school revenue is, of course, the amount contributed by the State.

School-district organization in Pennsylvania led to some difficulty in aggregating data to fit our unit of analysis—the municipality. All school districts in the area are independent of municipal governments, but most are coterminous with municipal boundaries. However, all school districts do not operate schools. There are many jointure arrangements whereby districts pool resources and students for the joint conduct of elementary schools, junior-, and/or senior-high schools, and sometimes complete educational programs. But the jointures are not self-supporting; they are supported by contributions from member districts based upon formulas negotiated by the participants. Furthermore, state aid is distributed to member districts and not to the jointure itself. Thus school revenues of districts, whether or not participating in jointures, were easily assigned to the municipalities in which they were located.

Union districts present a more difficult problem. Unions are formed by mergers of several districts which lose their separate identity. For the few union districts, revenues were apportioned to municipalities on the basis of market value and pupil ratios.

Despite the problem of data collection that it presented, the pattern of school-district organization simplified analysis by minimizing the effect of differences in size of schools upon costs of education. As intended, jointures and unions produce a not-too-unequal distribution of the number of pupils in each attendance unit.

We chose to measure school activity by revenues rather than expenditures. It simplified data collection, but this was by no means the sole reason. By using revenues, we acquired a sum that, when added to municipal revenues, produced a meaningful total to which tax effort and types of taxes levied could be compared. Furthermore, by using only "revenue receipts" and disregarding miscellaneous sources of income, we obtained a sum more representative of ongoing commitment to education than had we attempted to make adjustments for windfall receipts (such as property sales) and expenditures, and for borrowing when it did occur. Adjustments for tuition payments were also simplified by using revenues rather than expenditures. Finally, "revenue receipts" came closest to, and correlated best with, that amount of school expenditures devoted solely to instruction.

We did not use instructional expenditures alone, because we did not wish to involve ourselves in the discussion of what are frills or non-frills. Our concern was solely with the degree to which communities desire to invest in education, not with the purposes of that investment. For the most part, the school revenues were uniformly in proportion to both total revenues and expenditures. What variations did occur helped eliminate ambiguities in the analysis. We must emphasize, however, that the school revenues used in this study are of our own construction and *do not* compare directly with any compilation of school statistics. While the measure employed is that of revenues, in the discussion, we shall use the terms "school revenues" and "expenditures" interchangeably. It is the level of activity that is our concern, not revenues or expenditures. It is easier to describe activity as spending even though it is measured by revenues.

The market value of real property per student, a variable that is usually employed in analysis of school finance, is conspicuous by its absence in this study. Our decision not to use it for general purposes of correlation, but only for selected comparisons, is based on the fact that the measure is merely a composite of two municipal characteristics—wealth and pupil population—and does not in itself convey a meaningful image of a community. We doubt if a poor community considers itself any richer for the absence of children. True, the ratio of pupils to community wealth will affect the capacity to spend for education, but this is the result of the interaction of needs and resources, a process that is obscured in the measure "market value per pupil."

Measures of Tax Effort. Four measures were used to express tax effort or burden and the distribution of tax burden within municipalities. Two are in general use, two were designed for our data. The first, property tax collections as a percentage of total tax collections is an indication of the distribution of burden between property owners and other taxpayers. The second, tax collections as a millage of market value of property is a gross indication of tax effort. The third measure is the effective tax rate on residential property. It differs from the usual equalizations of real property tax rates since it is calculated on the basis of residential market value ratios alone.

The fourth measure will be described in greater length subsequently. Briefly, it attempts to consider taxes in relation to the marginal utility of personal wealth. It was derived from the ratio of residential tax rate to average household market value and is hereafter referred to as the *householder burden index*.

Statistical Methods

The statistical techniques used in this study are standard procedures that will be familiar to those with even modest training in this subject. They range from the simple tools of ranking and scatter diagramming to the more complex processes of multiple regression. While we do not wish to insult, bore, or confuse the reader, the following section on statistical methods may hopefully be of use to persons of varying acquaintance with statistics. To those who know statistics well, or not at all, a brief scanning is recommended. For the former, this will be sufficient to identify the methods used; for the latter additional effort may only contribute to a sense of frustration. For the person who is just rusty on the subject, the following few pages may deserve careful reading.

The Matrix of Simple Correlations. The preliminary procedure for identifying the degree of association between fiscal measures and municipal characteristics was the development of a simple correlation matrix composed of seventy two variables. (Appendix C lists all the variables employed in the study). Each of the seventy two variables were correlated with one another for the Suburbs, Towns, and Townships, and for the total four-county area. (The City of Philadelphia was excluded from all correlations). The simple correlations identified relationships deemed sufficiently significant to warrant further analysis through the application of additional statistical techniques.

The results of the correlations for the total area were of little use. Correlating the characteristics and responses of all 225 municipalities served primarily to highlight differences in urban and semi-urban behavior, differences that were evident during data collection and that led to the initial establishment of the Suburban, Town and Township classifications. Accordingly, the correlation analyses concentrate on variations within the three groups referring only occasionally and for purposes of illustration to the findings for the entire area.

Partial Correlations. Correlation analysis summarizes the relationship between two sets of variables where one is assumed to be dependent upon the other. The correlation coefficient indicates the degree to which variations in one variable are associated with variations in another variable for a given population—in this study, a group of municipalities. Apart from the theoretical question of the causality that can be inferred from correlation analysis, in no case can an independent variable in, and of itself, be considered determinative. Its association with a dependent variable suggests a relationship that can be accepted with more or less assurance as additional evidence is brought to bear on their association. Even were a perfect 1.0 correlation found between density and expenditures, for example, one would not be justified in asserting that increases in density (the independent variable) cause increases in expenditures (the dependent variable). It may well be that density is itself related to another independent variable, perhaps wealth, which is more responsible for inducing differences in expenditures. The correlation matrix indicated the association of independent variables with one another as well as with the dependent variables, suggesting a basis for distinguishing between factors affecting expenditures independently and those that were a reflection of the intervening influence of some other independent variable.

One method of testing for the independent influence of density is to hold constant for the factor suspected of intervening between the two. Controlling for wealth requires the grouping of all municipalities with identical wealth and then observing whether within classes of wealth, variations in density continue to be associated with variations in expenditures. This procedure was employed at several points in the analysis.

Holding constant is possible only when a large number of cases is being examined, especially if more than one variable is suspected of having intervening influence. With a small number of cases it would be difficult to find enough municipalities in a given wealth class to calculate meaningful correlations of density and expenditures.

Partial correlation is a statistical tool that approximates the effect of holding constant for intervening variables. It relates the coefficients obtained from correlating two or more independent variables with a dependent variable and with one another. In the example here used, the partial correlation coefficient is, in effect, the weighted average of the coefficients of correlation of density and expenditures that would have been obtained had they been calculated for the small number of cases in each class of wealth. The simple or zero-order correlation is a measure of the association of two variables. As additional variables are introduced for control, the order of the correlation is increased by their number. Thus a first order partial has one control, a second-order two.

Multiple Regression and Correlation. The calculation of partial correlations beyond the second-order is extremely difficult and time-consuming. Multiple regression and correlation simplifies the measurement of the association between two variables controlling for a large number of intervening variables. This technique summarizes the combined influence of a number of independent variables and in addition indicates the relative influence of each. The square of the coefficient of multiple correlation (R^2) is the coefficient of multiple determination and is interpreted as the percentage of the variation in a dependent variable that can be attributed to or "explained" by variations in two or more independent variables.

Multiple regression is essentially a technique .for prediction While correlations of any order show the direction and significance of the variation in one variable in relation to another, they do not measure its size. A perfect correlation of density and expenditures may suggest that every increase in density is accompanied by an increase in expenditures, but it does not indicate the size of the expenditure increase that may be expected from any given change in density. This regression analysis does.

Regression builds on the formula for a straight line $Y = a + bx$, where Y symbolizes the value of the dependent variable, X the independent variable and a is constant. The beta coefficient (b) is the amount of increase (decrease if its sign is negative) that accompanies a one-unit increase in X. Multiple regression extends the formula to $Y = a + bx_1 + bx_2 + \ldots bx_n$. Each of the beta coefficients represents the amount of change in the dependent variable associated with a change in one of the independent variables controlling for the effect of all the others. The beta coefficient is then very similar to the partial correlation coefficient. However, the size of the betas is affected by differences in the scales of the independent variables. Some of our measures are expressed as percentages and have a maximum possible range of 0-100. Others are monetary values with ranges in the thousands. The beta coefficients are not directly comparable until they are standardized for differences in the size and range of the independent variables. This is accomplished by expressing each coefficient in terms of the standard deviation of the variable it represents, producing a weighted beta (B). A hypothetical regression for the example being used might be:

$$Y \text{ (Expenditures)} = a \text{ (constant)} + .825\ X_1 \text{ (density)} + .514\ X_2 \text{ (wealth)}$$

Controlling for the effect of wealth, for each increase of one standard deviation in density, expenditures would increase by .825 of a standard deviation. For each increase of one standard deviation in wealth, controlling for the effect of changes in density, expenditures would increase by .514 of a standard deviation. Density has the greater effect on expenditures.

Beta weights and partial correlation coefficients are similar but somewhat different measures of association. Although their magnitudes differ, they will usually rank variables in the same order of importance. The beta weight has one additional property that led to its use even when partial correlations had previously been calculated. The square of the beta weight (B^2) represents the direct contribution of one variable to the coefficient of multiple determination, that is, the percentage of variation in the dependent variable accounted for by variations in the independent variable. The sum of the direct contributions of the independent variables plus their combined indirect effect is equal to the coefficient of multiple determination. If the R^2 for expenditures correlated with density and wealth had been .967, the relationship of the three factors might be summarized as follows:

Table III–1

Percentage of Variation in Expenditures Accounted
For by Density and Wealth

	B	B^2 Percentage Variation
Density	.825	68.0
Wealth	.514	26.4
Combined Indirect Effect		2.3
R^2 – Total Variation Explained		96.7

Here is a summary of the statistical techniques employed in the study. A simple correlation matrix was first computed. After inspection, significant relationships were further tested by holding constant for the effects of suspected intervening variables and by calculating partial correlations. Multiple regression and correlation were used to determine the combined effect and relative importance of a number of variables. The last procedure utilized beta weights for measurement of degrees of association, but not for prediction.

The symbols that will appear in the Chapters that follow illustrated by the example used throughout this section are:

r expenditures—density

The Pearsonion product-moment coefficient of correlation of density and expenditures.

r^2 expenditures—density

The coefficient of determination, the percentage of variation in expenditures "explained" by variations in density.

r_s expenditures—density

The Spearman rank-order coefficient of correlation of expenditures and density.

r expenditures—density; $k =$ wealth

The coefficient of correlation of expenditures and density controlling for the effect of variations in wealth. The symbol k indicates the independent variable under control.

R^2 expenditures—density and wealth

The coefficient of multiple determination, the percentage of variation in expenditures, "explained" by variations in both density and wealth.

B density

The weighted beta coefficient of density—the change in standard deviations of expenditures that will accompany a one-standard deviation change in density, controlling for changes in all other variables in the regression equation.

B^2 density

The percentage direct contribution to the coefficient of
multiple determination that
is accounted for by density.

The question of the statistical and interpretive significance of the
coefficients will be treated as they are reported. Unless otherwise
indicated each calculation was performed four times for a constant
number of cases—90 Suburbs, 41 Towns, 94 Townships, and 225
municipalities for the total area.

NOTES

1. John C. Bollens (ed.), *Exploring the Metropolis* (Berkeley:
University of California Press, 1961), Chapter 14.
2. The Penn Jersey Transportation Study supplied 1950 municipal
and 1951–52 school data which were derived from reports on file
with the Pennsylvania departments of Internal Affairs and Public Instruction. Municipal data for 1959 were taken from *Local Government
Financial Statistics, 1959* (Harrisburg: Bureau of Municipal Affairs,
Department of Internal Affairs, 1960). School data for 1959–60 are
from individual school district reports on file with the Department of
Public Instruction.
3. At best, this procedure resulted in a close approximation since
service profits and losses from utility enterprises could not be fully
isolated for a single year.

IV

Fiscal Responses: Municipal Programs

What factors explain differences in municipal expenditures? Do municipalities spend in relation to the abundance of their taxable resources, or do they spend because of the particular requirements of their physical environments? Are some types of citizens "more expensive" than others in that they demand more and better services? These are some of the questions that guide the following analysis of municipal operating expenditures.

Total Operating Expenditures

Total operating expenditures portray the recurring volume of business conducted by a municipality. Substantial amounts of activity are to be expected in large jurisdictions, for variations in total expenditures are primarily related to differences in population size. The coefficients of correlation of total operating expenditures and population are: Suburbs .909, Towns .945, and Townships .834. The correlations of expenditures and total market value of real property are of a similar order, for the latter is closely related to population size.

In Table IV–1 population and total market value are correlated with both total operating expenditures and total revenues. The use of total revenue yields even higher coefficients, for it is a more inclusive measure of the volume of municipal activity, comprising funds raised in support of both operating and capital outlays. The differences in the expenditure and revenue coefficients point to divergencies in the distribution of operating and capital expenditures. Regardless of the measure employed, however, the relationship is obvious—the larger the municipality the more it spends.

Table IV–1

Coefficients of Correlation: Total Operating Expenditures, Total Revenue and Population and Total Market Value

	SUBURBS		TOWNS		TOWNSHIPS	
	Op. Exp.	Revenue	Op. Exp.	Revenue	Op. Exp.	Revenue
Total Market Value	.869	.953	.910	.946	.873	.936
Population	.909	.935	.945	.971	.834	.918

Operating Expenditures Per Capita

The impact of municipal size is so great that variations in total operating expenditures cannot be related to other municipal characteristics. By using a per capita measure, size is somewhat controlled, enabling the influence of other factors to be measured. Table IV–2 summarizes the central tendencies for operating expenditures per capita in the three study groups—Suburbs, Towns, and Townships.

Table IV–2

Operating Expenditures per Capita, Central Tendency by Study Area

	Mean	S	V	Range
Suburbs	$23.40	$11.75	.502	$84.16–6.29
Towns	21.30	11.42	.536	47.26–6.10
Townships	9.08	4.03	.444	19.33–2.31
Philadelphia	98.84			

The need for sub-classifying municipalities that was suggested in Chapter II is here demonstrated by the extreme difference in the average expenditure of the Suburbs and Towns on the one hand, and the virtually rural Townships on the other. Indeed, the classification itself is a gross method of controlling for density within the extremely large classes of under°and above 500 persons per square mile. There is a critical point of development that distinguishes the urban from the rural environment. Yet within the framework of similar physical environments municipal expenditures continue to differ significantly, as suggested by the relatively high coefficients of variability for each of the groupings.

Expenditures per capita were correlated with each of the other seventy-one variables in the correlation matrix. Table IV–3 lists those variables that appear to be most related to expenditure variations as well as some that were suspected of being so related regardless of their coefficients. Suburban, Town, and Township expenditures appear to be influenced by different sets of independent variables.

Table IV–3

Coefficients of Correlation: Operating
Expenditures per Capita and Selected Variables*

	Suburbs	Towns	Townships
Market Value per Capita	.553	.268	.297
% Industrial and Commercial	.544	.348	.010
% Residential	−.515	−.270	−.401
% Single-family D. U.'s	−.432	−.464	.372
% Young Adults	−.405	−.433	−.092
Social Rank	.113	.035	.319
Density	.151	.481	−.093
Population	.114	.440	.047
Residential Value per Household	−.012	.040	.124

* Coefficients significant at .05 level are underlined.

The factors most associated with variations in expenditures are: for the Suburbs—municipal wealth, land-use composition, and age of the adult population (percent young adults refers to the percentage of persons 21 and over who are 25 to 34 years of age); for the Townships—municipal wealth, social rank and the amount of residential development; for the Towns —population size, density (and the closely related single-family dwelling measure, the percentage of dwelling units which are in single family structures), and age of the adult population. Some of the most important variables are obviously related to each other. Some, which yield low or even insignificant coefficients of correlation, cannot yet be dismissed; for their relevance may be obscured by intervening variables operating in opposite directions; or they may be of importance for selective Suburbs, Towns, or Townships but not for the classifications as a whole. Final judgment must await the introduction of some controls and further refinement of the classifications.

SUBURBAN EXPENDITURES

As Chapter II amply demonstrates there is no suburban prototype. Economic function, wealth, and social characteristics are mixed in diverse fashion. Nevertheless, there are some Suburban characteristics that are somewhat consistently related to one another. The interrelationship of Suburban independent variables is summarized in Table IV–4.

The two variables most associated with Suburban expenditure variations are market value per capita and the percentage of real property assessments in industrial and commercial use, the former a measure of municipal wealth, the latter of economic function. The matrix shows them to be related to one another as well as to most of the remaining independent variables. Con-

Table IV–4—Suburbs

Matrix of Correlation Coefficients of Independent Variables

	Market Value Per Capita	% Ind. & Com.	% Residential	% Single-family D.U.'s	% Young Adults	Density	Population	Social Rank
Residential value per HH	.376	-.360	.295	.555	-.153	-.439	.163	.845
Social Rank	.286	-.329	.374	.454	-.314	-.201	-.148	
Population	-.021	-.031	.057	.009	.006	.160		
Density	-.366	-.003	.145	-.688	-.538			
% Young Adults	-.274	-.046	.022	.183				
% Single-family D.U.'s	.078	-.393	.285					
% Residential	-.627	-.957						
% Ind. & Com.	.584							

trolling for market value per capita and percent industrial and commercial will permit closer examination of the independent influence of other variables.

Table IV–5 reports the partial correlations obtained for all variables controlling first for market value per capita, then for percent industrial and commercial and, finally, for both these variables. When an independent variable has a larger partial than simple correlation, this indicates a closer relationship for groups of municipalities as measured by the constant than for the Suburbs as a whole. Thus, the increase of the density coefficient from a .151 simple to a .454 partial with market value per capita controlled, suggests that there are a number of sparsely populated wealthy communities that spend more than densely populated poor communities, but that for Suburbs of similar wealth, increases in density are related to expenditure increases.

Table IV–5—Suburbs

Coefficients of Partial Correlation: Operating Expenditures
per Capita and Selected Variables Controlling for
Market Value per Capita and Percent Industrial and Commercial*

	Simple Coefficients	1st Order Partials k=MV/CAP.	1st Order Partials k=I & C	2nd Order Partials k=MV/CAP. I & C
Market value per capita	_.553_		_.345_	
% Ind. & Com.	_.544_	_.327_		
% Residential	_-.515_	_-.259_	.024	
% Single-family D.U.'s	_-.432_	_-.572_	_-.284_	_-.498_
% Young Adults	_-.405_	_-.316_	_-.453_	_-.287_
Density	.151	_.454_	.178	_.400_
Population	.114	.151	.156	.166
Social Rank	.113	.056	_.367_	.134
Residential Value per HH	-.012	_-.284_	_.234_	.242

* Coefficients significant at .05 level are underlined.

When an independent variable's partial coefficient is smaller than the simple, part or all of the variation in the independent variable is related to the factor under control. It would appear from the diminution of the coefficient for percent assessed value in residential use when industrial and commercial use is controlled, that the former is approximately the reciprocal of the latter.

Controlling only for market value, expenditures increase with increasing density and decreasing personal wealth (measured by household market value) and decreasing percentages of single-family dwelling units. To reverse the statement, the pattern suggests that low municipal expenditures are associated with the stereotyped, upper middle-class dormitory suburbs. However, this pattern may merely reflect the higher costs of servicing industry and commerce and the fact that these land-uses concentrate in areas of high density, low-priced, multiple-family dwellings. This surmise is verified to some extent. Controlling for industry and commerce alone, density and the percentage of single-family dwellings appear to exert little independent influence on expenditures. Indeed, variations in density appear to be sufficiently related to the land-use complexion that this first-order partial for density is no longer statistically significant. However, the partial coefficient for household market value has changed its sign, indicating that in functionally similar communities (industrial, residential etc.) higher expenditures are associated with higher-priced homes and wealthier individuals. Controlling for both municipal wealth and functional land-use allocations, density and the character of housing are meaningfully related to levels of municipal expenditure.

Several additional variables also appear to be related to expenditure policy when either or both municipal wealth and land-use allocation are controlled. Although the percentage of adults in the 25–34 year age bracket is related to the two control variables, there continues to be a tendency for expenditures to decline in those municipalities where young adults comprise a large proporation of the population. Social rank is also of interest. When land use alone is controlled, social rank is significant, although part or most of its influence may be related to market value per capita.

Two additional findings warrant emphasis at this time. Expenditures per capita are in no way related to population size for the Suburbs as a whole. Hypotheses about the effect of scale are given no support. Secondly, despite the interrelation of market value per capita and industrial and commercial land-use, they are independently related to expenditures. Expenditures rise with increases in municipal wealth regardless of whether residential or non-residential properties are the major tax resource. It is by no means obvious, however, that municipal expenditures are simply a matter of "those that have spend." Communities with large industrial and commercial holdings tend toward higher expenditures regardless of whether they are rich or poor. This relationship, too, is subject to more than one interpretation and will be discussed at greater length subsequently.

The partial correlations just considered demonstrate the relevance of several variables that appeared to be unimportant prior to controlling for market value per capita and percent assessed value in industrial and commercial use. The controls assumed that the latter two variables were the most determinative of variations in expenditures and were masking the possible influence of others. The procedure did not, however, suggest what influence the other variables had on the controls. Multiple correlation and regression summarizes the relationship of all the independent variables to expenditures per capita and to each other, answering, in effect, the question of the relative importance of each of the independent variables.

A multiple correlation was computed using five independent variables: market value per capita, percent industrial and commercial, social rank, density, and perecent young adults. The resulting coefficient of multiple determination (R^2) is .573 signifying that 57.3 percent of the variation in municipal expenditures can be attributed to variations in the five independent variables. The Beta weights listed in Table IV–6 suggest the change in standard deviations of expenditures that will accompany a standard deviation change in each of the factors, controlling for the effects of changes in all the others. The Beta squared represents the percentage of the total variation in expenditures accounted for by variations in each of the independent variables, or, in other words, the relative size of their independent contributions to the coefficient of multiple determination.

Table IV–6—Suburbs

Percentage of Variation in Operating Expenditures per
Capita Accounted for by Selected Variables

	B	Percent Direct Contribution to Total Variation (B^2)
Percent Ind. & Com.	.560	31.4%
Density	.274	7.5
Social Rank	.237	5.6
Percent Young Adults	−.235	5.5
Market Value per Capita	.152	2.3
Total Direct Contribution		52.3%
Combined Indirect Effects		5.0
Total Variation Explained (R^2)		57.3%

More than 31 percent of the variation in Suburban expenditures is attributable to the degree of industrial and commercial activity. The other four factors account for the smaller percentages indicated. The five variables account for more than 52 percent of the total expenditure variation with an additional five percent attributable to their combined indirect effect.

The most surprising result of this analysis is the fate of market value per capita. It now apears that the factor may "borrow" its effect from other municipal characteristics to which it is related, and that local decisions to spend are not simply a function of ability to pay. Expenditures are, instead, associated with particular kinds of wealth in particular kinds of municipalities.

Since the functional specialization of Suburbs affects their expenditures so greatly, a map of expenditure patterns reflects, in part, the geographic distribution of specialized economic activities (see Map V). The highest expenditure levels are in the industrial communities, a number of which are along the

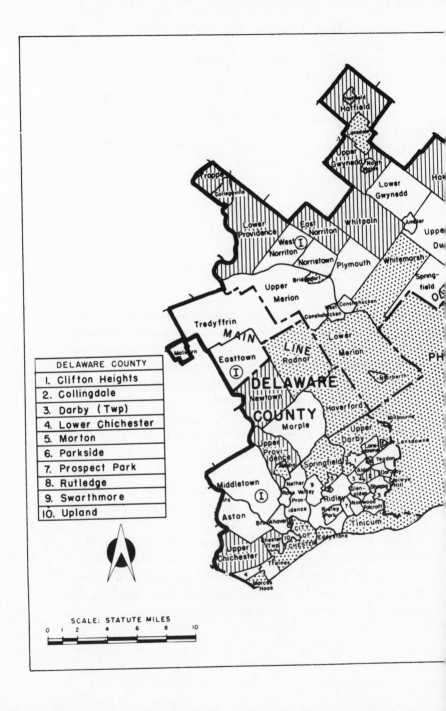

DELAWARE COUNTY

1. Clifton Heights
2. Collingdale
3. Darby (Twp)
4. Lower Chichester
5. Morton
6. Parkside
7. Prospect Park
8. Rutledge
9. Swarthmore
10. Upland

SCALE: STATUTE MILES

0   1   2   4   6   8   10

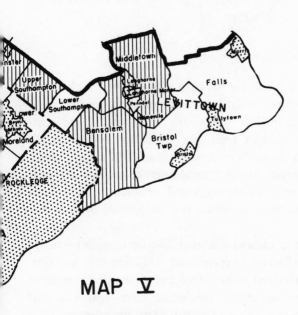

MAP V

SUBURBS

MUNICIPAL EXPENDITURES
PER CAPITA, 1960

HIGHEST	QUARTILE	($98.18 — $28.75)
MIDDLE	QUARTILES	($28.75 — $16.70)
LOWEST	QUARTILE	(#16.70 — #6.29)

river at the lower boundary of the study area. Other high levels of expenditure are in the higher social rank residential suburbs —at least those which are well developed. The more sparsely populated fringe areas have lower expenditure levels regardless of social rank. These patterns suggest the need for a more refined grouping of Suburbs.

A Suburban Land-Use Typology

Non-residential land use has been identified as the characteristic most associated with Suburban municipal expenditures. Moreover, municipalities specializing in industrial and commercial activity spend a great deal regardless of their wealth or other characteristics. We suspect that specialization in industrial and commercial activity generates service needs so compelling that differences in resources and preferences have but a slight impact on the expenditure policies pursued by such municipalities.

What of the residential Suburbs? The Beta weights indicate other factors influencing expenditures, although they are overshadowed by the effect of industrial and commercial specialization. Therefore, separating residential from non-residential Suburbs will permit closer examination of the selective influence of other characteristics. Rather than adhering to quartile or other arbitrary groupings, every effort will be made to type Suburbs according to those physical characteristics most meaningfully distinguishing them.

The most obvious distinction between Suburbs centers around their degree of industrial and commercial activity. Experimentation with a number of groupings indicates that when industrial and commercial assessments exceed one-third of total assessments a distinct set of policy responses can be identified. There are nineteen Suburbs evidencing this degree of industrial and commercial specialization. They are typed *Industrial and Commercial Centers*.

The remaining Suburbs either specialize in residences or are balanced in the ratio of their residential and non-residential activity. Although notice will be taken of differences in expenditures associated with their varying degrees of non-residential activity, they are all considered basically residential. The Beta weights suggest that density is an important determinant of expenditure variations in residential Suburbs. Accordingly *High-density* and *Low-density Residential Suburbs* are separated. One group appears to be sufficiently distinguished from the other non-industrial and commercial Suburbs to warrant a fourth classification. These are eleven densely populated, older boroughs incorporated years ago to set them apart from their rural surroundings, but recently engulfed by urban expansion. Each has become a Suburb only since 1940; most contain balanced amounts of residential and non-residential activity, and all appear to have been less affected by the growth of the urban area than their neighboring Suburbs, having retained most of their pre-Suburban characteristics. They are designated *Enclaves*. (see Map VI).

The line of demarcation between High- and Low-density residential suburbs is 2,000 persons per square mile. Densities above this level would be achieved in a fully developed municipality having average amounts of land in public and non-residential uses, with residential construction on lots of one acre or less. Densities below 2,000 represent either a municipality developed on large, residential lots or the presence of large, undeveloped areas.[1] There were 35 High-density and 24 Low-density Residential Suburbs.[2]

Table IV–7 summarizes the characteristics of each of the

DELAWARE COUNTY
1. Clifton Heights
2. Collingdale
3. Darby (Twp)
4. Lower Chichester
5. Morton
6. Parkside
7. Prospect Park
8. Rutledge
9. Swarthmore
10. Upland

SCALE: STATUTE MILES

0 1 2   4   6   8   10

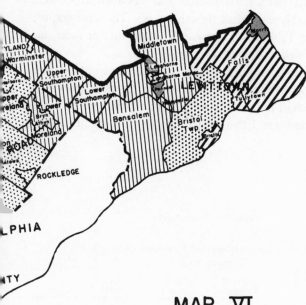

MAP VI

SUBURBS

[high density dots] : HIGH DENSITY RESIDENTIAL

[low density lines] : LOW DENSITY RESIDENTIAL

[diagonal hatch] : INDUSTRIAL AND COMMERCIAL

[fine dots] : ENCLAVES

four Suburban types. Industrial and Commercial Centers are clearly distinguished by their low social rank and their combination of the highest average municipal wealth with the lowest average personal wealth. Industrial and Commercial Centers spend considerably more than the other types. The semi-graphic presentation in Table IV–9 shows this to be true for most, individually, as well as for the average.

The variables previously correlated with expenditures per capita for all 90 Suburbs have been retested by rank-order correlation for each of the Suburban types. The coefficients of rank-order correlation are listed, where statistically significant in Table IV–8.

Table IV–7—Suburbs

Mean Values of Selected Characteristics by
Type of Suburb

	Industrial & Commercial Centers N = 19	High-density Residential N = 35	Low-density Residential N = 24	Enclaves N = 11
Social Rank	18.8	32.7	42.6	26.0
Market Value/capita	$5,507	$ 3,628	$ 4,465	$3,149
Residential Value/HH	$5,331	$10,458	$13,100	$8,764
% Ind. and Com.	60.6	13.1	12.9	19.8
Density, Persons/Sq. Mi.	5,139	7,192	1,087	3,366
% Young Adults	22.0	21.1	24.1	21.0
Population	12,058	17,956	11,067	2,857
Operating Expenditures/Capita	$34.63	$23.16	$18.39	$17.06

Table IV–8—Suburbs*

Rank Order Correlations: Operating Expenditures per Capita
and Selected Variables by Type of Suburb

	Industrial & Commercial Centers N = 19	High-density Residential N = 35	Low-density Residential N = 24	Enclaves N = 11
Social Rank	——	.770	.396	——
Market Value/capita	——	.687	.453	.600
Residential Value/HH	——	.518	.625	——
% Ind. and Com.	.430	.470	——	——
Density	——	——	——	——
% Young Adults	-.633	-.530	-.652	——
Population	——	——	——	.782

* Correlations underlined are significant at the 1 percent level, others at the 5 percent level.

Industrial and Commercial Centers. Although Industrial and Commercial Centers spend more than Enclaves or Residential Suburbs, the variation within this type is across a wide spectrum. Millbourne, the highest spender, is essentially a small cluster of houses huddled around a large Sears and Roebuck store located at a major transportation intersection on Philadelphia's western boundary. Upper Gwynedd, located on the outer edge of the urban area, spends the least. Tiny Millbourne has the highest density of the Centers and has been urbanized for many decades. Upper Gwynedd, a sprawling municipality, has just experienced enough population growth to qualify for inclusion in the suburban ring.

Municipal Density and Age. There is no correlation between expenditures and density in Industrial and Commercial Centers. However, for this type of Suburb, density is less a charac-

IV-9—Suburbs

Operating Expenditures per Capita
by Type of Suburb

Industrial & Commercial N=19		High-density Residential N=35		Low-density Residential N=24		Enclaves N=11	
Millbourne	$84.16	Lower Merion	$45.24				
Marcus Hook	52.72						
Lansdale	46.71						
Tinicum	45.17			Radnor	$40.31		
Jenkintown	45.09			Bryn Athyn	39.29		
Tullytown	41.84	Media	39.33				
Eddystone	41.00	Hatboro	34.74				
		Narberth	33.95	Whitemarsh	31.15	Morrisville	$30.05
Chester	33.23						
Bristol (Boro)	32.35						
		Cheltenham	30.30				
Bridgeport	29.62	Upper Darby	29.48				
		Haverford	28.91				
Norristown	28.22	Springfield (D)	28.75				
Trainer	27.98	Swarthmore	27.46				
Upper Merion	27.72	Yeadon	27.19			Ambler	25.40
Conshohocken	25.31	Abington	25.09	Rose Valley	24.94	Malvern	24.02
Sharon Hill	24.20			Lower Moreland	23.98		

Name	Value	Name	Value	Name	Value	Name	Value
Falls	20.39	E. Lansdowne	22.03	Upper Dublin	22.57	*SUBURBAN MEDIAN*	20.35
SUBURBAN MEDIAN	20.35	Prospect Park	21.39	Tredyffrin	20.94	North Wales	20.30
		Springfield (M)	21.33	*SUBURBAN MEDIAN*	20.35	Penndel	17.73
		Morton	21.17	Plymouth	20.22		
		Clifton Heights	20.93	Lower Southampton	17.52		
		Rutledge	20.82	Lower Gwynedd	17.20		
		Norwood	20.79	Aston	17.20		
		Upper Moreland	20.63	Marple	17.07		
		Ridley Park	20.46				
		SUBURBAN MEDIAN	20.35				
		Nether Providence	20.28				
		Lansdowne	20.15				
		Aldan	19.80				
		Glenolden	19.73				
		Folcroft	19.49				
		Ridley (Twp.)	19.45				
		Darby (Boro)	18.18				
		Bristol (Twp.)	18.10				
West Conshohocken	18.18						
Lower Chichester	17.39	Colwyn	16.95				

Upper Gwynedd	15.68		
	Brookhaven	16.88	Newtown (D)	16.41	Hatfield (Boro)	15.30

Upper Gwynedd | 15.68

Brookhaven | 16.88
Darby (Twp.) | 16.85
Rockledge | 15.87
Collingdale | 15.61
Parkside | 14.98
Chester (Twp.) | 13.52

Newtown (D) | 16.41
Horsham | 16.17
Upper
   Southampton | 15.09
Bensalem | 14.81
Whitpain | 14.15
Middletown (B) | 14.03
Upper
   Providence (D) | 13.18
Warminster | 12.43
Upper Chichester | 11.00
Hatfield (Twp.) | 7.97
East Norriton | 6.89
Lower
   Providence | 6.29

Hatfield (Boro) | 15.30
Trappe | 12.42
Langhorne | 11.96
Ivyland | 10.66
Hulmeville | 10.21
Collegeville | 9.66

terization of the life-style of residents than an indication of the size and nature of industrial and commercial installations. Low density Centers are generally those recently developed where housing and economic activities are physically separated and where non-residential structures are of more recent design and construction. These Centers are not faced with the high costs of plant deterioration and integrating residential and non-residential land-uses. For the most part, their large, newer-design industrial and commercial installations are less dependent upon municipal services than those in older, more densely developed Centers.

While there is no correlation between density, as such, and expenditures in Industrial and Commercial Centers, insofar as density is related to the character and age of industrial and commercial development (not necessarily the age of the community), the newer, less densely developed Centers spend less than older Suburbs similarly specializing.

Increasing Industrialism and Commercialism. Although the very basis for selecting this type is industrial and commercial specialization, expenditure variations continue to be affected by variations in the degree to which properties are devoted to residential and non-residential uses. The Centers with the greatest industrial and commercial activity have the highest expenditures, regardless of their market value per capita. Are industrial and commercial uses a cost factor, or do such uses merely prompt residents to take advantage of additional services that can be provided out of taxes borne disproportionately by industrial and commercial installations?

If the latter hypothesis were true one would expect wealth to act as a stimulant to higher expenditures as well. But expenditure levels are not at all related to levels of tax resources. Additional evidence that industrial and commercial uses are themselves a cost factor is presented in Table IV–10 where the distribution of expenditures by function is contrasted for the four types of Suburban municipalities.

Industrial and Commercial Centers spend more than the other types of Suburbs for each function, with the exception of planning, libraries, and refuse disposal. In the next chapter, school expenditures will also be seen to be lower for the Centers. Thus, for the Industrial and Commercial Centers, services which relate to residential amenities and to home and school environment receive somewhat less emphasis than the industrial and commercial property servicing functions, such as servicing of streets, and fire and police protection.

Young Adults. The characteristic most related to expenditure variations in Industrial and Commercial Centers is the percentage of adults in the 25–34 year age bracket. As the percentage of young adults increases municipal expenditures decrease ($r_s = -.633$). Table IV–8 points to a similar relationship in the Residential Suburbs.

Table IV–10—Suburbs

Mean Expenditure per Capita by Function by Type of Suburb

Function	Industrial & Commercial N = 19	High-density Residential N = 35	Low-density Residential N = 24	Enclaves N = 11
General Government	$ 4.61	$ 2.72	$ 2.48	$ 2.86
Libraries	.21	.30	.13	.07
Park and Recreation	1.30	.78	.33	.20
Police	9.51	5.68	5.29	4.69
Fire	2.22	1.16	.89	.76
Streets	5.08	3.10	3.49	3.52
Street Lights	1.97	1.38	.73	1.41
Planning	.29	.26	.47	.03
Sewer	4.33	2.98	2.01	1.16
Refuse Disposal	2.16	2.57	1.15	1.49
Interest	.82	.48	.21	.30
Total*	34.63	23.16	18.39	17.06

*Not a summary of enumerated items. Also includes miscellaneous expenditures.

It was originally hypothesized that young adults would favor low expenditures, during this stage of their lives when maximum earning capacities have not been reached and household expenditures claim a large share of their budgets. But the hypothesis cannot yet be considered verified in the Industrial and Commercial Centers, despite the high negative correlation of expenditures and young adults. Several of the lesser-spending Centers that have large concentrations of young adults (Upper Merion, Sharon Hill, Falls and Lower Chichester), also contain newer industrial and commercial facilities which are less costly to service than those in older places. Nevertheless, the correlation coefficient is large enough to suggest that, despite this coincidence of factors, the influence of the young adult population is to depress expenditures in Industrial and Commercial Centers.

In summary, expenditures in Industrial and Commercial Centers primarily reflect a response to the service needs of the economic activities that concentrate in this type of Suburb. The intensity of need is probably affected by the age, amount, and physical characteristics of the industrial and commercial installations. Service needs are rarely ignored, regardless of the municipal resources available. Population characteristics appear to have little influence on expenditures, except for the possible tendency of municipalities with large proportions of young adults to favor lower levels of public spending.

Residential Suburbs. The mean per capita expenditure of High-density Residential Suburbs is $23.16, Low-density $18.39. Low-density communities spend less for each function except planning. This emphasis seems perfectly consistent for areas with large amounts of undeveloped land. Many of the differences in expenditures are related to the physical differences of high- and low-density development. Low sewage disposal costs, small outlays for streets and street lighting, little attention to parks and recreation, all reflect the low-density environment's ability to escape the higher social costs of congestion, or to defer assumption of public responsibility for existing social costs.

In the High-density Residential Suburbs municipal expenditures range from a high of $45.24 in Lower Merion, to a low of $13.52 in Chester Twp. Lower Merion is the first Suburb adjacent to Philadelphia on the fashionable Main Line. It has been a dormitory for Philadelphia since the early days of railroad commutation, retaining a prestigous reputation despite a little dowdiness in a few older sections. It has been for many decades a pioneer among Suburbs in furnishing a full complement of "new," quality urban services. Chester Twp., at the other extreme, lies on the fringes of industrial Chester City. Its population is largely Negro. It has the lowest social rank and nearly the lowest level of community wealth of all the Suburbs. It represents the leavings of a century of annexation during which "better elements" have broken away to form new municipalities or to join others. High density is not a social or economic class category.

The Low-density Residential communities range in expenditures from a high in Radnor of $40.31, to a low in Lower Providence of $6.29. Radnor lies just a little further out the Main Line from Lower Merion. While portions of this Suburb lying around the train stations developed early and quite densely, those further from the rail stations have developed more recently with lower densities or have not yet been developed at all. Thus portions of the municipality have the service-need characteristics of a high-density community. At the other extreme, Lower Providence is a very sparsely developed Suburb, lying north of the old borough of Norristown. Its parsimonious municipal policy is not easily explained, for other communities as little developed spend over twice as much for municipal services.

Although the Low-density Residential Suburbs spend less than the high-density, their average wealth is greater in terms of both residential and municipal property resources. The social rank of their populations is higher and their adult populations are younger. The share of municipal wealth in non-residential uses is approximately comparable in both residential types. Despite their differences in levels of expenditure and demographic characteristics, the correlates of expenditure variation within both residential types are substantially the same.

Social Rank and Wealth. The correlation coefficients in Table IV–8 illustrate a pattern common to both High- and Low-density Residential Suburbs. Expenditures rise as populations increase in status, as residential values increase and as municipal wealth increases. This pattern seems to indicate that affluence expresses itself in preferences for the socialization of additional services, although at differing costs depending upon various patterns of physical development. The need for sewers in densely developed communities may have to be met regardless of the kind of people who are citizens, but in Low-density Suburbs, where alternatives do exist, high-status populations are more likely to assert their preference for public sewerage disposal systems than low-status. In High-density Residential Suburbs, other services may be involved, but the process of choice and emphasis is much the same. High-status municipalities generally spend more for those services commonly provided in all Residential Suburbs, and they are most amenable to extending the number and types of services included within the scope of public responsibility. That they are prone to do so is no doubt affected by the fact that high social ranking municipalities generally do not want for taxable resources.

Industry and Commerce in Residential Suburbs. A positive correlation between expenditures and percent industrial and commercial is indicated in Table IV–8 for High-density, but not for Low-density Residential Suburbs. Indeed, the six highest spending High-density residential Suburbs are also the highest in percent assessed value in non-residential uses. The absence of a correlation for low-density municipalities is understandable in light of the nature of the industrial and commercial installations in these areas. Most are newer and of a low cost-generating type. In addition, while some of the Low-density Residential Suburbs have considerable proportions of their total assessments in industrial and commercial uses, this does not necessarily signify a great amount of economic activity. It is doubtful whether industry and commerce make an impact upon municipal budgets until they generate substantial centers of activity. Of all the Low-density municipalities, only in Radnor is there a major central business section.[3] Radnor spends more than any other Low-density Suburb.

Young Adults. The tendency for expenditures to decline with increasing precentages of young adults that was noted in Industrial and Commercial Centers is also evident in both High- and Low-density Residential Suburbs. Here, however, it is possible to test the question of whether this pattern reflects some attribute of this age group or whether it reflects their concentration in municipalities of a particular type of development that generates few service needs. The Low-density Residential type is, in effect, a control group; for all municipalities in this class are "new," having experienced most of their population growth and development since World War II. The negative correlation of expenditures and young adults within this group indicates that the age of the residents of municipalities is iteslf a meaningful factor differentiating levels of municipal expenditures. It appears that young adults prefer to do without, or to have lower levels of municipal service. As adult populations become older, expenditures increase. Perhaps this marks the passage of the marginal mortgage holder, the school-oriented parent, or the transient with few ties to the community.

In Residential Suburbs, then, the physical characteristics of communities (that is, their land-use patterns), and the age and nature of residential and non-residential development generate a set of responses similar to those observed in the Industrial and Commercial Centers. But residential Suburbs are more able to choose the expenditure policies they will pursue, since they are not affected by the overwhelming demands of industrial and commercial activity. In residential communities, municipal wealth and the preferences associated with population character- istics emerge as significant determinants of the range of activi- ties conducted by municipal governments and the degree of financial support afforded them.

Enclaves. More than half the 90 Suburbs are small boroughs that have been urbanized for many decades. Some of the Sub- urban boroughs have been functionally part of the metropolitan area from their very outset, having begun as commuter outposts in the railroad era. It has been assumed that boroughs long within the influence of the center city have been subjected to the forces of specialization and are therefore not politically dissimilar to the larger Suburbs. The eleven Enclaves, however, are all boroughs whose corporate existence arose independently of the influence of metropolitan Philadelphia. They are akin to the Towns in every respect save that of having been recently engulfed by continued urban penetration into once rural areas. They are, naturally, located on the outer suburban fringe.

The Enclaves are typical of the traditional small town or vil- lage that once served as a service-center for a rural hinterland. They do not specialize in either economic functions or popula- tions. They mix residential and non-residential property uses, and, due to their small areas are generally high in density. Of the four Suburban types, the Enclaves have the least municipal wealth and the smallest populations, but they exceed the In- dustrial and Commercial Centers in social rank and residential property values. Their range of expenditures is small, from a high in Morrisville of $30.05 to a low in Collegeville of $9.66. The mean Enclave expenditure of $17.06 is the lowest of the four types.

The Enclaves spend less than one would expect from municipalities of their density. Variations in their expenditures are not related to the factors found to be significant for Residential Suburbs. Table IV–8 shows their expenditures to be related significantly only to the size of population and market value per capita. Of the Suburbs, only in the Enclaves is size related to expenditures, a characteristic they share with Towns. Most Towns and all the Enclaves are boroughs, and boroughs are extremely varied in size. The smallest are indeed very small, Ivyland for example having only 425 persons. The small Enclaves provide very few services for their residents; the larger ones supply nearly a full complement. Thus, the most significant distinction between their expenditures is the range of services they provide, which in turn is virtually dependent upon their size.

The Functional Distribution of Suburban Expenditures

Budgetary decisions involve three types of judgments: (1) evaluations of the intrinsic value and productivity of individual governmental activities or programs (2) comparisons of the competing claims for larger shares of the budget by the many programs judged to be productive and of value, and (3) a decision as to the total level of funds to be allocated to governmental action. In smaller jurisdictions, particularly where, as is typical of most local units in metropolitan Philadelphia, executive and legislative powers are combined in one body, the budgetary process is sufficiently uncomplicated to enable continual simultaneous consideration of the three.

The analysis of Suburban expenditures has to this point emphasized the total level of governmental activity, with some attention given to the components contributing to total expendi-ures. This section is concerned with the support given various types of activities by Suburbs of differing characteristics. Cor-relations are again the major analytic tool. While it would have been desirable to apply the correlation technique to functional expenditures in each of the four Suburban types, it was techni-cally inadvisable, since some municipalities reported no ex-penditures for a number of functions, which reduced the sam-ple size to a number too small for statistical reliability.

Correlations were instead calculated for each of ten func-tional classes of expenditures and selected municipal character-istics for the 90 Suburbs. The influence of the percent industrial and Commercial variable and municipal wealth are again held constant. The resulting coefficients of partial correlation are summarized in Table IV–11. The procedure does not eliminate the interdependence of all the variables, nor are the coefficients very large. They are to be interpreted not in a determinative sense but as an expression of those functional emphases most associated with particular municipal characteristics. If they are read in conjunction with the mean functional expenditures by type of Suburb listed in Table IV–10, some inferences may be made as to policies favored by differing types of Suburbs.

For the most part, high-spending Suburbs spend relatively large amounts for all functions. Table IV–11 points to those functions particularly emphasized by Suburbs of selected char-acteristics, All coefficients are statistically significant to at least the 5 percent level. Those underlined represent the more im-portant responses associated with each of the characteristics.

Table IV–11 may be construed as a fiscal profile of certain types of municipalities. These results corroborate the inferences drawn from Table IV–10 that Industrial and Commercial Cen-ters favor programs oriented toward the physical characteristics and service needs of industrial and commercial specialization. Police and fire protection, streets and street-lighting are services of great importance to industrial and commercial uses. The negative correlation of planning expenditures and density reflects the fact that sparsely populated, sparsely developing areas give relatively more support to this municipal service.

The Low-density Residential Suburbs are characterized by two independent variables: density and percent single-family dwelling-units. The latter is probably a better measure of subdivision and housing patterns than the former. It shows a consistent lack of dependence on municipal services other than planning in these newly developing municipalities. The more densely populated Residential Suburbs spend considerably for public refuse disposal, partly due to the circumstances of their environment, partly as Social Rank indicates, as a result of the preferences of the high-status populations that abound in some High-density Residential Suburbs.

High-social-rank municipalities show consistent concern for public libraries, but the association of library expenditures and social rank is confined to High-density Residential Suburbs. Where young adults predominate, libraries as well as most other public activities are de-emphasized.

Among the Residential Suburbs, only the more populous (not necessarily the most densely populated), and those with relatively wealthy homes spend more for parks and recreation. These communities also spend large amounts for planning, particularly if they still contain underdeveloped territory. While physical characteristics appear to be most influential in shaping the fiscal profiles, influences of population characteristics cut across suburban types to temper needs with preferences and to produce varying patterns of policy responses.

In summary, Industrial and Commercial Centers spend for activities that serve the needs generated by their specialized economic role in the metropolitan area. Residential Suburbs

Table IV-11—Suburbs

Coefficients of Partial Correlation: Functional Expenditures per Capita and Selected Independent Variables, Controlling for Percent Industrial and Commercial and Market Value per Capita

	General Government	Libraries	Parks and Recreation	Police	Fire	Planning	Sewage	Refuse Disposal	Streets	Streetlights
First Order Partials										
Per Cent Industrial and Commercial, $k = MV/CAP$	.382			.232	.363	-.220				.408
Market Value per Capita, $k = \%I\ \&\ C.$	.392	.261		.396		.338				
Second Order Partials $k = MV/CAP$ and $\%I\ \&\ C.$										
Density	.260			.334	.235					
Social Rank	.203	.467		.394	.227	-.267	.215	.412	.253	.232
% Young Adults	-.367	-.314		-.321	-.289			.250		-.312
Residential Value per Household						.383		-.410		
% Single-family Dwelling Units			.369			.318				-.342
Population	-.502	-.267	.310	-.374	-.300	.273	-.280	-.258		-.271

Table IV-12—Towns

Operating Expenditures per Capita by Type of Town

Industrial and Commercial Towns 17		Residential Towns 18		"Suburban" Towns 5	
Coatesville	47.26				
Doylestown	41.45				
Sellersville	39.33				
Quakertown	34.19				
Royersford	33.57				
Downingtown	32.94				
Kennett Square	31.98				
West Chester	31.69				
New Hope	29.80	Soudertown	29.41		
South Coatesville	28.06				
Phoenixville	27.63				
Pottstown	26.69				
Spring City	25.59				
Oxford	22.16				
Newtown (Bucks)	20.05				
		Yardley	19.64	Valley	19.70
		Telford	19.36		
		Avondale	17.38		
Town Median	16.72	*Town Median*	16.72	*Town Median*	16.72

	Pennsburg 16.06	
	Green Lane 15.63	
	West Grove 14.67	West Pottsgrove 14.61
	Parkesburg 13.69	
	Riegelsville 13.25	
	Richlandtown 12.77	
	Atglen 12.62	
Schwenkesville 11.24	Dublin 11.15	
Honeybrook 10.94	Red Hill 10.34	Lower Pottsgrove 10.35
	East Greenville 10.22	
	Silverdale 9.40	
	Trumbauersville 9.08	
	New Britain 9.05	Modena 8.61
	Chalfont 7.95	West Goshen 6.10

differ in expenditures according to their development patterns. Low-density Residential Suburbs have little need for most services, but do evidence concern for planning. More densely populated Residential Suburbs, regardless of their wealth or status, respond to congestion by developing more services. Wealth and status generate higher service demands, reflecting preferences for more and better amenities. Where young adults predominate, there is a general emphasis on low expenditures that is reflected in particular functions according to the development patterns of the municipalities in which they locate.

Town Expenditures

The Towns developed to serve specialized needs that were non-metropolitan. Founded in the last century and often situated at strategic transportation intersections, they originated as commercial centers for agricultural hinterlands or as manufacturing places. From their outset, these communities have served as employment centers, while at the same time providing ancillary residential areas within their boundaries. Thus they developed as balanced communities largely unspecialized as to population, providing places of both work and residency.

With the passage of time, the Towns have met with varying fortunes and a kind of specialization among them has appeared —specialization based upon their comparative success. Some Towns have failed as commercial or industrial centers for any of a number of reasons. Today they are essentially little residential clumps on the countryside. They are low in density as they contain many arrested subdivisions. Their Main Streets remain dormant or decline. Their factories are often vacant or under-utilized. Time and technology have made them poor locational choices for new business enterprises. Thus they are largely residential Towns.

The Towns that succeeded have larger percentages of assesments in industrial and commercial use, reflecting their continued vitality. Several have been sufficiently successful so that their growth has spilled over their boundaries into neighboring townships. The latter, no longer rural in character, are included in the Town classification, but are in essence "suburbs" of other Towns. There are then three types of Towns: Industrial and Commercial Towns,[4] Residential Towns, and "Suburban" Towns.

Municipal operating expenditures per capita for the forty Towns [5] varies from a high of $47.26 in Coatesville, to a low of $6.10 in West Goshen. To explain this variation, Town expenditures were correlated with the same independent variables previously used in the Suburbs. According to the simple correlations presented in Table IV–13, density and the related percentage of single-family dwelling units are the most important factors associated with expenditure variations. Unlike the Suburbs, for the Towns, population size appears to be a statistically significant variable. Young-adult percentages are again significant, as is the land-use variable, percent assessed value in industrial and commercial use.

Table IV–13—Towns

Coefficients of Simple and Partial Correlation:
Operating Expenditures per Capita and Selected Variables*

	Simple Coefficients	First Order Partials k = Dens.	k = Popu.
1. Density	.481		.288
2. % Single Family D U's	-.464	-.281	-.378
3. Population	.440	.196	
4. % Young Adults	-.433	-.324	-.388
5. % Ind. and Com.	.348	.356	.250
6. % Residential	-.270	-.294	.177
7. Market Value/cap.	.268	.181	.269
8. Residential Value/H.H.	.040	.150	.033
9. Social Rank	.034	.025	.015

* Coefficients underlined significant at .05 level.

The partial correlation procedure was repeated controlling for density and population size. When both were controlled no other variable yielded a statistically significant correlation coefficient. Most of the large Towns are also densely populated. Expenditures are higher the larger and more densely populated the Town, but no other characteristic tested could explain expenditure variations at any given density or size.

The weighted Betas were again calculated to sort out the relative importance of several municipal characteristics. The results in Table IV–14 show density to be the most influential factor, accounting for half the more than 43 percent of expenditure variation attributable to the five characteristcs. The large size of the combined indirect contribution suggests that the statistical technique has not been able to separate the close interdependence of several variables. Through the use of a scatter diagram their interrelationship and its effect on expenditures can be examined more closely.

Table IV–14—Towns

Percentage of Variation in Operating Expenditures per Capita
Accounted for by Selected Variables

	B	Percent Direct Contribution to Total Variation (B^2)
Density	.468	21.9%
Percent Young Adults	.216	4.7
Market Value/Cap.	.200	4.0
Percent Ind. and Comm.	.171	2.9
Social Rank	.033	.1
Total Direct Contribution		33.6%
Combined Indirect Effects		10.0
Total Variation Explained (R^2)		43.6%

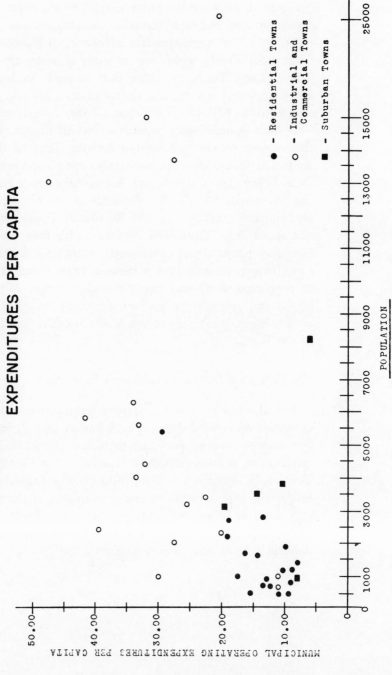

TOWNS

POPULATION SIZE AND MUNICIPAL OPERATING EXPENDITURES PER CAPITA

● - Residential Towns

○ - Industrial and Commercial Towns

■ - Suburban Towns

POPULATION

MUNICIPAL OPERATING EXPENDITURES PER CAPITA

Figure II, showing the relationships between expenditures, populaton, and economic specialization, demonstrates several points. (1) The larger spenders are almost all Industrial and Commercial Towns which are, in turn, generally the larger Towns. Large Towns are those that "succeed" as Industrial and Commercial centers, and success exacts a price in greater service costs. (2) The "Suburban" Towns spend modestly. They have younger adult populations, which we have seen is characteristic of newly developed Suburbs. Four of the five are largely industrial in tax base, representing a spillover from the successful Towns they border. Just as in the newer industrial and commercial Suburbs, these installations are not dependent on municipal services. (3) The Residential Towns are small and spend little. This seems consistent with their functional failure as industrial and commercial centers. (4) Within each type, there is no relationship between expenditures and size of population. It appears that the original simple correlation of size and expenditures has been explained away. Size is related to expenditures only in that it reflects other characteristics of the Towns.

The Functional Distribution of Town Expenditures

The allocation of resources to municipal functions is a prime expression of political choice. The Suburban analysis indicated relationships between particular municipal characteristics and emphases on selected services. A repetition of this analysis for Towns is less meaningful. Many of the Towns, particularly the residential, appear barely to recognize municipal government as a necessary or worthwhile urban institution. Their level of municipal activity is akin to that of the rural hinterlands. A different type of analysis is necessary for the Towns.

Table IV–15 distributes Town expenditures per capita to each of ten functions. The left side of the table indicates the number of Towns by type that spend any money (even one cent) for each function. The right side averages the per capita expenditures for each function for those Towns in which each is performed.

None of the Residential Towns provide a full complement of services. Some spend nothing for fire protection, a third collects no refuse, two-thirds have no sewers, no parks, and only a handful plans or provides any library service. Even where services are provided, expenditures are lower than in the Industrial and Commercial Towns or even their suburbs in some cases.

Table IV–15—Towns

Distribution of Functional Expenditures by Type of Town

	Number of Towns Having Service			Mean per Capita Expenditure For Towns Having Service		
	Ind. & Com. N = 17	Res. N = 18	"Suburbs" N = 5	Ind. & Com.	Res.	"Suburbs"
General Government	17	18	5	$3.30	$2.74	$1.59
Libraries	8	5	0	.33	.20	—
Parks & Recreation	14	7	1	1:05	.70	.04
Police	17	18	5	6.32	2.07	2.21
Fire	17	14	5	1.36	1.00	.42
Streets	17	18	5	5.17	3.41	4.87
Streetlights	17	18	5	2.02	1.84	.97
Planning	9	2	2	.33	.21	.29
Sewer	13	6	2	5.85	1.61	3.47
Refuse Disposal	16	12	3	1.86	1.35	1.23

In brief, overall Town expenditures, as well as those for

specific functions, appear to be related to the amount of economic activity in the Towns. Towns that continue to fulfill their function of serving a larger economy develop municipal enterprises that are more active on all fronts than those of Towns that have lost their original function. In terms of municipal services, the Residential Towns are but slightly distinguished from their rural hinterlands.

Many of the Industrial and Commercial Towns are large and relatively wealthy. But expenditures do not appear to be related to these factors *per se*. The economic functions performed in the larger, more wealthy Towns, and their pattern of physical development, including density, appear to be the primary factors associated with their expenditures.

Interestingly, all government services, including libraries, parks, and planning, receive greater attention in the Industrial and Commercial Towns than in the Residential Towns. The latter are generally quite small and like the small Suburban Enclaves provide minimal services. Although sometimes only slightly larger, the Industrial and Commercial Towns must enlarge their governmental enterprise in order to service industrial and commercial needs. Recognition of a more active role for government often extends to undertaking a fuller range of municipal services even if at minimal operational levels. This pattern suggests that size cannot completely be dismissed as a determinant of expenditures. There is a size difference between Chalfont and Philadelphia. Its effect on expenditures is not merely that of economies or diseconomies of scale. Small municipalities develop neither the ongoing political and administrative institutions nor the range of citizen interest necessary to support and conduct large scale governmental operations. The point in size at which these factors come into play is apparently lower for non-residential than residential places.

TOWNSHIP EXPENDITURES

The Townships, the rural portion of the metropolitan area, provide only minimal municipal services. Their operating expenditures range from $19.33 to $2.31 per capita, a substantial spread, though in a range lower than for any of the other groupings. The bulk of their expenditures is for roads, with general government invariably the second-largest expenditure. About half the Townships support police activities, and several more make small financial contributions to volunteer fire companies. Only one of the 94 spends any money for libraries, 2 for parks and recreation, 18 for health, 38 for planning, and 29 each for streetlights and refuse disposal. Even where such services are provided, expenditures are often only a few cents per capita.

None of the independent variables tested could explain variations in Township expenditures. This may reflect the fact that the variables were selected with regard to an urban setting and have little relevance to rural conditions. One tendency might be pointed out. Generally, the higher-social-ranking Townships provide more services and spend more than the lower-social ranking Townships. Planning appears to be the activity most emphasized by the former, although planning is generally emphasized in those municipalities ringing the suburbs.

For the most part, Townships have not yet developed to the point where their needs differ, nor where the preferences of their populations for various services generate sufficient demand to bring about governmental activity. The services they provide are minimal, traditional, and a product of indigenous experiences and conditions. The one policy that reflects their place within a metropolitan setting is their planning activity. This specialized service, essentially a mechanism for controlling incursions into the rural setting is largely a reflection of geography rather than social or economic differentiation.

Table IV–16—Townships

Operating Expenditures per Capita

*	1	Solebury	$19.33		48	*Schuylkill*	$8.11
*	2	Upper Makefield	18.53	*49	East Marlborough	8.07
	3	Highland	16.81	50	West Brandywine	8.04
	4	West Fallowfield	16.22	51	*Sadsbury*	7.64
	5	West Marlborough	16.12	52	New Britain	7.54
	6	*Willistown*	15.95	53	East Coventry	7.54
	7	*Montgomery*	15.83	54	Worcester	7.47
*	8	Newtown (Bucks)	15.73	55	Bridgeton	7.38
	9	Tinicum (Bucks)	15.31	56	*North Coventry*	7.32
	10	Warwick (Bucks)	15.14	*57	London Britain	7.31
*11	*Lower Makefield*	14.69	58	Elverson Borough	7.23
12	West Caln	14.56	59	Birmingham (D)	7.22
*13	*Northampton*	14.38	60	Warwick (Ch.)	7.03
14	Honeybrook	14.33	61	West Bradford	6.77
*15	*Buckingham*	14.15	62	West Nantmeal	6.74
*16	Pennsbury	14.02	63	Kennett	6.66
17	Upper Oxford	13.89	*64	East Bradford	6.50
18	Salford	13.84	65	Elk	6.43
19	New Garden	13.56	66	*Upper Providence*	6.35
*20	West Vincent	13.50	67	West Sadsbury	6.23
21	Upper Uwchlan	13.44	68	East Fallowfield	5.97
22	Durham	12.97	69	*East Pikeland*	5.87
*23	East Whiteland	12.50	70	Richland	5.84
24	Londonderry	12.22	71	Hilltown	5.83
25	East Nottingham	11.61	72	Concord	5.76
*26	East Nantmeal	11.36	*73	Birmingham (Ch.)	5.72
27	London Grove	11.32	74	Springfield (B)	5.71
28	West Rockhill	11.17	75	Milford	5.59
*29	Uwchlan	10.86	76	Penn	5.59
30	West Nottingham	10.43	77	Plumstead	5.54
*31	Pocopson	10.24	78	New Hanover	5.39
32	Upper Salford	10.13	79	*Limerick*	5.22
33	*Warrington*	10.10	80	*West Whiteland*	5.02
34	New London	9.98	*81	Wallace	4.99
*35	West Pikeland	9.90	82	South Coventry	4.80
36	Perkiomen	9.19	*83	*Towamencin*	4.75
37	Lower Salford	9.17	84	*Upper Pottsgrove*	4.70
38	Franconia	9.04	85	*Bedminster*	4.65
*39	Doylestown	8.96	86	Lower Frederick	4.65

40 Douglas	8.84	*87 Charleston	4.45
41 Nockamixon	8.78	88 Lower Oxford	4.32
*42 Bethel	8.77	89 Westtown	4.16
*43 Wrightstown	8.74	90 Upper Frederick	3.97
44 Franklin	8.65	91 East Rockhill	3.60
45 Marlborough	8.53	92 East Goshen	3.56
46 Haycock	8.42	93 East Brandywine	2.47
47 Upper Hanover	8.13	94 East Caln	2.31

Municipalities marked with an (*) are high in Social Rank—35.0 or above.

Municipalities in italics evidence urban-penetration densities of 300 persons per square mile.

Summary

Are municipal policies related to patterns of socio-economic differentiation in a metropolitan area? The foregoing analysis has shown such a relationship to exist. Civic policies—municipal choices—are the product of an interplay of values, circumstances, pressures, and past events. We have categorized selected measurable aspects of these factors as needs, resources, and preferences. The classification is operational and some variables shift from one category to another in the context of specific analysis. The general findings are that needs are the most important bases of policy, preferences the next most important, and resources the least. The distinction between needs and resources is crucial to these findings.

Needs. The major test contrasting the influence of needs and resources was to correlate both property wealth and land-use patterns with variations in expenditure levels. Expenditures varied more directly with the percentage of property in industrial and commercial use than with municipal wealth *per se.* Even poor industrial communities had relatively high expenditures. Non-residential uses represent costs to municipalities, especially in older industrial and pre-shopping-center commercial areas. These facilities generate needs met through municipal services regardless of the taxable resources available. This was seen to be operative in both the Suburbs and Towns. Whether the cost of providing services to non-residential properties works a hardship on residents is a question treated in Chapter VI.

Density was initially posited as a likely need factor on the assumption that certain development patterns require greater social services and controls. Density was a factor explaining expenditure variations in both the Suburbs and Towns, but more particularly in the latter. Many of the more densely populated residential areas were also poor and low in Social Rank, characteristics that appear to be related to low expenditures. Despite these countervailing forces, the needs generated by density were so great that a separation between high- and low-density residential municipalities was necessary to clarify other relationships. It was not merely that high-density municipalities spent more, they also spent in different ways. Density reflects differences in styles of living and the preferences associated with them, as well as differences in physical needs.

Resources. The literature and lore of local government delight in depicting "tax grabs" where, through adroit manipulation of municipal boundaries, large tax-producing properties are yoked to a modest number of homes whose residents "milk" these bountiful resources for substantial services to themselves. Such cases conjure up the image of a calculating and politically sophisticated citizenry. There probably are exceptions, but for the most part, industrial and commercial wealth is not used in Philadelphia's Suburbs to finance amenities for local residents.

Wealth, whether in residential or non-residential property was not a good barometer of expenditures. Expensive homes can boost the taxable resources of a community just as can big factories and commercial streets. Home values are closely related to the social status of their occupants. In several analyses, it appeared that social rank was a more discriminating characteristic of expenditure variations than home value. Here again, it appeared that a resource *per se* contributed less to expenditures than a non-resource characteristic to which it was related.

Generally, municipal expenditures are not simply a matter of "those that have, spend." This may stem from the fact that the local portion of school expenditures is closely related to municipal wealth because of the equalizing character of the state school subsidy. The resulting local school expenditures in wealthy communities may "use up" local resources which might otherwise have been devoted to greater municipal outlays. This question, too, will be treated in Chapter VI.

Preferences. Our findings indicate that municipal expenditures generally rise as communities become more specialized in providing homes for wealthy high-social-ranking populations. This was true for both high- and low-density residential Suburbs, but not for industrial and commercial centers. The latter economic functions are apparently a more inflexible determinant of needs than residential development patterns.

Social rank and personal wealth as measured by home value, though closely related, do not influence expenditures identically. The shade of difference between the two is indicated by their association with selected functional expenditures. Library expenditures were related to social rank, but not to wealth. On the other hand, municipalities with higher home values were clearly more concerned with planning and land-use controls, while no significant relationship was found between ths expenditure and social rank.

A more accurate statement of the social rank and personal wealth findings can be made in negative terms. No municipality with high social rank or with wealthy citizens eschewed public services. Private assumption of services or "doing without" is not a feature of the high-toned Suburbs.

There is a high incidence of eschewing services wherever young adults congregate, and congregate they do. Generally they exercise a locational preference for newer subdivisions in less congested municipalities. This colonizing pattern often results in a glut in the school systems of certain municipalities. Perhaps these schools are absorbing the tax resources of the areas in which young adults concentrate. Or possibly these families have a pioneering zest for inconveniences. At any rate, where the young assemble municipal expenditures decline, not only in Residential Suburbs, but in non-residential Suburbs and Towns as well.

Locational Choices. Specialization of populations in the Suburbs obviously stems from locational choices. People choose their places of residence as they choose their style of clothes, brand of liquor and public policies. Many urban residents are highly mobile, willing and able to move. Political choice is expressed by moving van as commonly as by municipal budgets and ballot boxes. Of course, some individuals are less mobile than others, being rooted by old associations, lack of resources or inertia.

The exercise of locational choice is the very basis of urban spatial differentiation. Needs, resources, and preferences, as we have defined them, are merely products, viewed at one point in time, of accumulated locational choices of individuals and enterprises. Hence, when we say that needs are more closely related to expenditures than are preferences, we are not attributing causal consequence to the inanimate factory which leads to demands for service. Need represents a legacy of choices which become enshrined in a particular physical environment. Tolerance of that environment remains a passive choice underlying contemporary local policy.

It is not by chance that the Industrial and Commercial Suburbs are, with the exception of the newer areas of industrial and shopping center location, all extremely low in social rank. Neither is it accidental that their expenditures do not appear to be affected by the slight variation in social rank that does exist among these Suburbs. Tolerance of the existing level of services and their distribution between residential and non-residential recipients is a characteristic of those that have chosen to locate in these communities.

If all the people of Swarthmore were to move to Marcus Hook, the politics of that Industrial and Commercial Suburb would be as much affected as its social rank. But the residents of Swarthmore will not abide the smell of refineries nor tolerate a lack of amenities and beauty in environment. Apart from physical surroundings,until sufficient change in Marcus Hook's policies, particularly with regard to education, is brought about, it is not likely that those now resident in Swarthmore would even consider Marcus Hook as a possible place of residence. Expenditure policy is not only a reflection of locational choice it is also an element in the latter process.[6]

The present citizens of Marcus Hook are either less articulate or have other values than those of Swarthmore, and one or both of these alternatives partially accounts for their being where they are. Because the citizens of Marcus Hook make few demands, industrial needs essentially shape public policy. It is in this sense that a locational choice underlies all our generalizations and variables.

Most communities are very aware that the people and land uses that they attract or allow have profound consequences for their public policies. Hence, land-use controls and policies are of prime concern in suburban politics. Each municipality tries to shape its character and density by little domestic immigration laws called zoning ordinances. This dimension of political choice is the subject of a later chapter.

NOTES

1. Study Commission of the Philadelphia Metropolitan Area, *A Metropolis Expands* (June, 1958).

2. One municipality, Upland, was eliminated at this point in the analysis because of probable errors in its financial report.

3. *Delaware Valley Shopping Centers, 1959,* published by The Philadelphia Inquirer.

4. Because few Towns develop the extreme differentiation of functions evident in the Suburbs, Towns were deemed to be specializing in industrial and commercial activities if assessments for industrial and commercial property exceeded 25 percent of all assessed property.

5. The Town of Perkasie was eliminated on suspicion that its financial reports mixed capital and operating expenditures.

6. See the leading statement of this hypothesis, — Charles M. Tiebout, "A Pure Theory of Local Expenditures," *Journal of Political Economy,* Volume 64 (October, 1956).

V

Fiscal Responses: School Revenues

Public education in Pennsylvania is, in many ways, a thing apart. Public school policy is politically, organizationally, and financially separated from other activities locally conducted. Moreover, for many people it is of greater personal concern than other local activities. Its financial importance is obvious— all communities, outside of Philadelphia, spend more for schools than all other municipal activities combined, some from six to eight times as much.

The state is partly responsible for the public school's unique position in local government. It requires all municipalities to provide public education, closely supervising and directly participating in local school management and finance. The unique organizational and financial characteristics of public education merit discussion prior to analysis of policy differentiation in the metropolitan area.

School District Organization

Pennsylvania's school districts are autonomous political subdivisions, authorized, subject to state supervision, to conduct and finance public education at the primary and secondary levels. Most school-district boundaries are coterminous with those of municipalities. The district system originated along township lines. When portions of townships incorporated as cities or boroughs, they formed their own school districts. This splintering process often worked hardship on the rural remnant of the township. There are, however, two boroughs in this sector that never formed their own school districts, Rose Valley and Modena. Both are included in the school district of the municipalities from which they separated, Nether Providence and East Fallowfield respectively.

All of the other municipalities in the sector at one time constituted autonomous school districs. The movement for reducing their number has, in Pennsylvania, as elsewhere, led to the employment of organizational forms that have consolidated some districts and decreased the number that actually operate schools.

Union districts result from the merger of previously independent units. In merging, the former districts lose their identity but retain one concession to their individuality. One member of the union's school board is elected from each of the former districts and the remainder necessary to complete the number required by law are elected at large.

The union's method of finance is by far its most significant feature. One tax rate is levied upon the combined tax bases of all municipalities in the district. Each municipality shares in school costs in the ratio of its tax base to the total district tax base, regardless of the number of pupils it sends to school. It is possible for one of two municipalities in a union to have sixty percent of the district's tax resources and forty percent of its pupils. Such extreme discrepancies do not exist in the sector's six union districts, possibly because no district would merge under such conditions. But there are sufficient imbalances in the distribution of resources and pupils for tensions to be evident in several unions.

The source of discontent is not always to be found in the wealthier municipality's resentment at paying for the cost of other childrens' education. Tension in at least one union can definitely be traced to the municipality favored by having a greater proportion of the district's pupils than resources. In this case the favored municipality has shown continued reluctance to support the higher expenditures that its partner demands for the district.

There are six union districts in the sector (not including the Nether Providence and East Fallowfield Districts, which are not technically unions). They comprise sixteen municipalities, four merging three units each and two merging two units.

The so-called independent district is another type that disregards municipal boundaries. It differs from a union only in that its components are not whole municipalities or former districts, but parts of one or more municipalities. The Swamp and Fagleysville Independents, for example, each consist of a small portion of New Hanover. The other two independents in the sector cross municipalities. Line Lexington includes portions of Hatfield, Hilltown and New Britain Twps., Independent Number One is composed of parts of Kennett and East Marlboro. Thus, while the unions decrease the number of administrative units in the sector, the independents add a few more.

There are, then, a total of 230 school districts serving the 238 municipalities in the sector. Of these 211 are fully coterminous with municipal boundaries. Not all operate schools. Most participate through contract in one or more *jointures* whereby some or all of their pupils are combined with those of neighboring districts in a joint elementary, secondary, or complete educational program. The school districts of Salford and Upper Salford, for example, contract with one another for a joint ele-

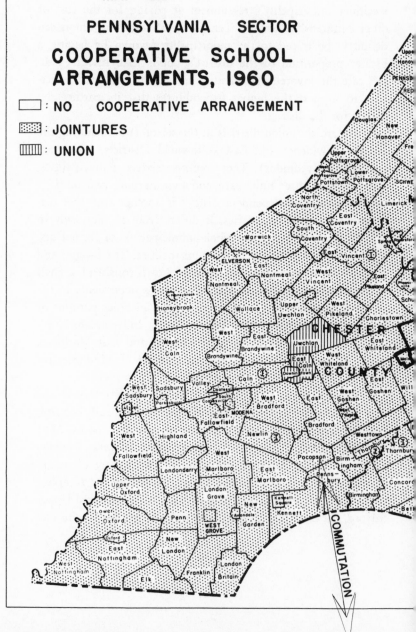

MAP VII

PENNSYLVANIA SECTOR

COOPERATIVE SCHOOL ARRANGEMENTS, 1960

☐ : NO COOPERATIVE ARRANGEMENT
▦ : JOINTURES
▥ : UNION

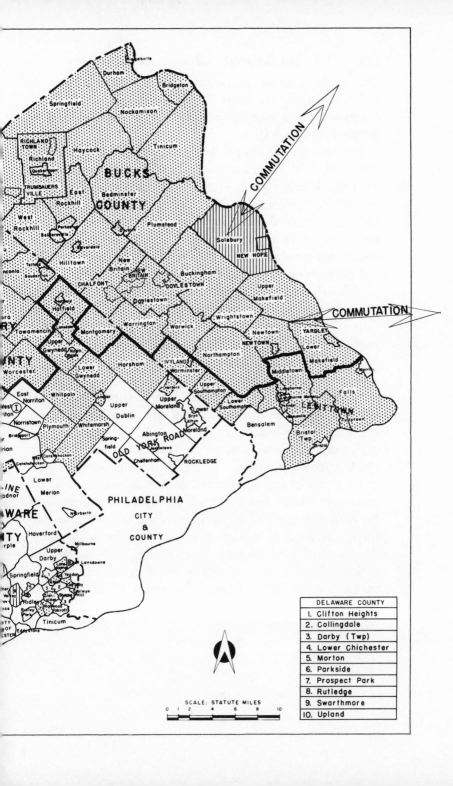

SCALE: STATUTE MILES
0 1 2 4 6 8 10

DELAWARE COUNTY
1. Clifton Heights
2. Collingdale
3. Darby (Twp)
4. Lower Chichester
5. Morton
6. Parkside
7. Prospect Park
8. Rutledge
9. Swarthmore
10. Upland

mentary program and participate with four other districts in
a high school jointure. Every Town and Township in the sector
is a member of at least one jointure. The jointure pattern is illustrated in Map VII.

Jointures operate schools, but do not constitute school districts; and, most important, they have no independent financial
authority. They are governed by boards representing the school
boards of the contracting districts, often composed of all members of the latter. Participating districts contribute to the jointure's expenses by mutual agreement. The financial agreement
usually, but not always, takes into consideration both the wealth
and the number of pupils of each participant.

Although unions and jointures share the objective of elimina-
ing small schools, their impact upon school administration reflects critical differences in their organization and finance. The
jointure permits individual districts to enjoy the advantages of
central schools without forfeiting their financial independence
and possibly advantageous resource-pupil ratios. Although the
jointure is looked upon by some as a forerunner of merger, to
others, it appears to operate as a most effective means of reducing merger incentives.

A complete examination of the local public school system
should procede from investigation of the difference in alternative forms of organization and finance. Moreover, even for
an analysis limited to expenditure policy, the appropriate unit
for analysis might well be the jointure and not individual districts. The focus of this study is, however, the municipality.
The effect of jointures must be considered, and, indeed, the
policy of forming jointures will be treated extensively in Chapter IX, but, for the most part, this analysis is confined to the
expenditure policy of individual school districts and the municipalities they embrace.

State Participation in School Finance

The Commonwealth of Pennsylvania has sought to stimulate school-district consolidation by granting monetary rewards to districts that close schools, participate in jointures, or merge to form unions. These reorganization incentives are but a few of the many recurring grants that, in total, account for the state's payment of approximately half the cost of local education throughout the Commonwealth. The basic subsidy "on account of instruction" given to all schools for operating expenses accounts for about 70 percent of all special and general grants. Its equalizing features are typical of many of the special grants.

The subsidy "on account of instruction" is based on a formula that distributes aid inversely to local resources. At the time of this study, the formula equalized to an expenditure of $5800 per teaching unit. A teaching unit is composed of 30 elementary pupils or 22 high school pupils. The Basic Account Standard Reimbursement Fraction formula is:

$$\text{BASRF} = \frac{\$5800 - \dfrac{\textit{Market Value}}{(\text{No. of Teaching Units})} \quad .004375}{\$5800}$$

The .004375 that is multiplied by market value per teaching unit represents a minimum tax effort ($4\frac{3}{8}$ mills). The BASRF is multiplied by the number of teaching units in the district and by $5800 to arrive at the amount of the state subsidy.

Fifty-eight hundred dollars per teaching unit is not viewed as a goal, but rather the maximum amount to which the state will equalize. For elementary pupils alone, it represents an expenditure of only $193 per pupil. All school districts actually spend much more. The tax effort employed in the formula is similarly far from that actually levied. The median school tax rate in the state was approximately 10 mills in 1960.[5] Nevertheless, the subsidy and other grants do provide a considerable portion of the revenue of many districts.

To illustrate the formula in operation, it will be converted to a pupil basis, considering each teaching unit to consist of 25 pupils. The reimbursement fractions for Lower Merion and for Chester Twp. would then be:

$$\text{Lower Merion} = \frac{\$232 - (50{,}418)\ .004375}{\$232} = .049$$

$$\text{Chester Twp.} = \frac{\$232 - (\$8{,}562)\ .004375}{\$232} = .838$$

Lower Merion, with more than $50,000 in maket value per pupil would be eligible to receive approximately five percent of the first $232 it spends per pupil from the state. Chester Township would receive 84 percent. Both districts spend considerably more, reducing the proportion of state aid to total expenditures per pupil. The equalizing character of the formula is reduced, however, by a guaranteed minimum subsidy of $1,000 per teaching unit. For all districts, then, the subsidy "on account of instruction" provides at least 17 percent of the first 5800 spent per teaching unit.[2] Map VIII indicates the extent to which state aid is relied upon by Suburban, Town and Township Schools.

Urban and Rural Schools

Since all municipalities are required to provide public education, and since the state acts to lessen disparities in the balance of local resources and needs, there is some justification for

Table V-1

Measures of Central Tendency for Selected
School Variables by Study Area

	Suburbs			Towns			Townships		
	Mean	S	V.	Mean	S	V.	Mean	S	V.
Total Revenue/Pupil	$ 499	79	.159	$ 471	68	.144	$ 479	68	.142
Local Revenue/Pupil	$ 368	116	.315	$ 267	68	.254	$ 281	89	.317
Market Value/Capita	$4130	1760	.426	$3360	1100	.327	$3770	1270	.337
Social Rank	31.2	20.9	.670	20.7	9.4	.454	28.2	11.8	.418
% Population in School	15.2	4.1	.272	18.6	3.7	.200	19.9	3.1	.155
% Tot. Rev. from State Aid	28.7	12.5	.438	42.8	10.8	.254	41.7	12.3	.296

abandoning the Suburban, Town, and Township classifications for the analysis of school finance. Indeed, in recent studies of metropolitan Cleveland and St. Louis, no distinction was made between more-and-less urban school districts in the analysis of school expenditures, although the municipalities were classified for purposes of analyzing municipal expenditures.[3] We fear that metropolitan Philadelphia includes so wide a range of urban and rural sections, that the extreme diversification characteristic of the Suburbs may distort statistical findings for the sector as a whole.

For example, Table V–1 indicates that Suburban school districts, as a class, are quite different from Towns and Townships. The average Suburb has fewer children in public school relative to total population, is wealthier, of higher social rank and raises more local revenue per pupil. It receives less state aid, yet contributes enough local funds to devote more total revenue to each pupil. There is generally little variation in expenditures within each of the classifications, despite the extreme variation in Suburban social and economic characteristics.

It appears that urbanism as such is at least partly responsible for differences in school expenditures. Perhaps the difference between average Suburban, Town and Township revenues is due to a need for school construction and/or higher costs, and not to any difference in choice of policy. Examination of rental payments covering costs of school construction does show many rapidly growing Suburbs to be spending larger amounts for school construction, but construction cost does not explain differences in expenditures between Suburbs, nor does it fully account for the fact that Suburbs as a class spend more for education than Towns or Townships. Differences in the cost of similar activities conducted by all school districts are not that easily disposed of.

To anticipate conceptual and methodological problems stemming from the number of units employed for correlation and regression analysis, two separate bases were selected. One contains all municipalities in the sector, a second separates school districts into a Suburban and semi-urban group.[4] If all municipalities are viewed as the universe for policy decisions, any correlations found within the universe should be relevant as well for a sample number of units. To be sure, Suburbs, Towns and Townships are not random samplings. It is precisely for this reason that differences in correlations are of interest. What characteristics influence the amount of support given public education thrloughout the sector? Is their influence uniformly operative, or are there other factors associated with the Suburban or semi-urban environment that affect school policies?

Following the procedure used for municipal expenditures, school revenue was first correlated with aggregate municipal characteristics. As was expected, school-district revenue is closely associated with pupil enrollment. Enrollment is itself a function of total population, which in turn is related to the total market value of property. The latter is also highly correlated wtih revenue. The correlations appear as well when local revenue is used as the dependent variable. Almost all the variation in both total and local school revenue can be attributed to differences in district size, measured by enrollment, or by marekt value.

Table V–2

Coefficients of Correlation: Total School Revenue,
Local School Revenue and Enrollment and Market Value

	Suburbs		Towns		Townships	
	Total	Local	Total	Local	Total	Local
Revenue & Enrollment	.986	.921	.978	.985	.965	.933
Revenut & Market Value	.959	.985	.977	.988	.939	.975

The effect of controlling for market value or for enrollment is suggestive. Table V–3 lists the coefficients of partial and multiple determination for enrollment and market value. When market value is held constant, differences in enrollment account for a greater percentage of the variation in total revenue than local revenue. When enrollment is held constant, differences in market value account for more of the variation in local revenue than total revenue.

Table V–3

Coefficients of Multiple and Partial Determination:
Total School Revenue, Local School Revenue and
Enrollment and Market Value

	Suburbs		Towns		Townships	
	Total	Local	Total	Local	Total	Local
Coefficients of Partial Determination						
Revenue & Enrollment; k=Market Value	84.6	39.9	41.5	22.6	73.4	10.3
Revenue & Market Value; k=Enrollment	64.5	83.2	22.6	53.9	27.7	70.7
Coefficient of Multiple Determination						
Revenue & Enrollment & Market Value	99.2	98.3	96.9	97.9	96.9	95.5

The effectiveness of the state's equalization formula is apparent, even in these gross terms. The larger school systems are not necessarily those with the most market value. In distributing aid inversely to the ratio of pupils to market value, the state counteracts the tendency for resources to be the dominant determinant of school revenue, relating revenue more closely to the number of pupils served.

Correlates of Revenue per Pupil

When school revenues per pupil are examined, the size of school districts loses its significance. There is no relationship between total or local revenue per pupil and municipal size, or the size of jointures in which municipalities participate. School systems with both large and small enrollments are to be found throughout the sector. Scale does not appear to affect levels of school support.

A number of characteristics are significantly associated with variations in revenue per pupil. Most are themselves related. Three appear to be dominant. Although they were not preselected for this purpose, each represents one of the three factors that were hypothesized as affecting expenditure variations— needs, resources and preferences. The most important independent variables associated with differences in revenue per pupil throughout the sector and within the suburbs and the semi-urban group are the percentage of total population in public school (hereafter pupil percentage), market value per capita, and social rank.

The first two characteristics are the basis for the state-aid formula. Increases in municipal wealth lighten the effort required to support public schools. But increases in the number of pupils attending school burden the financial resources of municipalities. The market value per pupil ratio of the aid formula combines the need-resource relationship into one mathematical expression. But in their effect upon school expenditures, the two work in opposite directions. Increases in municipal wealth are accompanied by higher revenue per pupil. Given the same amount of resources, increases in enrollment are accompanied by lower revenue per pupil. At any level of resources and needs, higher revenues per pupil are associated with higher social rank.

The relative importance of the three characteristics for all school districts in the sector is indicated in Table V–4. Of most interest is the difference in their contributions to variations in local and total revenue per pupil. Almost 70 percent of the variation in local revenue per pupil is attributed to the three variables, but only 41 percent of the variation in total revenue per pupil. Moreover, more than half the variation in local revenue is explained by combinations of wealth and enrollment, but these two factors are decidedly less important than social rank in explaining variations in total revenue per pupil including state aid.[5]

Table V–4

Percentage of Variation in Total and Local
School Revenue per Pupil Accounted for by Resources,
Needs and Preferences for the Entire Sector, N=223

| | Percent Direct Contribution to Total Variation | |
	Tot. Rev/Pupil	Local Rev/Pupil
Market Value per Capita	3.1%	26.3%
Percent Population in School	6.6	24.4
Social Rank	29.2	10.7
Total Direct Contribution	38.9	61.4
Combined Indirect Affects	2.3	7.4
Total Variation Explained (R^2)	41.2	68.8

It would be less than realistic to suggest that the pattern of influences upon local revenue per pupil represents what could be expected were no state aid available. The aid formula itself requires greater local contributions from wealthier districts and those with fewer pupils. All districts know the exact amount of aid to which they are entitled in advance of budget preparation. Is state aid merely a supplement to the revenue that school boards have previously decided to allocate to public education; or do school boards supplement state aid with the amount of local funds required to maintain their desired levels of expenditure? The latter seems a more adequate description of the budget process. But whether larger local contributions from the wealthier districts are a result of the state formula or whether they represent a "natural" pattern of school financing, the fact is that after state aid has been distributed, neither resources, nor need, but social rank separates the high- from the low-spending districts.

This finding compares interestingly with those of the St. Louis and Cleveland studies. In St. Louis, where "the state of Missouri contributed very little to the local school districts on an equalization basis," average assessed valuation of real property per pupil was found to be the variable most associated with differences in school expenditures among 27 districts.[6] A measure comparable to social rank was not used, however. In metropolitan Cleveland, where a state foundation program existed, Sacks and Hellmuth found that "the availability of resources does not guarantee high expenditures, but the high personal wealth, correlated as it is with high assessed valuation per student does."[7]

The Cleveland measure of personal wealth, we suspect, would correlate well with Social Rank. Indeed, the measure here employed to approximate personal wealth, residential market value per household, does. Our conclusions correspond to those of both the St. Louis and Cleveland studies. In the absence of state equalization, school expenditures in metropolitan Philadelphia would probably be influenced most profoundly by the availability of resources. Municipal wealth, personal wealth, and social rank often go hand-in-hand. The equalization process, however, diminishes the range of differentiation in resources elevating differences in social rank to the most discriminatory position.

Urban and Semi-Urban School Support

The relative importance of needs, resources, and preferences are altered when the sector is analyzed by Suburban and semi-urban components. The association of social rank and revenue per pupil is statistically insignificant for Towns and Townships separately considered or combined. The amount of variation in both total and local revenue explained by the three variables is quite similar, but only in the Suburbs does their pattern of influence approximate that found for the entire sector.

Table V–5

Percentage of Variation in Total and Local
School Revenue per Pupil Accounted for by Resources,
Needs and Preferences for Suburban and Semi-Urban Districts

	Percent Direct Contribution to Total Variation (B^2)			
	Suburbs N=88		Semi-Urban N=135	
	Tot. Rev/Pup.	Loc. Rev/Pup.	Tot. Rev/Pup.	Loc. Rev/Pup.
Market Value	13.5	32.0	10.3	33.3
Percent Population in School	9.9	30.1	17.7	22.2
Social Rank	20.3	18.4	2.2	4.6
Total Direct Contribution	43.7	80.5	30.2	60.1
Combined Indirect Affects	+5.2	−2.9	+7.6	+6.3
Total Variation Explained (R^2)	38.5	77.6	37.8	66.4

A comparison of Tables V–4 and V–5 raises two questions. Why does social rank exert a preponderance of influence over total revenue per pupil when all districts are viewed as the universe, slightly less for the Suburbs, and a negligible influence for the semi-urban group? Why do the Suburban and semi-urban groups differ so markedly?

Suburban differentiation underlies the answer to both questions. The highly differentiated Suburbs provide the mathematical weight for the relationships in Table V–4. The Suburbs are extremely varied in social rank. Only in the Suburbs are social rank and market value per capita clearly distinguished from one another. Only in the Suburbs are districts not participating in jointures to be found. In part, social rank's influence on variations for the sector as a whole is a statistical quirk stemming from the extreme differences between Suburban and semi-urban districts.

Social rank is not a significant differentiator of Town and Township school policy. These municipalities are relatively unspecialized with regard to the status of their residents. Furthermore, what differences do exist between municipalities is often subsumed in the jointures to which all belong. A later chapter will demonstrate that jointure policy is iteslf affected by social differentiation. Nevertheless, in Towns and Townships, the historic emphasis and need for rural consolidation has produced a network of contractual relationships that limits the expression of social differentiation.

Social rank differences, the most critical aspect of urban differentiation, are compromised, of necessity in the semi-urban area, in the joint support of school programs. Differences in the availability of resources and the pressure of pupil populations do manifest themselves in varying levels of financial support for education. Although jointure partners differ in both social rank and resources, since state aid is distributed to participants and not to the jointure their need-resources inequalities are reduced. As a result, whole jointures spend more for education when the collective resources of their members is great. Social rank preferences have little opportunity for expression in school expenditures, except in so far as they are associated with resources.

Many Suburbs are free from all jointure ties. Others, if not completely free to shape their school destinies are, at most, compelled to compromise with no more than one or two partners. The character of the older Suburbs has long been stable. Partners in a school agreement are likely to be not too dissimilar socially. The resulting distribution of school expenditures represents deliberate policy choices made by relatively independent districts.

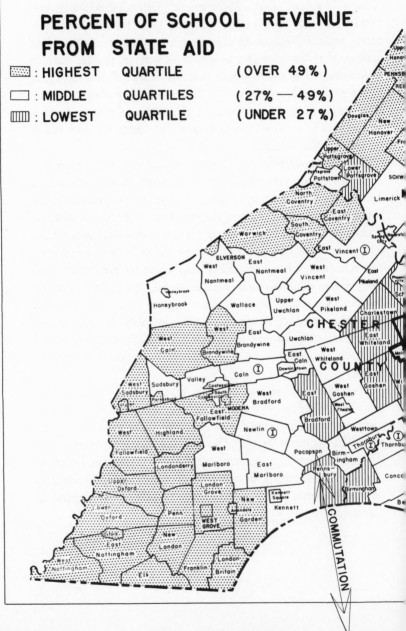

MAP VIII

PENNSYLVANIA SECTOR

PERCENT OF SCHOOL REVENUE
FROM STATE AID

▒ : HIGHEST   QUARTILE   (OVER 49%)

☐ : MIDDLE   QUARTILES   (27% — 49%)

▥ : LOWEST   QUARTILE   (UNDER 27%)

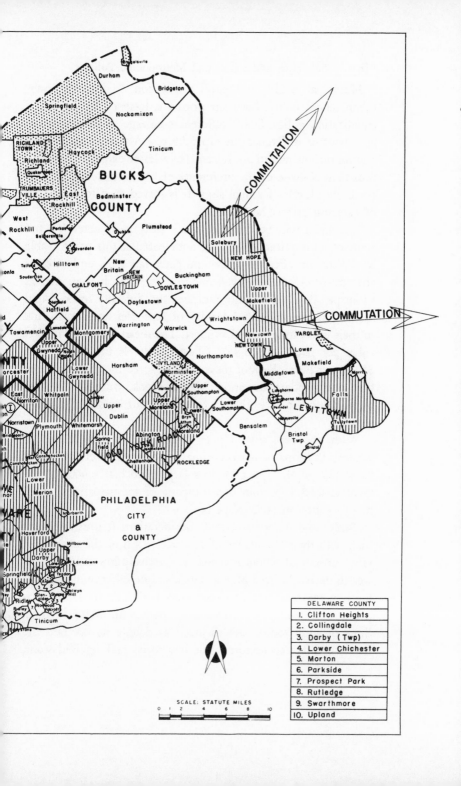

DELAWARE COUNTY
1. Clifton Heights
2. Collingdale
3. Darby (Twp)
4. Lower Chichester
5. Morton
6. Parkside
7. Prospect Park
8. Rutledge
9. Swarthmore
10. Upland

SCALE: STATUTE MILES
0 1 2   4   6   8   10

Municipal wealth and pupil population do influence Suburban school policy, but their impact is lessened by the state's equalization policy. Status differences emerge as the major determinant of differences in expenditures. Although social rank and municipal wealth are related (to a lesser extent in the Suburbs than elsewhere) the preference of high status communities for higher levels of school support is served even to the extent of exerting greater tax effort.

Tax effort will be discussed more fully in Chapter VI, but some of its implications may be anticipated at this point. Table V–6 lists the effective school property tax rates and selected characteristics of the eleven Suburbs with the highest market value per pupil. The table indicates the diversity to be found in the Suburbs and the interplay of resources and social rank in their effect upon school support. The mean Suburban market value per pupil is $26,353. Chester Twp. is the lowest with $8562 per pupil. Each of these eleven exceed the mean by more than one standard deviation, Marcus Hook, with $70,149 per pupil being the "wealthiest" for school purposes in the entire sector.

With one exception, Upper Darby, each of the eleven is wealthy in terms of market value per capita as well as market value per pupil. Upper Darby's large parochial school enrollment enables it to join this company of municipalities, much more wealthy in other respects.

Table V–6 deserves careful consideration. It illustrates first that, with their abundance of resources, each of the eleven can raise substantial school revenues at relatively low tax rates. As wealth decreases from Marcus Hook's high, other municipalities must increase tax rates to keep pace with Marcus Hook's expenditures. Some more than keep pace with Marcus Hook; those of high social rank as much as double its tax rate and far exceed its expenditures. The low social ranking Eddystone,

Table V–6

Revenue per Pupil and Selected Characteristics
of Eleven Suburbs with the Highest Market Value per Pupil

	Social Rank	School Tax Rate	Tot. Rev/Pupil	%I & C	MV/Pupil
Tinicum	5.5	5.5	$507	72	$42,608
Eddystone	5.9	9.5	477	62	59,015
Marcus Hook	6.2	6.6	513	87	70,149
Trainer	7.6	8.4	381	72	37,841
Plymouth	17.9	13.9	555	32	39,347
Upper Gwynadd	35.1	12.3	497	54	44,382
Upper Darby	36.9	11.1	540	21	36,793
Jenkintown	50.8	14.6	650	41	41,995
Whitemarsh	52.9	15.1	584	26	36,565
Radnor	58.4	12.1	674	17	45,360
Lower Merion	68.8	11.6	644	20	50,417

Tinicum, and Trainer continue to levy low rates and fall below
Marcus Hook in expenditures, Tinicum spending as much as it
does only through receiving approximately $100 per pupil
from the federal impacted area program.

Upper Gwynedd and Plymouth deviate from expectations,
the former spending less than its social rank would indicate,
the latter more. In both cases, the effect of jointure influences
are evident. Plymouth is linked to wealthy, high social ranking
Whitemarsh in a junior-senior high school jointure. Upper
Gwynedd's six partners include Townships as well as Suburbs,
none nearly as wealthy as Upper Gwynedd and all varying considerably in social rank.

The table illustrates yet another aspect of urban differentiation, the two sources of municipal wealth. Although it is obvious that to qualify as a wealthy municipality some balance of
industrial and commercial activity is usually required, the high
social rank municipalities count for their wealth upon the income of their residents and the value of their homes. Wealthy,
low-social-rank municipalities are industrial places. Only occa-

160   Suburban Differences and Metropolitan Policies

sionally in the past has it been possible for a Jenkintown to combine high-status residences with large amounts of commercial activity. (Commerce, is of course more amenable to such mixing than industry.) But now we find newly developing Upper Gwynedd apparently able to balance large amounts of industry and high social rank.

Upper Gwynedd's social rank does not yet make it a Lower Merion, nor even a Whitemarsh. But what of the future, and more particularly what will be its appeal to the locational preferences of high-status individuals in light of the school policy it presently pursues in cooperation with six poorer, lower-social-ranking partners? One might predict that jointures on the fringes of the metropolis, conceived as rural solutions, will have stormy days ahead, as the process of urbanization drives a wedge between the urban and rural districts.

Religion and School Policy

As previously suggested, there were more than a few variables associated with differences in revenue per pupil. Most could be related to social rank or to either or both market value per capita and percent population in school. Religion, however, although significantly related to all three, appeared to influence policy somewhat independently. Religion has already been noted in regard to Upper Darby's emergence as a "wealthy" municipality. Parochial school enrollment affects school policy in several ways. Large parochial school enrollments result in districts' having high ratios of total population to children in public schools. The effect on market value per pupil is often to place these communities among the more wealthy in terms of the state-aid formula. Many, but not all of the municipalities with substantial parochial school enrollments, are among the lowest-social-ranking Suburbs. (There is a correlation of −.306

between social rank and parochial school enrollment.) While the aid formula requires moderate to large amounts of local revenue from them, these communities all raise less revenue than others with comparable market value per pupil.

When social rank is also held constant, the municipalities with large parochial school enrollments spend as do others within their range of resources and social rank, almost always, however, standing at the bottom of their range. Parochial school enrollment appears, then, to have only a slightly inhibiting influence on school expenditures. It is an inhibition consistent with the level of preferences expected from communities of varying social rank and is manifested in a most understandable manner, considering the personal sacrifices necessary for the support of two school systems. Districts with high parochial school enrollment always levy lower school tax rates than communities with comparable market value per pupil and social rank.

Summary

Differentiation in the metropolitan area is reflected in varying degrees of support for local schools. A community's level of school support is initially related to the resources available to it and to the number of pupils in its public schools. By reducing disparities in resource-need ratios, state aid lessens their influence upon expenditure levels and enables preferences associated with populations of differing social ranks to emerge in the Suburbs, and throughout the sector, as the most discriminating characteristic affecting school expenditures.

But the influence of social rank, and of resources and needs as well, is modified by the numerous Suburban and, especially semi-urban jointures. Cooperation, of necessity, must compromise diversity. Whether it can be achieved only at the level of the lowest common denominator is a question of obvious concern to the many Suburbs currently engaged in resisting school-district consolidation. That it will become of concern to semi-urban municipalities, as yet undifferentiated, but soon to feel the effects of urbanization, is equally obvious. But more of this later.

NOTES

1. This millage is an interpolation of data contained in several reports of the Governor's Committee on Education. No median is available, but ten mills is probably a very close approximation.

2. Thus stated, there is an implication that each district must spend $5800 per teaching unit to receive its full share of state aid. The formula also may be interpreted as requiring a 4 3/8 mills tax levy before state aid is forthcoming. Neither is true. The allocation determined by formula is distributed by the state, regardless of the actual expenditures or taxes of the local districts. But since all spend at least $5800, it is convenient to view the subsidy as a percentage of the first $5800 of expenditures.

3. Metropolitan Cleveland is analyzed in Seymour Sacks and William F. Hellmuth, Jr., *Financing Government in a Metropolitan Area* (Glencoe: The Free Press of Glencoe, Inc., 1961). Metropolitan St. Louis is analyzed in John C. Bollens (ed.) *Exploring the Metropolis* (Berkeley: University of California Press, 1961).

4. Two Suburbs were eliminated from the school analysis, Bryn Athyn and Millbourne. Both are extremely small and send their few children to schools of neighboring municipalities, although they do have school boards.

5. A test was run using market value per pupil and social rank instead of the three variables here reported. The resulting influence of social rank and the combined resource-need measure was much the same.

6. Bollens, *op. cit.*, p. 323 and pp. 327–330.

7. Sacks and Hellmuth, *op. cit.*, p. 123.

VI

Fiscal Responses: Tax Policy

Expenditure analysis has identified and sought to explain variations in municipal and school-expenditure policies. Tax analysis has complementary, but not identical objectives. Expenditures indicate who spends, why, and what for. Tax analysis asks at what price. It is particularly relevant to questions of the relationship between expenditures and resources, and of the extent to which tax considerations influence policy decisions. The concept of tax effort underlies examination of these questions.

Tax policy can also be viewed independently of expenditure decisions. Having decided to pursue various programs, how do municipalities distribute the burden of their support? Burden is not synonomous with effort. The latter is a communal concept, the former personal. The distribution of burden undoubtedly influences tax effort and in turn has a feed-back effect on expenditure decisions. But in light of their distributive effects, decisions to employ alternative types of taxes are a distinct and significant form of political choice.

Tax effort and burden are two focuses of this chapter. A third is the comparison of emphases upon school and municipal services. This comparison is better served through analysis of tax effort than expenditures, for both services use identical tax bases and are therefore in direct competition for revenue.

Post World War II Revenue Needs

In the years immediately following World War II, local governments throughout the country were forced to increase revenues to meet the accumulation of deferred capital improvements and salary increases, the need for adapting older urban environments to the auto age, the pressure of increasing costs in older areas, and to provide basic services for the new suburbs. States were repeatedly called upon to help solve "local" financial problems. Most did so by recognizing that the problems were more than local and increasing grants-in-aid and shared taxes. Pennsylvania responded by, in effect, throwing the problem back to local units through its so called "tax-anything law." To be sure, the state did increase its share of school support, but in response to demands for additional aid, the legislature granted school districts and municipalities authority to use their own ingenuity in finding new tax sources.

Act 481 of 1947

Prior to passage of the "tax-anything law," local governments had enjoyed limited access to non-property tax sources. Although some municipalities in the area were levying occupation taxes, the only widely used non-property tax was the school district's per capita tax. Philadelphia, of course, had pioneered in local income taxation and used other non-property taxes, by permission of the legislature.

Act 481 of 1947, as subsequently amended, permitted all municipalities and school districts to employ any tax, not otherwise prohibited, that was not being used by the state. If the state enacted a tax subsequent to its use by local units, the local tax ordinances would be vacated immediately, unless expressly permitted by the legislature. Thus, the many municipalities that had adopted a one percent Deed Transfer Tax prior to 1951 were permitted to continue its use when the legislature elected to levy a state-wide Realty Transfer Tax in that year, and the State tax did not foreclose future applications of the Deed Transfer Tax by localities.

Act 481 and its amendments identified most of the taxes that would be used and some of the jurisdictional and rate conflicts that might arise. The act stipulates rate limits and calls for the sharing of taxes when levied by coterminous jurisdictions upon the same object, person, or transaction. The maximum per capita rate that can be charged any one individual under Act 481 is $10. This is in addition to a $5 rate authorized to school districts by earlier provisions of the School Code. Coterminous school districts and municipalities may both levy Act-481 per capita taxes, but at a combined rate not to exceed $10. They may agree to divide the rate in any way, but, should both seek the maximum, the rate must be equally divided. Per capita rates in the area range from none to $15. Where the maximum is charged, at least $5 is going to the school district under the School Code. The remaining $10 levy is ordinarily divided equally by the school and municipal governments, although occasionally only one government will levy the entire $10.

The major Act 481 revenue producer in the state is the local income or wage tax. Its maximum rate is one percent. The rate may be apportioned through the agreement of coterminous units or equally shared should their combined rates add up to more than one percent. The income tax is subject to further jurisdictional complications. While school districts may tax the income of residents only, municipalities may tax both residents and non-residents. But no taxpayer may be required to pay more than one percent. Where rate conflicts exist, Act 481 gives precedence to the place of residence.

In areas of commutation, local income tax administration is extremely complicated. Metropolitan Philadelphia is spared such confusion, for the tax is virtually unused outside of the central city. Act 481 gives precedence to the place of residence where more than one unit seeks to tax income at the maximum rate, but neither the precedence nor the rate limitation apply to income or wage taxes levied under authority of a statute other than Act 481. Where Act-481 income taxes conflict with Philadelphia's wage tax, precedence is given to the city. Because the city's rate is more than one percent, any neighboring municipality or school district that levied an income tax under Act 481 would have to exempt those of its residents who work in Philadelphia. It is generally believed that this precedence accounts for the fact that only a handful of units on the outskirts of the metropolitan area levy income taxes.

In addition to the few income taxes and the widely used deed transfer and per capita levies, other Act-481 sources of revenue in the area are occupations, mercantile transactions, amusements, trailers and mechanical devices. Their use and productivity vary, but come nowhere near that of the deed transfer and per capita taxes. Almost all municipalities and/or school districts levy one Act-481 tax; some use as many as six.

Real Property Tax Dependence

The post-war expansion in governmental activity continued through the decade of the 50's. Between 1950 and 1960 revenue raised for both school and municipal services doubled on a per capita basis. Table VI–1 compares mean Suburban, Town and Township per capita revenues in 1950 and 1960. School revenue per capita is a misleading figure for it does not take into account the fact that most Suburbs have lesser numbers of pupils relative to total population than Towns or Townships, nor does it take into account changes in the ratio of pupils to total population between 1950 and 1960. Nevertheless, the additive per capita revenues do indicate a substantial increase in school and municipal activity and costs, with a larger school increase everywhere but in Philadelphia.

Table VI–1

Mean School and Municipal Revenue per Capita
by Study Area, 1950 and 1960

	School Revenue		Municipal Revenue		Total	
	1950	1960	1950	1960	1950	1960
Suburbs	$37.99	$76.08	$16.75	$28.20	$54.74	$104.28
Towns	38.92	88.59	15.05	25.91	53.97	113.50
Townships	38.17	95.68	9.45	16.26	47.62	111.94
Philadelphia	27.75	49.95	57.79	123.79	85.55	173.62

Where did the additional revenue come from? Grants-in-aid helped, but the proportions of total revenue derived from intergovernmental sources increased only slightly between 1950 and 1960. (See Table VI–2). Non-tax revenues constitute about the same proportions of total revenue in both years. The major increase has come from local taxes, a sizeable, but not preponderant amount from the new-found taxing power of Act 481. Little use had been made of the act by 1950. The primary non-property taxes then employed were the occupation and school per capita levies. By 1960 Act-481 revenues had become a substantial element in the tax structure of many municipalities.

Table VI–2

Intergovernmental Revenue as a Percent of Total Revenue
by Study Area, 1950 and 1960

	School Aid as a Percent of Total School Revenue		All Aid as a Percent of School & Municipal Revenue	
	1950	1960	1950	1960
Suburbs	28.0	29.3	21.7	23.7
Towns	42.6	42.9	33.1	35.7
Townships	41.6	42.1	41.2	45.9
Philadelphia	13.4	32.8	7.5	11.4

Table VI–3

Real Property Tax Revenue as a Percent of Total School
and Municipal Tax Revenue by Study Area, 1950 and 1960

	Mean of the Percentages for Each Unit		Mean for the Area as one Unit	
	1950	1960	1950	1960
Suburbs	94.9%	86.6%	94.0%	90.1%
Towns	81.9	76.1	84.6	80.7
Townships	79.7	76.9	79.5	73.7
Philadelphia			62.1	57.7

In Table VI–3, the percentage of tax revenue derived from
the real property tax is calculated in two ways. One shows the
average of each municipality, the other shows the real property
tax percentage of total Suburban tax revenues, Town tax revenues and Township tax revenues. The differences in the two
calculations indicate that the effect of non-property taxation is
selective. While some municipalities may derive as much as
40 percent of their revenues from non-property tax sources,

the real property tax continues to supply 90 percent of the tax revenue raised throughout the Suburbs. Moreover, the effect of non-property taxes is more pronounced in municipalities that raise lesser amounts of revenue, accounting partially for the differences in the two sets of percentages.

The doubling of revenues for the ten-year period reported in Table VI–1 ignores the effects of inflation and fails to distinguish between increases in governmental activity and mere increases in cost. However, by any measure of inflation or real cost, the increase in revenues per capita is quite real. In terms of the householder's budget, constant dollar revenue increased approximately 70 percent. Viewed from the perspective of what local governments could buy for the additional dollars, the increase was about 45 percent. This differential in part reflects the severity of the financial squeeze in which local governments are caught. Governmental costs have risen more rapidly than Gross National Product, the general price index, or the consumer price index.

Real property taxes have supplied most of the additional revenue. The property-tax base, however, has not increased as much as revenues. Between 1950 and 1960, market value per capita increased 35 percent in the Suburbs, 37 percent in the Towns, and 42 percent in the Townships. These values were also affected by inflation. Application of a property-value deflator requires adjustments taking into account local assessment practices, the amount and timing of new construction between 1950 and 1960, and other information not easily acquired. Even in current dollar value, however, the growth of the property-tax base has not kept pace with the revenue increase in constant dollars. As most householders can attest, real increases in property tax rates have been required to support the growth and increased costs of governmental activities.

Table VI–4

Market Value per Capita Increases by Study Area, 1950–1960

	1950	1960	Percent Increase
Suburbs	$3,052	$4,132	35%
Towns	2,432	3,328	37
Townships	2,644	3,750	42
Philadelphia	2,569	2,871	12

Property Tax Rates in the Metropolitan Area

The property tax rate is a product of three factors: expenditure levels, the size of the property-tax base, and the availability of non-property tax revenues. Increasing the tax base at a given expenditure level will permit a lowering of the tax rate. Similarly, at a given expenditure level, the larger the proportion of expenditures that can be supported by grants, non-property taxes, and other revenue, the lower the tax rate will be.

Property tax rates throughout the area vary much less than do wealth, expenditures, and the proportions of school and municipal revenue derived from non-property tax sources. This testifies, in part, to the success of the school aid formula. The combined school and municipal tax rates on residential property are summarized in Table VI–5.

Table VI–5

Effective Residential Property Tax Rates,
Central Tendency by Study Area

	Mean	S	V	Range
Suburbs	19.4	3.8	.196	6.1–25.1
Towns	18.9	4.9	.259	10.1–27.9
Townships	16.9	3.6	.213	9.1–23.1
Philadelphia	23.3			

The difference in mean Suburban, Town, and Township rates might have been anticipated in Table VI–3. There, dependence upon the real property tax was found to decline from a Suburban high to a Township low. It is in the lesser spending municipalities that non-property taxes can have the greatest impact on property tax rates. Townships generally have low tax rates, because their municipal expenditures are slight and because grants and non-property taxes constitute large portions of their total revenue needs. Low-density Residential Suburbs also spend sparingly, but their low tax rates also reflect their relatively high market value per capita. Despite extensive use of non-property taxes, most Towns lack a sufficient property-tax base to support their relatively high expenditures with low tax rates. As a class, their tax rates are exceeded only by the High-density Residential Suburbs. The lowest of all tax rates are shared by Townships and some of the wealthier Industrial and Commercial Centers.

Property-tax rates are a true measure of neither tax effort nor burden. They do, however, represent the largest and most direct portion of the householder's payments in support of local governmental activities. In the absence of a more adequate measure, they will be used as an index of comparative tax effort.

The most commonly used measure of tax effort is total revenue expressed as a millage of market value. It yielded no results when employed in this study. We believe that the measure is misleading. It really indicates what property tax rates would be if all revenue were raised from property taxes. But as a measure of current tax effort, it is inadequate; for non-property taxes often bear no relationship to the size of the property tax base. For example, it is possible, although very unlikely, for both of two municipalities to derive all their revenue from per capita taxes. If one had large amounts of non-residential property in its assessments, its revenue expressed as a millage of market value would be much lower than that of the other. But would this represent a lower tax effort? Individuals in both municipalities are paying the same amount of taxes, and these amounts are not at all related to the character or size of the property-tax base. The relationship of tax payments to property values may say something about relative burdens associated with comparable tax efforts, but, as a measure of effort, the fact that non-property taxes calculate to a high or low millage on market value is illusory if not meaningless.

For all its shortcomings, the equalized or effective property tax rate does indicate what basic taxes are paid by owners of the same type of property in different jurisdictions. In short, it is an accurate, if not complete, measure of tax effort and will be so employed hereafter, noting where necessary the effect on property-tax rates of other revenues. The analysis of effort that follows is descriptive rather than mathematical. For the sake of manageability, and to avoid the highway-aid complications of rural revenues, it will deal solely with Suburban tax effort.

Suburban Municipal Tax Effort

In the Suburbs, residential tax rates for municipal purposes range from 7.6 mills in High-density Residential Narberth to 1.4 mills in Low-density Residential Lower Providence. In Table VI–6, the Suburbs with the ten highest and ten lowest municipal tax rates are identified by type and their expenditures per capita shown in parenthesis.

There is little difference in the high- and low-taxing municipalities' use of non-property taxes. In fact, contrary to what might have been expected, all of the high rate municipalities

Table VI–6—Suburbs

Ten Highest and Ten Lowest Municipal Tax Rates

High Rate 7.6 - 5.3 Mills	Low Rate 2.3 - 1.4 Mills
H.D. Narberth ($38.95)	I & C Upper Gwynedd ($15.68)
H.D. Darby Boro (18.18)	I & C Tinicum (45.17)
H.D. Upper Darby (16.88)	I & C Upper Merion (27.72)
I & C Jenkintown (45.09)	L.D. Upper Providence (13.18)
I & C Bridgeport (29.62)	L.D. East Norriton (6.89)
I & C Norristown (28.22)	L.D. Hatfield Twp. (7.87)
I & C Chester City (33.23)	L.D. Treydyffrin (20.94)
H.D. Bryn Athyn (39.29)	L.D. Middletown (14.03)
H.D. Lower Merion (45.24)	H.D. Chester Twp. (15.87)
H.D. East Lansdowne (34.74)	L.D. Lower Providence (6.29)

use one or more Act-481 taxes, while two of the low rate jurisdiction rely solely on the property tax. The difference in tax
rates is not explained by the availability of non-property tax
revenues.[1]

Although there is an obvious relationship between tax rates
and expenditures, it is not uniform. Industrial and Commercial
Centers are among the highest and lowest taxers, but even those
with low rates spend quite highly. Of the four high-taxing
Centers, three are extremely poor. Despite their lack of resources, they spend well, at the expense of high tax rates. The
fourth, Jenkintown, is quite wealthy, but its expenditures are
so high as to require considerable tax effort. All of the low-
taxing Industrial and Commercial Centers are extremely
wealthy. While two have recently been developed and therefor
have, as yet, low expenditure requirements, all are capable of
deriving large amounts of revenue from low tax rates. While
wealth affects the ease with which industrial and commercial
Centers support their municipal services, it does not determine
the level of services maintained. The older Centers respond to

their physical needs by spending, if necessary, at the expense of high tax rates.

The pattern for the Residential Suburbs supports the proposition that expenditures are not merely a product of wealth. Those low in density, generally spend little. Some are quite wealthy and require minimal tax rates to fulfill their limited revenue needs. High-density Suburbs spend more. The poorest can do so only by levying high tax rates. But some of the wealthiest are also among the high taxers. For all its wealth, Lower Merion must levy high taxes to support the services it has decided upon. Jenkintown, in addition to its industrial and commercial activity is also high in social rank. This perhaps accounts for its extremely high expenditures and tax rates. Although it is not among the ten highest taxers, Radnor has the highest expenditures and tax rate of the Low-density Suburbs. For the Suburbs and the area as a whole, while wealthy municipalities spend more than poor municipalities, the difference in their expenditures is greater than the difference in their wealth. Large expenditures do require high tax rates.

The foregoing suggests that tax rates are merely the outcome of the interplay of expenditure decisions and the availability of resources. Is this to say that tax rates in and of themselves do not influence expenditure decisions? Obviously not. But it does indicate that tax sensitivity is of less importance than those characteristics identified in Chapter IV. Need appears to be the primary determinant of expenditures, and depending upon the availability of resources, of tax effort. Industrial and Commercial Centers and High-density Residential Suburbs spend more; thus, for the poorest among them, this means tax rates are out of proportion to the amounts of revenue actually produced by their tax base. Despite their wealth high social rank municipalities demand service levels of such magnitude as to require high tax rates.

Suburban School Tax Effort

In addition to expenditure levels, wealth, and the availability of other revenues, school-district property-tax rates are influenced by the equalizing feature of the State's grant-in-aid formula. Assuming substantial similarity in the use of non-property taxes and ratios of pupil to total population, the formula requires a higher tax rate of the wealthier of two municipalities having the same expenditure per pupil. There is a definite tendency, particularly evident in the Suburbs, for school-property tax rates to increase with wealth and with revenue per pupil. The former relationship may be attributed to the equalization formula, but the latter goes far beyond its requirements. Generally, school districts that spend more do so by exerting greater tax effort.

The Suburban school districts with the ten highest and ten lowest tax rates are listed in Table VI–7, with their revenue per pupil shown in parentheses. Wealthy districts are to be found on both sides of the listing. The prevalence of High-density Residential Suburbs among the high taxers is significant not because of the density of these municipalities, but because they are almost all high in social rank. The seven Industrial and Commercial Centers among the low taxers are all low-social-ranking, as are the three Residential Suburbs that complete the list. (Millbourne has again been excluded from the list as has Bryn Athyn. Both operate no schools. The latter has very few pupils in public schools.)

The high-rate municipalities in Table VI–7 are generally wealthier than the low-rate, although Marcus Hook, Tinicum, Trainer and Eddystone are among the wealthiest municipalities in the metropolitan area. Marcus Hook's and Tinicum's wealth enable them to maintain substantial school programs at extremely low tax rates. On the other hand, Upper Merion, also

Table VI–7—Suburbs

Ten Highest and Ten Lowest School Tax Rates

High Rate 21.2 - 16.6 Mills		Low Rate 9.6 - 5.5 Mills	
H.D. Rutledge	($607)	H.D. Clifton Hts.	($444)
H.D. Swarthmore	(607)	I & C Eddystone	(477)
H.D. Parkside	(434)	H.D. Colwyn	(396)
H.D. Cheltenham	(590)	I & C Conshocken	(489)
H.D. Upper Moreland	(558)	I & C Lansdale	(460)
H.D. Abington	(578)	I & C Trainer	(381)
E. Morrisville	(618)	I & C Chester City	(434)
I & C Upper Merion	(606)	L.D. Warminster	(448)
H.D. Springfield (M)	(524)	I & C Marcus Hook	(513)
H.D. Darby Twp.	(508)	I & C Tinicum	(507)

wealthy, but high in social rank and with a greater proportion of pupils to total population takes greater advantage of its valuable industrial and commercial property, through a higher tax rate, and thus maintains higher school expenditures. So too, do the other wealthy high social ranking municipalities.

When tax rates are correlated with revenue per pupil for all Suburbs, the obvious association of effort, social rank, and program level shown in Table VI–7 becomes less clear. Nevertheless, without any controls, there are significant, but small positive correlations between tax rates and revenue per pupil and social rank. Resources, which figured prominently in differences of revenue per pupil, bear no relationship to tax effort.

Wealthy districts can and do sustain higher levels of school support than poor districts with no greater effort. Wealthy, high-social-ranking municipalities do exert greater effort to increase programs even more. Few wealthy districts reduce their tax rates to the point where their expenditures equal those of the poorer communities. Those that do are *never* high in social rank. Although some high-social-ranking districts such as Lower Merion have enough wealth and enough children in private schools to support extensive school programs at "bargain" tax rates, for most high-social-rank districts, educational expenditure preferences require high tax rates. On the other hand, many low-social-ranking districts with moderate tax bases and large numbers of children in parochial schools, reduce tax rates much below Lower Merion and devote little revenue to those of their pupils in public schools. Wealth provides the foundation for the structure of differentiation in school support; social rank adds the roof.

Competition in School and Municipal Tax Effort

Chapter IV referred more than once to the possibility that the pressure of school needs operated to reduce municipal expenditures or that, conversely, large municipal expenditures might have a depressing effect on school support. The question can be put in terms of the classic argument for school fiscal independence. There is a widespread belief, institutionalized in the independent taxing powers given most school districts, that schools would suffer without fiscal independence. Indeed a current controversy over the control of Philadelphia's school finances bears evidence of its continued popularity. The argument for independence contains overtones of political reformism and distrust of organized political decision-making processes, but most practically, a basic assumption that two needles are better than one in drawing blood from a stone.

The argument against educational separatism has usually rested on grounds of political responsibility and coordination of local services and has usually ignored the matter of financial support. But a theory of school-municipal integration has been advanced that challenges the financial assumption of those advocating separation. It asserts that where school and municipal budget requests are jointly considered by one representative political body, the process of compromise-and-support building that is the essence of politics, may actually result in greater financial support being given to both functions.[2]

We hesitate to draw a causal connection, but school revenue per pupil and municipal expenditures per capita are positively and significantly correlated in each of the municipal classifications and throughout the metropolitan area. The association becomes even more significant when the high municipal spending Industrial and Commercial Centers are excluded. The process of exclusion high-lights the selective nature of school and municipal competition; for only in the low-social-ranking communities do wide discrepancies between school and municipal tax effort appear.

These findings suggest that the question of comparative support for school and municipal services is related more to the social characteristics of differing political units than to their integrated or separated policy making mechanisms. The question is not what institutional arrangement increases or decreases competition, but what kinds of people are apt to perceive and react to competition between school and municipal tax demands. Outside of Philadelphia, all the metropolitan school districts currently enjoy fiscal freedom. We suspect that there would be little difference in relative tax shares were both functions combined. If schools suffered, that result would probably be confined to low-social-rank municipalities, for those of high social rank tax and spend highly for both purposes.

Although school and municipal policies represent responses to different sets of conditions, one social characteristic is associated with high expenditures for both services—high social rank. There is not a single example of a high-social-rank Residential Suburb spending considerably for municipal services and spending relatively little for education. Nor is there a school district with high expenditures, whose coterminous municipality does not either spend or tax highly. Even in Low-density Residential Suburbs, where municipal expenditure requirements are ordinarily low, there is no apparent choosing between school and municipal programs when both expenditures and tax rates are considered.

In contrast, there is a decided favoring of municipal services in low-social-ranking Industrial and Commercial Centers. Their resources and tax effort combine to produce either high municipal expenditures at low rates or moderate expenditures at high rates, but their school-tax rates and revenue per pupil are almost uniformly low. Low-social-ranking municipalities are very likely to have lower than average school-tax rates and average or above municipal rates.

Whether this tendency reflects a greater tax sensitivity in low-social-rank municipalities and a consequent willingness to sacrifice school support in the face of competition for limited resources, or whether it represents differences in influence and access to policy making enjoyed by various interests within these municipalities, is a question worthy of further research. In either event, it is evident that in so far as tax rates influence expenditure decisions, and to the extent that municipal and school policy-making bodies compete for the use of identical tax bases, low-social-ranking municipalities are most likely to respond to the pressure of tax sensitivity by sacrificing school to municipal programs.

The Real Property Tax Burden

It is not necessary to repeat here descriptions of the real property tax's regressivity. The burden of the tax is relevant to this discussion in considering two questions: To what extent does the burden of the property tax lead to diversification of tax policy? To what extent does the burden affect tax effort? The first leads to examination of the use of Act 481 in the metropolitan area. The second returns to the question of the impact of tax rates upon expenditure decisions.

The householder burden index was constructed to measure the personal sacrifice associated with varying tax efforts. Municipal and school real property tax rates were expressed as a ratio of average residential market value per household. The latter, it was assumed, roughly approximated differences in personal wealth. The index then, relates intermunicipal tax rate differentials to intermunicipal wealth differentials. A 10 mill tax on an average household value of $10,000 yields an index of 100; the index for the same rate on a value of $15,000 is 67. The higher the index, the greater the burden of the tax rate. A $100 tax, payed by the owner of a $10,000 home, is probably a greater sacrifice than a $150 payment by the owner. of a $15,000 home.

The householder burden index correlates negatively with social rank, municipal wealth and personal wealth. The relationship to industrial and commercial specialization is not clear. Combined, these observations suggest that the high tax rates of high-social-ranking and wealthy residential areas are probably a lesser burden to their residdents than the lower tax rates of the low-social-ranking wealthy or poor Industrial and Commercial Centers. Intermunicipal differences in personal wealth are greater than differences in tax rates.

The distinction between effort and burden may explain the apparently greater tax sensitivity of low-social-ranking municipalities and the absence of evidence of residential "milking" of industrial and commercial tax bases. Municipalities of low social rank, including almost all the Industrial and Commercial Centers, have extremely low average household values. Even where the presence of highly valued non-residential property permits servicing municipal and school needs through low tax rates, the burden on owners of inexpensive homes is substantial.

Despite the fact that a rate increase will, at times, produce as much as three non-residential to one residential property tax dollar, the burden on the home-owner appears to be sufficient to forestall rate increases. That this burden should stimulate tax sensitivity is understandable. That tax sensitivity results in an apparent willingness to sacrifice school to municipal programs reflects the value preferences assigned these services in low-social-ranking municipalities.

Tax Diversification

The burden of the property tax offers a point of departure for viewing community efforts at tax diversification. If diversification affords the opportunity of trasferring or shifting burdens from one group of tax payers to another, then the property tax burden and its distribution among various interests will obviously influence decisions regarding the adoption of non-property taxes.

To what extent does Act 481 redstribute the burden of govenrmental support ordinarily associated with the real property tax? The major Act-481 taxes available to municipalities and school districts in metropolitan Philadelphia are Deed Transfer, Per Capita, Occupation, Mercantile and Amusement taxes. The prospects for shifting or capitalizing actual tax payments vary, but no extended economic analysis is necessary to observe several predominant features of these tax alternatives.

The Act-481 taxes provide greater tax relief to industrial establishments than to any other class of property owners, because Act-481 taxes replace real property taxes. At the same time industrial processes are not taxable under its provisions. Indeed, industrial interests throughout the state were very active in supporting the passage of Act 481 in 1947.

Only two taxes, the Mercantile and Amusement levies enable

municipalities to "export" governmental costs to customers coming from other communities. The Deed Transfer Tax is somewhat exportable. Chargeable to either sellers or buyers, it is popularly viewed as a form of initiation fee for new residents in a community, or as a severance charge upon those leaving. Its widespread usage testifies perhaps to its lack of impact upon residents already committed to municipalities.

Per capita and occupation taxes are burdens upon individuals. While they may alter the proportionality of taxes otherwise paid solely on the basis of property holdings, their greatest effect is upon the distribution of burden between home-owners as a class and owners of non-residential property.

Self-interest should lead the residents of municipalities with regional commercial or amusement activities to favor mercantile or amusement taxes. Industrial and Commercial property-owners should opt for those taxes affecting individuals rather than property, although the former have much to gain from all non-property taxes. Each or all of the Act-481 taxes may not actually relieve homeowners from tax payments. But if the tax comes in a different form, or even if the bill comes in a different envelope, it may be more acceptable to a taxpayer who feels hard-pressed by the regular property-tax bill.

In deciding tax policy, local governments must be aware of their competitive relationships with other municipalities. High taxes may reduce property values, drive away customers, or penalize local development in other ways At least this is the presumtion

The above discussion suggests several hypotheses that may explain the use of property tax alternatives: (1) Tax diversification increases as the real property tax burden on home-owners increases. (2) The distribution of property between Industrial, Commercial, and Residential uses will affect the choice of Act

481 taxes and the extent of their use. (3) Diversification is related to geographic location.

These hypotheses are not mutually-excluding, nor can they take into account, with the data available, differences in the political structure and control of municipalities. It obviously makes a great deal of difference in considering a mercantile tax, if the local council is or is not controlled by Main Street merchants. Subject to these limitations, the hypotheses may be tested in the suburban portion of the metropolitan area.

How is diversification to be measured? A community may attempt to diversify by levying a number of non-property taxes. But the productivity of the latter may be so low, and the revenue requirements of the municipality so great, that the effect of the non-property taxes upon property-tax rates and the percentage of revenue derived from property taxes is almost negligible. On the other hand, municipalities with extremely low expenditures may support most of their activities with the proceeds of one well-administered non-property tax. Diversification may, then, be taken to mean either intent or success. Since the focus of this study is choice, we are more interested in the former, and, hence, the number of taxes levied, but their actual impact on local finances cannot be ignored.

Tax Diversification and Tax Burden. The first hypothesis suggests that the householder burden index may correlate with the use of non-property taxes. A significant, although not very large correlation, does appear after certain controls taking into account the other hypotheses are introduced. There is no relationship between the actual tax rate and diversification; nor does any pattern emerge based upon tax revenue expressed as a millage of market value. Both the tax rate and the potential rate, if all revenues were to come from the property tax, would be affected by expenditure levels. But diversification is not related to expenditures, tax rates now levied, or potential rates.

Diversification's association with household burden is supplemented by a general tendency for municipalities with few resources to use Act-481 taxes. For most municipalities, low market value per capita is virtually synonymous with inexpensive homes. The householder burden index relates home value to tax rates, which are in turn affected by expenditure levels. But poorer communities, regardless of tax rate and burden index, display a decided tendency to diversify. The foregoing suggests that it is not burden, as such, that leads to diversification, but that prevailing attitudes in poorer communities may create an environment conducive to great sensitivity with regard to property-tax rates among local officials.

The suspicion that diversification among poor municipalities is due less to the burden of the property tax than to attitudes toward tax rates in general is given further support by examination of the financial effect of non-property taxes. In municipalities with large expenditure obligations, Act-481 taxes provide small proportions of total revenue needs, yet poor industrial and commercial centers diversify despite the shift in burden from industrial property thus entailed. Poor residential communities diversify despite the fact that the possibilities of diversification for them represent a change in the form of the tax bill rather than a shifting of costs from homeowners to other groups. In fact the major property tax alternative employed by these municipalities, the per capita tax, is even more regressive than the property tax.

Wealthy residential communities levy fewer numbers of taxes than poor ones, even though many of the former levy high tax rates. Whether this reflects attitudinal differences, a lesser burden perceived, or a realization that diversification would do little to change total tax payments for most homeowners, the difference in behavior is significant.

Tax Diversification and Non-Residential Land Use. Wealthy Industrial and Commercial Centers do not diversify, even though the value of their homes is often very low and the householder's burden from the property tax quite high. This is especially true for wealthy industrial centers. If the previously discussed diversification in poor industrial centers is a product of industrialists' pressure on local officials to relieve them of property tax burden, one would expect such pressure to be applied in wealthy industrial areas as well. But a contrary pressure appears to be operative in the wealthier industrial centers. Although homeowners may not be milking industry, they are sufficiently self-interested not to employ taxes that spare industry at the expense of homeowners. Several levy nothing but the real property tax.

Commercial activity affords the opportunity of shifting costs to non-residents through the use of mercantile and amusement taxes. The Towns, municipalities that developed primarily as sub-regional commercial centers, use these taxes extensively. In the Suburban portion of the metropolitan area, their use is sporadic and by no means extensive. The amusement tax represents a small financial contribution to the fiscal structures of those municipalities where it is employed. The mercantile tax, even at low rates, provides substantial revenues for some municipalities.

The tax relief that can be gained through the mercantile tax can only be realized in municipalities with considerable amounts of commercial activity. Several municipalities wth large shopping centers appear to be attempting to export their governmental costs, but many more, especially those with large property-tax bases and those that are high in social rank are not. Once again, wealth (communal or personal) appears to be related to acceptance of the property tax and a disinclination to diversify.

Tax Diversification and Geographic Location. No clear-cut pattern is evident, but it is more than likely that the use of mercantile taxes is affected by geographic location and the nearness of competitors. Widespread Town use of the tax does suggest that isolation from competition is a factor.

Geographic location appears to be related to the use of other taxes as well. Delaware County municipalities and school districts use Act 481 with the least frequency. Bucks County's Suburbs, Towns and Townships are prolific in their use of non-property taxes. This grouping by counties may reflect the community of opinion shaped in county organizations of local officials.

Act 481 has been most useful to communities having modest revenue needs. However, as an aid to most urban communities, the "tax-anything law" has been singularly unhelpful. Non-property taxes act as buffers to the property-tax burden in a few specialized commercial centers that can tap sales made to non-residents. Most of the other taxes yield little and merely substitute one type of homeowner's tax payments for another. Although the substitution may have other significant redistributive effects, they operate primarily to the disadvantage of homeowners.

The availability of broad taxing power has beckoned invitingly to the poor Suburbs. Many have succumbed to the temptation, but the results in terms of revenue have been meager.

NOTES

1. Millbourne, with the lowest tax rate in the area relies primarily on the mercantile tax, but it has been excluded from this table because of its deviant characteristics described above.

2. Julius Margolis, "Metropolitan Finance Problems: Territories, Functions, and Growth;" National Bureau of Economic Research, *Public Finance Needs, Sources and Utilization,* (Princeton, N.J.: Princeton University Press, 1961).

VII

Land-Use Policy

This chapter is concerned with suburban land use. It examines the allocation of land to industrial, commercial, and residential uses and the density of residential development. Granting the somewhat determinative nature of history, topography, and access to transportation; communities do, nevertheless, choose planning, zoning, and subdivision policies which may influence their future development. In the final analysis, no matter how wide or narrow a range of alternatives is available to municipalities, it is only through their action that legal designations of land use are made.[1]

The availability of choice is perhaps best attested to by the heated debates and unpredictable outcomes that characterize suburban planning and zoning hearings. Indeed, a perusal of suburban weeklies in the Philadelphia metropolitan area suggests that of all municipal activities, zoning changes command the greatest attention of local residents.

In recent years, several classifications have been employed to distinguish cities and suburbs according to their economic function.[2] The classification here used, percent of land zoned industrial, commercial or residential, is considered the most appropriate reflection of public policy. Others, such as the size or the ratio of labor force to resident population, the size of commercial and industrial establishments, the gross volume of sales or output, all involve decisions and activities which lie beyond the direct control of the municipality. The amount of land zoned for a particular use *is* a public decision.

This analysis is confined to the Suburbs as defined in Chapter II; for these are the municipalities that have made or are making basic land-use decisions. Large portions of the Townships are still in agricultural use. The majority, as yet not having felt development pressures, are unzoned. Towns were excluded because of the unique pattern they represent. Most small, older boroughs, were fully developed years ago and have had little opportunity to respond to urban expansion through land-use controls.

Two of the 90 Suburbs in the sector are located in Chester County. They were eliminated because the analysis is by county and two is too small a number to work with. Seven other Suburbs for which data were not available were also excluded, resulting in an examination of 81 Suburbs. Thirty-nine are in Delaware, 29 in Montgomery, and 13 in Bucks County.[3]

The data were organized by county for several reasons. First, municipalities in each of the three counties are generally in different stages of growth. A majority of Delaware's Suburbs are old, most having reached urban densities by 1920. More of the Montgomery and Bucks Suburbs, and especially the latter, are still in the early stages of growth. Secondly, two of the three county planning commissions have important responsibilities in subdivision approval. In all three, county staff aid for local planning is potentially influential for certain types of planning decisions. In addition to these formal activities, county government can set the tone and atmosphere in which local planning takes place. Finally certain types of data were available only in Delaware County. (Most of the data useful to land-use analysis are collected at the county level, where there are few common procedures for collection or classification.)

Social Rank and Land Use

Suburban communities have generally displayed an ambivalent set of reactions to proposals to allocate land for industrial uses. While industry is often looked upon as bringing tax advantages to a locality (especially if its workers reside elsewhere), the mention of industry often conjures up images of congestion, unsightliness, and activities generally discordant with residential amenities. Hence one might expect to find high-social-ranking Suburbs—those least pressured for tax sources—giving industry a cool reception. There is indeed a high correlation between social rank and the percentage of land zoned residential. The rank-order correlation, on a county by county basis, is Delaware .832, Montgomery .770, and Bucks .651. The higher the social rank of a municipality, the greater is the proportion of land zoned residential and, conversely, the lower the percentage of land zoned for industrial or commercial use.

Industrial Use. There is a negative correlation between social rank and land zoned for non-residential use, but it is larger for industrial than for commercial zoning, suggesting that commercial uses of land have been more acceptable to high-status communities than industrial uses. Nevertheless, a few high-social-ranking municipalities do have 5 or more percent of their land zoned industrial.[4]

In recent years, high-social-rank municipalities have been increasingly permitting industry to enter. This may be partly attributable to the assumed favorable industrial ratio of taxes to service demands. However, high-social-ranking communities' current and increasing receptivity to industry stems not only from financial concerns, but also from the changing nature of industry itself. Industry no longer connotes the ugly factory with noxious odors, air pollution, unpleasant noise, and a low-class labor force. Many Suburbs have found that they can attract industries that employ a professional labor force and take pride in beautifully landscaped and architecturally subdued locations. Moreover, the continued growth of the metropolis and its highway network has enabled Suburbs to house industry while excluding its lower income employees, thus not only taking advantage of the more pleasing aspects of modern industrial plants, but also enjoying even more favorable cost-revenue ratios.

One might expect increases in the number of industries capable of meeting rigid performance requirements to lead to these industries' locating in high-social-ranking communities. Zoning data does not afford a breakdown on type of industry. However, a survey of selected municipalities indicates more rigid industrial performance requirements in high-social-ranking than in low-social ranking municipalities. It is only since World War II that industry has provided "high-status" plants in any sizable numbers.

The changing nature of industry is reflected in an interesting pattern of zoning for industrial use in high-social-ranking municipalities. Older high-social-ranking municipalities zoned their land to exclude, or severely limit, industrial uses. Newer high-social-ranking communities provide for industrial parks and invite selected high-class industries to enter. Delaware County, for example, has the oldest group of municipalities in our study. Of its 19 highest-social-ranking municipalities (the top half), 16 passed their first zoning ordinance prior to 1945, and only one of the 16 has over 5 percent of its land zoned industrial (see Table VII–1). Of the three high social ranking municipalities that passed their first zoning ordinance after

1945, two have over 5 percent of their land zoned industrial.

Fewer Bucks and Montgomery County municipalities had pre-1945 zoning ordinances. But the pattern for the higher-social-ranking municipalities within each county is similar to Delaware's. High-social-ranking municipalities that passed zoning ordinances after 1945 zoned more land for industrial use than those that passed zoning ordinances prior to 1945.

Table VII–1

Year of First Zoning Ordinance and Percent of Land Zoned
Industrial in High-social-ranking Suburbs by County

	First Zoning Ordinance Before 1945		First Zoning Ordiance After 1945	
	Over 5%	Under 5%	Over 5%	Under 5%
Delaware	1	15	2	1
Montgomery	2	8	3	1
Bucks	0	1	3	2
Total	3	24	8	4

Table VII–1 is based on the top-social-ranking Suburbs in each county. If all suburbs are grouped together, and the 39 highest in social rank are chosen without regard to counties, a somewhat different group is obtained (16 from Delaware, 19 from Montgomery, and only 4 from Bucks), but the results are the same. The comparable totals for this group are:

Table VII–2

First Zoning Ordinance Before 1945		First Zoning Ordinance After 1945	
Over 5%	Under 5%	Over 5%	Under 5%
6	22	8	3

The percentages of land zoned industrial are based upon ordinances in effect in 1960. Some of the municipalities that first zoned prior to 1945 have, then, had the opportunity to amend their classifications. However, some may have become fully developed quite early and thus were faced with little vacant land to allocate later to industrial usage. It is also generally easier to zone previously unzoned land than to change classifications. Nevertheless, these considerations suggest that those high-social-ranking municipalities that zoned prior to 1945 allocated even less land to industry then than they do today.

Zoning policies do not necessarily reflect actual land usage. However it was our observation that the recent zoning policies of high-social-ranking municipalities intended to allocate more land for industry actually had that effect. The percentage of total assessed value in industrial property is a measure of usage. Again viewing the 39 highest-social-ranking suburbs, their distribution with regard to industrial usage and year of first zoning ordinance is:

Table VII–3

First Zoning Ordinance Before 1945		First Zoning Ordinance After 1945	
Over 1% Assess. in Ind. Use	Under 1% Assess. in Ind. Use	Over 1% Assess. in Ind. Use	Under 1% Assess. in Ind. Use
9	18	8	4

The data lead us to conclude that high-social-ranking municipalities are more amenable to industrial development today than they have been in the past.

There is no such pattern among the lower-social-ranking municipalities. Many of them have always been highly industrialized and do not appear to have followed today, or in the past, any particular policy of industrial encouragement or exclusion. Their age and the timing of their first zoning ordinance bear no relation to amounts of land zoned industrial.

The total assessed value of a community is a good measure of its resources and the potential effort required to provide local services. In the past, the service preferences of high-status communities have been satisfied through tapping a rather wealthy residential tax base, although often through the exertion of considerable tax effort. Low-social-ranking municipalities have, at times, been able to provide equal levels of service with little effort through enjoying a virtual monopoly of the industrial tax base. Our data suggest that industrial property will be more widely distributed in the future. With an industrial tax base added to the higher residential values of the high-social-ranking municipalities, the gulf between them and their lower-social-ranking neighbors may become even wider.

Residential Use. The choice to zone residential necessitates further decisions likely to affect the character of a municipality. Most important is the determination of the lot sizes upon which homes may be built. This choice affects not only the density of the municipality, but, in many instances, the type of people who will live there. The latter consideration is based on the assumption that large lots will have more expensive homes than small lots and will, therefore, attract higher income residents.

There is ample evidence that this assumption is implicit in the reasoning that leads to large-lot zoning and that lot-size requirements are frequently favored as a device to insure the construction of homes of a certain cost.[5] There are, indeed, more efficient ways to influence housing prices, but Pennsylvania courts have been uncooperative in this endeavor. They have ruled both minimum-cost requirements and minimum-habitable-floor-area requirements unconstitutional when tied to zoning.[6] Many municipalities previously using these methods have, in the face of judicial decisions, turned to minimum lot-size provisions.

Tests were made to determine whether there is in fact a correlation between lot size and the price of new homes within municipalities. The price of individual homes by lot size was available only for Delaware County.[7] However, only 8 municipalities experienced enough subdivision activity between 1955 and 1960 to provide a range of prices and lot sizes. In 6 of these 8 municipalities, the product-moment correlation of the price of new, single-family dwellings and lot sizes is between .594 and .773. In Upper Providence, the correlation is a barely significant .447 and in Upper Darby it is not significant at all.

Upper Darby and Upper Providence both show the effect of the immediate spillover of populations from densely populated urban centers. Upper Darby is adjacent to Philadelphia and much of Upper Providence's development is an extension of Media, the old and densely populated county seat. In both municipalities, new construction is occurring on lots that are exceedingly small by Suburban standards. Yet prices of new homes vary considerably; hence the absence of a home-price–lot-size correlation.

In brief, the question of the relationship of lot size to home price is qualified by two distinct "styles" of suburban development. In the more remote and undeveloped suburban areas, lot size is related to home price. In municipalities immediately adjacent to older urban centers and in communities close to railroad commuter stations, most development is high-density and the price decision of the builder is strongly influenced by locational factors rather than by lot size. The locational importance of the commuter stations is less evident today than a few decades ago: nevertheless, the pattern of high-density development at a relatively high price, appealing to high-status individuals, still perists in a few cases.

In the Suburbs, then, lot size and its corresponding demographic characteristic, density of development, is related to a number of factors among which are location and the desire to restrict development to expensive homes. Two additional factors help explain residential densities: social rank and the time at which development took place. A survey of the Suburbs sub-stantiates this point.

Delaware County. Of the 39 municipalities in Delaware County, only seven have any land zoned for 16,000 square feet or more. These seven are all among the 10-highest social-ranking municipalities in the county. Of the other three high-social-ranking municipalities, two (Swarthmore and Lansdowne) lie entirely within one mile of a commuter railroad station.

We may conclude, then, that zoning for minimum lots of 16,000 square feet or more in Delaware County is a phenomenon associated with high social rank. No low-social-ranking municipality zones so restrictively, and, with one exception, all high-social-rank communities not lying along commuter railroad lines zone some land at that density.

If we consider zoning policies pertaining to smaller lot sizes, 9,000 to 16,000 square feet, again it appears that local choices are largely a function of social status and time of development. There are 20 municipalities in Delaware County that do not lie entirely along commuter railroad lines. Of these, 9 are in the upper half of the County's social rank and 11 in the lower half. Of the 9 high in socialrank, 7 have land zoned for 9,000 square feet or more, Springfield and Upper Darby being the exceptions. Among the 11 low in social rank, only three have zoned at 9,000 square feet or more.

All of the high-social-ranking communities adopted their ordinances prior to 1945. All 3 of the low-social-ranking municipalities with 9,000 square feet zones adopted their first zoning ordinances after 1945. All 3, in addition, have public water and sewers, so larger lots were not necessary as health measures. Of the 8 low in social rank with no land zoned 9,000 square feet, 3 adopted their first zoning ordinances before 1945.

Table VII–4—Delaware County

Municipalities Not Lying Entirely Within One Mile of Commuter
Stations Zoning Land at 9,000 Square Feet or More by
Social Rank and by Year of First Zoning Ordinance

| | First Zoning Ordinance Before 1945 | | First Zoning Ordiance After 1945 | |
	Some Land Over 9,000	No Land Over 9,000	Some Land Over 9,000	No Land Over 9,000
High Social Rank	7	2	0	0
Low Social Rank	0	3	3	5

Montgomery County. Municipalities in Montgomery County
have larger land areas than those in Delaware. Most of their
development is Post World War II, and much more of their
residential land is zoned for minimum lot sizes of 16,000
square feet or more. Again looking at municipalities not lying
entirely within one mile of commuter stations, social rank and
the year the first zoning ordinance was adopted are significant
variables. None of the seven municipalities within one mile of
railroad stations zone for 16,00 square feet, whether high or
low in social rank. The remainder vary by time and social rank.

Table VII–5—Montgomery County

Municipalities Not Lying Entirely Within One Mile of Commuter
Stations Zoning Land at 16,000 Square Feet or More by
Social Rank and by Year of First Zoning Ordinance

| | First Zoning Ordinance Before 1945 | | First Zoning Ordinance After 1945 | |
	Some Land Over 16,000	No Land Over 16,000	Some Land Over 16,000	No Land Over 16,000
High Social Rank	7	0	4	1
Low Social Rank	2	3	4	1

Much the same pattern emerges looking at zoning for lots of
9,000 square feet. All but one low-social-ranking municipality
zone for 9,00 square feet or more. All but one of the high-social-ranking have more than 60% of their land zoned at this

density, and that one zoned before 1945. The year of the first zoning ordinance separates the low-social-ranking municipalities that have over 60% of their land in this zone as well.

Table VII–6—Montgomery County

Municipalities Not Lying Entirely Within One Mile of Commuter Stations Zoning Land at 9,000 Square Feet or More by Social Rank and by Year of First Zoning Ordinance

	First Zoning Ordinance Before 1945		First Zoning Ordinance After 1945	
	Over 60% Zoned 9,000	Under 60% Zoned 9,000	Over 60% Zoned 9,000	Under 60% Zoned 9,000
High Social Rank	6	1	4	1
Low Social Rank	1	4	4	1

Bucks County. In Bucks County, it is impossible to show a similarly neat pattern. Lower Bucks is newly developed. It experienced little urban growth prior to 1945, hence it is not surprising that only three zoning ordinances were passed prior to that year. Two of these were in low-social-ranking municipalities and provided no zones over 9,000 square feet.

The great urban growth that has taken place in Lower Bucks was spurred by the giant Levittown and Fairless Hills developments. Here, zoning did not express a reaction to development pressures. To the contrary, these huge developments came in on their own terms, among which were zoning allowances that would permit them to build at densities for which they were most proficient. Subsequent development in Bucks has been more in keeping with the pattern established by Suburbs in other counties.

Thus, in Philadelphia's Suburbs, the size of the residential lot has become an attribute of status as measured by social rank. Most high-status municipalities were zoned prior to 1945. Many limited the densities at which they would be developed

by restrictive lot-size requirements. It has not been possible to
calculate their social rank at the time their ordinances were
passed. One may well speculate as to whether their current
social rank is not, then, more a result of their early zoning
decisions than a factor that influenced their past choice. But
sufficient land still remains undeveloped to suggest that social
rank did then and does today influence zoning decisions. Since
World War II, large lots have been a characteristic of most
housing developments, but while most high-social-ranking municipalities seek to retain zones of 16,00 square feet, the low-
social-ranking seem content to hold the line at 9,000 square
feet.

Delaware County: Zoning, Lot Size and Home Prices

The price an individual will pay for a new home is a reflection of his income and his life-style values. If the latter influence land-use policy, then one would expect to find a relationship between the prices of homes and land-use policy. However, our data, organized by counties, represent averages. By
analyzing the sales price of all new homes, we are able to observe the composition of the average. Do municipalities specialize in high- or low-priced homes? Do the prices of homes within municipalities tend to be similar or varied? Are differences
in these respects related to land-use policies and/or to other
municipal characteristics? Only in Delaware County could data
be obtained for an examination of these questions.

The Price of New Homes. There are 39 Suburbs in Delaware County. Only 20 have had substantial building activity between 1950 and 1960 (5 or more subdivisions approved during
this period). Among these 20, two types of new-home pricing
emerged. These were municipalities in which all new homes
were relatively similar in price, and a group in which wide vari-

ations in prices could be found. The former are designated narrow-range communities, the latter wide-range.

Twelve were narrow-range—the smallest difference between the highest- and lowest-priced home within a municipality was $1,800 in Chester Twp., and the largest difference was $8,000 in Ridley. The narrow-range municipalities specialize in moderate or inexpensively priced homes. In them, no home was priced higher than $20,000. Price differentials in the 8 wide-range municipalities ranged from a low of $14,000 in Springfield to a high of $34,000 in Radnor, even after eliminating either the highest or lowest priced subdivision.

While the 8 wide-range municipalities offer a wide choice of prices, in all but Radnor and Upper Providence the prices cluster toward the bottom of the range. That is, at least 75 percent of the new homes for sale could be bought at a price less than midway between the lowest- and highest-priced home. In Nether Providence, for example, prices ranged from $12,000 to $39,000, but 75 percent of the homes could be bought for $18,000 or less.

Table VII–7 lists the prices and other characteristics of wide- and narrow-range municipalities; Figure III graphically depicts the price differentials and the lowest price at which 75 percent of new homes could be purchased in the wide-range communities.

Running through the heart of Delaware County is the West Chester commuter railroad. In the pre-war years (often Pre-World War I), high-density communities grew along this and other commuter lines. Our analysis is largely concerned with post-war, automobile-oriented development. This growth filled in the spaces between the railroads.

The wide-range communities generally lie to the north of the West Chester line, spreading up to, and including Main Line areas. These communities have predominantly single-fam-

FIGURE III

RANGE OF PRICES FOR HOMES BUILT BETWEEN 1950 AND 1960 IN WIDE RANGE MUNICIPALITIES AND LOWEST PRICE RANGE FOR WHICH 75 % SOLD

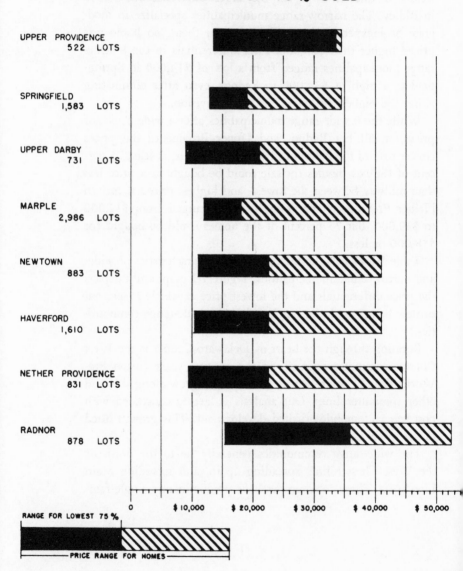

Table VII–7

Zoning and Selected Characteristics of Delaware County Suburbs
Communities with a Narrow Range in the Price of New Homes

Municipality	Price Range in Thousands	Density per sq. Mile	Percent Residential Land Lost Zoned for Minimum Sizes of: 16,000 Sq. ft. or More	9,000 Sq. ft. or More	9,000 Sq. ft. or Less	Percent Adults 25-34 Years of Age	Percent Land Zoned Com. and Ind.	1960 per Pupil School Revenue	Repub. Percent Vote for Gov. 1958	1960 Social Rank	1960 per Capita Municipal Operating Expenditure
Darby Twp.	8.5–13.4	7,874	0		69.2	30.7	37.6	$508	44.4	17.5	$16.85
Chester City	9.0–14.7	13,261	0		54.2	45.8	19.8	433	57.0	10.6	33.23
Folcroft	9.6–15.6	5,009	0		72.2	27.8	41.0	398	48.4	14.5	19.49
Brookhaven	10.3–17.9	3,106	0	82.2	8.9	8.9	28.5	479	55.8	21.8	16.88
Ridley Twp.	10.4–18.5	7,065	0		75.0	25.0	30.1	463	50.7	19.6	19.45
Ridley Park	10.5–14.0	7,387	0		80.0	20.0	22.4	404	62.8	33.7	20.46
Parkside	10.5–15.2	12,130	0		93.0	7.0	20.4	653	56.3	18.2	14.98
Upper Chichester	11.0–17.8	1,424	0	22.7	44.0	33.3	26.3	424	45.6	8.2	11.00
Chester Typ.	11.6–13.4	2,572	0	0	53.0	47.0	26.0	325	38.9	1.0	13.52
Sharon Hill	11.7–13.1	8,904	0	0	62.5	37.5	23.1	494	55.2	21.2	24.70
Darby Boro.	13.0–18.4	17,574	0	0	81.0	18.7	20.6	396	51.0	13.0	18.18
Communities with a Wide Range in the Price of New Homes											
Aston	13.0–20.1	1,796	0	49.0	31.0	20.0	32.9	368	50.6	20.7	17.20
Upper Darby	9.0–34.5	12,258	0	0	81.5	18.5	18.1	$540	59.3	36.9	$29.48
Nether Prov.	9.5–44.5	2,257	52.2	95.1	1.7	3.2	14.4	484	74.2	57.4	20.28
Haverford	10.5–41.0	5,402	22.1	36.8	56.8	6.3	16.5	516	65.4	51.6	28.91
Newtown	11.0–41.0	918	74.9	74.9	20.6	4.5	23.3	508	68.1	50.0	16.41
Marple	12.0–39.0	1,896	50.5	78.2	16.8	5.0	24.7	474	60.0	53.0	17.07
Springfield	13.0–34.5	4,243	0	0	93.5	6.4	19.3	504	66.0	55.7	28.75
Upper Prov.	13.5–34.5	1,026	84.8	84.8	10.4	4.8	2.9	551	74.2	52.1	13.18
Radnor	15.5–52.5	1,572	79.6	86.4	9.8	4.6	17.9	674	74.7	58.4	40.31

ily developments on land zoned for lots of 16,000 square feet or more. Generally, little land is zoned industrial or commercial.[8]

The narrow-range municipalities lie to the south of the West Chester line and border on the industrial belt along the Delaware River. Some of the narrow-range communities have substantial Negro populations (5 have over 10 percent). This is never the case in the wide-range communities, which have only the smallest fractions of non-whites in their populations. The narrow-range communities have a younger adult population than do the wide-range. In 7 of the narrow-range, 25–34 year olds exceed 25 percent, and in the other 5 they are between 20 percent and 25 percent. In the wide-range, 5 of the 8 are below 20 percent, and only three between 20 percent and 25 percent.

Only one of the 12 narrow-range communities (Ridley Park) gave the Republicans 60 percent or more of its vote in the 1958 gubernatorial election. Nine of them gave the GOP 55 percent or less. By contrast, all of the 8 wide-range communities voted 60 percent or more Republican and, in 7 of them, 65 percent or better.

With respect to social rank, all wide-range communities were higher than all narrow-range municipalities. The differences in social rank are pronounced. These differences existed in 1950 as well, indicating that the homes built from 1950 to 1960, and the people who moved into them, did not change the municipalities' basic character.

Most interesting, while the narrow- and wide-range municipalities evidenced differences in social rank and other characteristics, 75 percent of the new homes built in most of the wide-range communities between 1950 and 1960 sold within a range of prices generally available in the narrow range communities. In fact, the difference in the average price of new homes in several wide-range municipalities, even with the bias introduced by their few expensive homes, did not greatly exceed the average price of new homes in narrow-range communities. The average price of homes in narrow-range Brookhaven, $16,999, was higher than that of wide-range Springfield, $16,938, or Upper Darby, $16,435.

Social Rank and Housing Choices. It appears that populations of high social rank chose to locate in the wide-range municipalities and that those low in social rank located in the narrow-range communities, despite the fact that, at least in terms of price, homes were available to them elsewhere. But it is possible that the differences in social rank between narrow- and wide-range municipalities and the differences in their measured behavior are attributable to residents who occupy the expensive homes in wide-range municipalities. That is, of the adults moving into the 25 percent of the homes that could not have been purchased in the narrow-range municipalities, all had one or more years of college education and the males were all employed in managerial, professional, and sales occupations; while those who bought the less expensive homes were similar to those who located in the narrow range-communities.

The data available do not permit testing this possibility without making a number of far-reaching assumptions. Let us assume that the differences in the number of adults with a year or more of college education, and in the number of males employed in high-status occupations between 1950 and 1960, are accounted for by new residents entering each municipality and purchasing new homes. Social rank can then be calculated for new residents only.[9] By making the additionally restrictive assumption that purchasers of the expensive homes in wide-range municipalities were all of high status, we can compare the social rank of the new residents in the less expensive, new homes in wide range-municipalities with the new residents in the narrow-range municipalities.

Table VII–8 presents the occupational score of the residents moving into 9 narrow-range, and 7 wide-range communities between 1950 and 1960 (Upper Darby, Chester City, Chester Twp., and Sharon Hill, could not be included, because of net population declines or other circumstances that provided non-comparable data). These scores are the increases in the number of males in managerial, professional and sales occupations expressed as a percentage of the increased number of employed males. The second column lists the occupational score of the residents who purchased the less expensive homes in the wide-range communities, assuming that those who bought the more expensive homes were all in the high-status occupational categories.[10]

Table VII–8

Occupational Scores of New Residents Purchasing Homes in Narrow-range and Wide-range Municipalities between 1950 and 1960

	Percent New-employed Males in High-status Occupations	Percent New-employed Males in High-status Occupations Less 25% Assumed to Have Purchased More Expensive Homes
Narrow-range Municipalities		
Darby Boro.	33.5	
Brookhaven	30.4	
Aston	30.0	
Upper Chichester	28.6	
Ridley Twp.	28.5	
Darby Twp.	28.3	
Ridley Park	26.6	
Parkside	25.0	
Folcroft	18.6	
Wide-range Municipalities		
Nether Providence	70.2	52.6
Radnor	62.4	48.7
Marple	61.0	45.7
Springfield	59.8	44.9
Upper Providence	56.3	41.3
Haverford	53.6	40.1
Newtown	49.5	37.2

The new residents in the wide range-communities who purchased homes at prices available in the narrow-range municipalities have higher occupational scores than the new residents
of the narrow-range municipalities. A similar calculation for
educational scores results in little difference between the two
types of municipality. However, given the admittedly rigorous
assumption that all occupants of the more expensive homes
completed at least one year of college, the possibility that differences do exist cannot be ruled out. *It is at least evident that,
given different occupations, people willing to spend similar
amounts for new homes, choose to locate in different types of
communities.*[11]

The Stable Communities of Delaware County. In addition to
those Delaware County suburbs which are described above,
there are another 19 which had virtually no subdivision activity
in the 1950–1960 decade. While two of these, Rose Valley and
Swarthmore, are the highest-social-ranking communities in this
study, the other 17 are generally among the lowest. Their social
rank and residential market value per household indices are almost identical with the narrow-range communities. The difference from the narrow-range communities is in the age of the
adults. These are the places of residence of the older adult
suburban dwellers. One is inclined to see in them the narrow-
range suburban style one generation removed.

Summary

Land-use controls are the primary way in which communities
themselves may shape their physical environment. Here is a
crucial policy area which may be more important than any other
in setting the life-style of a community. But our own findings
indicate that choices exist only under limited circumstances.

The first limitation is the very permanency of land-use policies. Many Suburbs are faced with a physical environment created in an era of differing technology by generations with differing values than the present one. In this respect, many Suburbs are no different than older cities. They are attending a Mad Hatters tea party with most of the guests eating from the dirty plates of a past generation. However, of all urban dwellers, the suburbanite alone has the rare opportunity of obtaining a clean plate—the undeveloped fringe-area land.

Social and economic differentiation has a real chance to be translated into land-use policies in the "clean plate" areas of the fringe. No doubt this helps explain the large planning expenditures in areas that evidence little other municipal activity. It is also in these newer areas where lot sizes and new-home-prices show a decided relationship. Here the low-density style apparently finds full expression in an ample house on spacious grounds.

Differentiation expresses itself not only in a variety of preferences but even more in variation in the realization of preferences. Since the development of F.H.A. financing and the post-war unleashing of the automobile, a pervasively-held image of the proper residential situs has been disseminated by all media of mass communication. The daily auto commute should end in a low-density residential community with lawns to be mowed, fully detached homes to be weatherproofed and painted, and happy, smiling, exuberant children to be herded indoors from their outdoor play.

While low-density development characterizes the common preference, higher-social-ranking communities have been more determined in seeking its attainment and have realized it to a greater extent. Any inference that this pattern is simply a product of personal resources as they relate to social rank, is not substantiated by the findings. Lot size or even the price of

homes is not the only means through which social-status segregation takes place; even where people are apparently in a position to "buy their way up" the social ladder, they do not always
do so. The vehicle of social differentiation in Suburbs is not
simply a by-product of economics. Occupational and perhaps
educational segregation takes place between communities with
similarly priced homes.

Early suburban development resulted in a spatial separation
of urban functions. Indeed, part of the incentive for suburban
development was the search for a residential escape from the
blighting and distracting influences of industrial and commercial activities. In the large and spacious municipalities where
more recent development is taking place, conscious planning is
creating more balanced land uses without the old consequences.
Drawing upon the lessons of older uni-functional Residential
Suburbs, with their scanty tax bases, newer Suburbs of both low
and high social rank have been led to this new diversity. Technological changes have made this achievement possible.
Through proper screening, high-class residential communities
can select compatible industrial and commercial neighbors who
can now control their unsightly or disturbing effects on their
environment. Thus the new mixed suburb is in competition
with older industrial and commercial centers for non-residential
tax bases.

This development has two implications. Functional specialization by Suburbs will probably decline as lower-social-ranking
Suburbs lose their present predominant share of non-residential
activities. But while functional differentiation may decline, even
greater tax-resource disparities may be anticipated. This will be
most likely to occur if the new low-social-ranking Suburbs fail
in the new competition for industry. There are some indications
that this is happening.

NOTES

1. Some choice of policy is almost always available. Since Firey's study of Boston, social scientists have been inclined to accept the notion that social values can maintain and even transform land use in the face of contrary environmental pressures. Walter Firey, *Land Use in Central Boston* (Cambridge: Harvard University Press, 1946). Willhelm's study of zoning in Austin, Texas, specifically contrasts social values with "materialistic" considerations, concluding that the former are most useful to an understanding of land-use policy. Sidney M. Willhelm, *Urban Zoning and Land Use Theory* (New York: Free Press of Glencoe, 1962). For specific studies of how land use can be manipulated by human agencies, see: William H. Form, "The Place of Social Structure in the Determination of Land Use; Some Implications for A Theory of Urban Ecology," *Social Forces,* Vol. 32 (May, 1959), pp. 317–324, and Charles S. Liebman, *Some Factors Influencing the Distribution of Land Use in the Main Line Area* (Fels Institute of Local and State Government, University of Pennsylvania, mimeo, 1961).

2. For a selected bibliography and summary of that literature, see Leo F. Schnore, "The Functions of Metropolitan Suburbs," *American Journal of Sociology,* Vol. 61 (March, 1956), pp. 453–458.

3. Land-use data are derived primarily from the Appendix to the Zoning Volume of *Planning Measures and Controls in Southeastern Pennsylvania,* 1960). The categories used for classifying lot sizes and other zoning practices in this chapter are taken from this volume.

4. Five percent is a convenient cut-off point for municipalities in this metropolitan area. A municipality devoting less than 5 percent of its zoned land for industrial use shows virtually no interest in industry. In this, and in all subsequent discussions of zoning percentages, we are referring to the percentage of zoned land devoted to particular uses, never to total land area.   ,

5. James G. Coke and Charles S. Liebman, "Political Values and Population Density Control," *Land Economics,* Vol. 37 (November, 1961), pp. 347–361.

6. 28 *Wash.,* 221 cited in *Medinger Appeal,* 337 *Pa.* 217.

7. The data for Delaware County were obtained from the records of the Delaware County Planning Commission which by state law is required to review all subdivisions in the County before they may be recorded. The records maintained by the Planning Commission indicate, among other things, the number of lots in the subdivision, lot size, the lot frontage, the availability of public water and sewers, and

in most instances the price at which the homes would be sold. This
included all subdivisions reviewed from 1951 to 1960. The accuracy
of the sales-price data was confirmed through interviews with the
Planning Commission staff, conversations with certain builders, and
a spot check of ten subdivisions where the prices seemed far out of
line with similar developments in the same general area. With one
exception, the prices listed by the subdividers were within $1,000 of
the actual basic sales prices and whatever bias existed was always on
the low side. One unusually large subdivision where prices were far
out of line with what would be expected and where, in fact, very few
homes had been sold over a four year period, was excluded. Constant
prices were obtained from price deflators for new, residential, non-
farm construction found in *Economic Report of the President, 1961*,
Table C-5 "Implicit Price Deflators for Gross National Product 1929–
1960," p. 132.

8. Upper Darby deviates from this generalization for reasons stated
above.

9. The assumptions follow a complex chain of reasoning, partially
verified by testing 1950 and 1960 tracted municipalities, that must
account for the many possible combinations of new and old residents
who might have purchased the new homes. One possibility is that the
new homes in all municipalities were purchased by previous residents
of these municipalities, and the homes that they vacated were purchased
by in-migrants of either high, low, or mixed status. It is also possible,
but highly unlikely, that the new homes were occupied by older low-
status residents whose vacated homes were purchased by in-migrants of
high status. Many combinations of in- and out-migration and home
purchasing are possible. The data necessitate making the simplest of
assumptions. The findings are presented, then, as illustrative, but in
no sense proven.

10. This is done by subtracting 25 percent of the total population
from both the dividend and the divisor. In other words, if a municipality gained 10,000 employed males between 1950 and 1960 and
has, in 1960, 5,000 more employed in high-status occupations than
it did in 1950, the occupational score of the new residents (again after
making several assumptions) is calculated as 5,000/10,000 or 50 percent. Assuming that those who purchased the 25 percent of more
expensive homes were all in high-status occupations would give the
purchasers of the less expensive homes a score of 2,500/7,500 or 33.3
percent.

11. The choice, of course, may not be entirely voluntary. Private
groups such as neighborhood associations, builders and particular
realtors, may restrict entry to different types of individuals. In addi-

210   Suburban Differences and Metropolitan Policies

tion, people do not choose their residence from a wide alternative of suburbs. As was noted in more detail elsewhere, even the highest-status business and professional leaders selected their place of residence from among very limited alternatives. None of them even considered all the exclusive and high-status suburbs as reaonable alternatives. This is no doubt much more the case among the lower classes whose access to information is so much more limited. For related findings on the location of different occupational groups see Otis Dudley Duncan and Beverly Duncan, "Residential Distribution and Occupational Stratification," *American Journal of Sociology,* Vol. 60 (March, 1955), pp. 493–503. For a discussion raising similar problems see James M. Beshers, *Urban Social Structure* (N.Y.: The Free Press of Glencoe 1962), pp. 96–97.

VIII

Attitudes, Opinions and Local Policies

In designing this study, choices were made with regard to the selection of independent variables. Alternative methods of both measurement and analysis were available. We have already discussed several measures of need and resources that were considered and rejected. Alternative methods of measuring preferences were also explored.

Preference is the collective term we have used to refer to population characteristics, particularly social rank, that may affect perceptions and policy choices. In effect, we suspected that different kinds of people would have different preferences. When we find some population characteristic, social rank for example, to be correlated with variations in policy, we assume that social rank reflects and/or structures attitudes and opinions, and that preferences associated with the latter affect the institutional behavior of relevant political organizations—municipal and school governments.

An alternative and more direct method of isolating and measuring differences in preferences is to poll attitudes and opinions of representative population samples. This is, of course, a more expensive procedure than correlation analysis, although it endeavors to serve much the same purpose. For example, instead of correlating expenditures with social rank and then inferring that the consistently larger expenditures of higher-social-ranking municipalities reflect their higher preference standards, one could ask people from high- and low-social-ranking communities what their preferences are.

Such a direct approach has conceptual as well as economic disadvantages. The literature of social science generally indicates that the relationship between opinion and action is problematic. For the individual as well as for governments, the situs of opinion-expression and action are sufficiently removed that the former can only be regarded as a predisposition to action. Other factors intervene between opinion and action to alter the influence of predispositions. When the actor is a government and the expressers of opinions are individuals or groups of individuals, the conceptual difficulty is compounded. Not only do opinions fail to take into account the effect of resources and needs when they are included in the background for municipal action, they offer no evidence of the responsibility or representativeness of government policy makers. It is possible for the absence of political responsiveness to result in discrepancies between popular predispositions and governmental action.

Since our study is concerned with the actual behavior of governments, the opinion-survey method was rejected as a major analytic tool. However, several surveys were conducted on a small pre-test basis. While the design and the sample areas they employ differ from those finally selected for our major investigation, their results were sufficiently interesting, comparative, and corroborative to warrant inclusion in the study.

This chapter reports on two attitude and opinion surveys. In effect, it measures differences in the values that predominate in subareas of the metropolitan area. It uses survey techniques but retains the basic social-area orientation of the study. Specifically, the chapter measures differences in attitudes and opinions of residents and elected officials from municipalities of varying social rank and then relates these differences in predisposition to the policy differences that have been previously described. Secondly, the chapter examines the representativeness of the elected officials who constitute a municipality's formal policy makers. Representativeness in this sense refers to whether or not officials are similar to and share the value systems of their constituents. The broader question of public responsiveness and responsibility is reserved for later discussion. Finally, this chapter reports the results of a survey of opinions about metropolitan cooperation both in the abstract and in regard to specific areas of intergovernmental cooperation.

Two separate surveys were conducted using 3 samples. Two of the samples consisted of respondents from 16 Suburbs in Delaware County. Delaware County was chosen for this pretest because it contained the full range of municipal types found in the metropolitan area. The 16 municipalities were chosen as an analytic sampling of separate social types of suburban communities. Six municipalities were high in social rank, five municipalities were among the lowest in socal rank, and five municipalities close to the median on the social rank scale were selected.[1] Questionnaires were distributed to elected public officials (all councilmen) in each of the 16 municipalities at official borough and township meetings. The return from these 105 officials totaled 52 or 49.5 percent.

The second group of respondents (hereafter referred to as residents) were drawn from a random telephone-book sampling of residents in the same 16 municipalities. Of the 340 members of this sample, 123, or 36.2 percent, responded.

The third sample, to which somewhat different questions were addressed, was drawn exclusively from business and professional leaders in the metropolitan area, all of whom work in the central part of Philadelphia.[2] Of the 464 members of this sample, 186, or 40.1 percent, responded.

Returns were grouped by type of respondent (public official, resident, and business and professional leader) and by social rank of the respondent's municipality. Inferences from these grouped returns were made only for the specific sub-populations represented. The question of bias in an analytic sampling is whether or not the characteristics of the grouped respondents vary in any consistent and relevant manner from the characteristics of the subpopulations represented. In the case of all 3 samples, characteristics of the respondents reflected the known characteristics of members of the total sample.[3]

Suburban Residents and Public Officials: Attitude Differences

Five attitude batteries were used. Suburban residents and public officials were tested for local-cosmopolitan attitudes, nonpartisanship, anomie, conservatism, and ethnocentrism.

A local-cosmopolitan attitude test differentiates between types of persons with contrasting involvement and identification. The local is parochial, confined in his interest to one community, and preoccupied with local problems to the virtual exclusion of problems and events in any larger social setting. The cosmopolitan, on the other hand, identifies and relates himself to issues, events, and organizations outside the local community. Nonpartisanship refers to a distaste for Partisan political activity, a preference for individual rather than party identification, and a refusal to recognize cleavages in the parties' positions. Anomie is a lack of involvement and a feeling of helplessness before state and national political institutions. Conservatism is measured by support for the status quo and support for only minimal government activity in economic and social affairs.

Ethnocentrism consists of stereo-typed negative imagery and hostile attitudes toward all out-groups.

As Table VII–1 shows differences between respondents from high-social-ranking and low-social-ranking communities with respect to scores on local-cosmopolitan scales, anomie, conservatism, and ethnocentrism, were in the expected direction.

Table VIII–1

Attitudinal Scores of Public Officials
and Residents by Social Rank of Municipality

	Social-rank Grouping of Municipality		
	Upper	Middle	Lower
Public Officials	N = 23	N = 14	N = 15
Residents	N = 60	N = 35	N = 28
Localism			
Public Officials	18.3	20.0	22.0
Residents	16.3	17.2	19.4
Conservatism			
Public Officials	22.4	16.0	14.1
Residents	20.0	17.5	13.7
Anomie			
Public Officials	14.6	15.3	16.4
Residents	16.7	17.3	17.7
Ethnocentrism			
Public Officials	16.1	17.7	21.5
Residents	16.9	18.6	20.2
Non-Partisanship			
Public Officials	15.2	16.0	15.9
Residents	18.2	19.1	19.1

Scores increase in the direction of the attitude specified: that is, a score of 20 on the localism battery is a more localistic score than a score of 18. These scores were derived from a Likert type-scoring system. Respondents were asked to express their degree of agreement or disagreement with a series of statements designed to reflect the attitudes under investigation. Responses were converted to scores on each statement in the following manner: agree srongly—6, agree somewhat—5, agree slightly —4, disagree slightly—3, disagree somewhat—2, disagree strongly—1. Each attitude battery contained five statements; thus the possible range of scores on each battery was from 5 to 30. Figures in the table above represent the mean scores of the groups identified. Differences with respect to local-cosmo-politanism, conservatism, and ethnocentrism were above the .01 level of significance.

Residents of high-social-ranking communities, then, were on the average, significantly more oriented to national affairs, were more opposed to government activity in the economic and social spheres, and were less hostile to out-groups than residents of low-social-ranking communities. In addition, attitudes of respondents with low-social-ranking characteristics who lived in high-social-ranking communities were more different from attitudes of low-social-ranking respondents from low-social-ranking communities than were the attitudes of respondents with high-social-ranking characteristics in high-social-ranking communities. In other words, low-social-ranking respondents in high-social-ranking communities over-conform to the dominant values of their communities. There were insufficient respondents of high-social-rank characteristics living in low-social-ranking communities to draw any conclusions.

Suburban Residents and Public Officials: Opinion Differences

The outstanding fact that emerges from a study of opinions of suburban respondents is that residents of different areas have very different opinions about governmental activity. First of all, residents of high-social-ranking communities have different expectations of local government. They expect their governments to do different kinds of things and they become aroused over different kinds of issues. Secondly, as one might expect from the foregoing, place of residence serves to differentiate respondents in their replies to questions about specific metropolitan issues.

Differing Expectations. On the basis of respondents' replies to the questions of which goals they felt were "very important" for local government, 3 distinct images or roles for government emerged: providing amenities, securing a low tax rate, and maintaining the social characteristics of the community. Respondents who thought that the goal of maintaining improved public services and the goal of providing esthetic amenities were very important goals for local government were judged to have amenity expectations. As indicated in Table VIII–2 respondents from high-social-ranking municipalities were more concerned with amenities than respondents from low-social-ranking communities.

Table VIII–2

Percentage of Residents and Public Officials Who Judged It Very Important for Government to Provide Amenities

	Social-rank Grouping of Municipality		
	Upper	Middle	Lower
Residents			
Maintain improved public services	44.8	41.2	35.7
Provide esthetic amenities	50.0	38.2	32.1
Public Officials			
Maintain improved public services	56.5	46.6	50.0
Provide esthetic amenities	47.8	33.3	28.5

Residents were also asked about issues which were likely to get their community "most aroused." From high-social-ranking communities 58 percent of the residents said poor public service was such an issue. Only 49 percent of the residents from middle-social-ranking communities and 43 percent of the residents from low-social-ranking communities thought so.

Emphasis on the second value or role for local government, that of securing a low tax rate, was ascertained by determining which respondents thought the goals of acquiring business and industry and keeping tax rates down were very important goals for government. Respondents from high-social-ranking communities were not as concerned with this goal as respondents from low-social-ranking communities.

Table VIII–3

Percentage of Residents and Public Officials Who Judged It Very Important for Government to Secure Low Tax Rates

	Social-rank Grouping of Municipality		
	Upper	Middle	Lower
Residents			
Acquire business and industry	8.6	23.5	50.0
Keep tax rate down	56.9	79.5	82.0
Public Officials			
Acquire business and industry	13.0	26.6	64.3
Keep tax rate down	43.5	80.0	79.0

From high-social-ranking communities, 41 percent of the residents thought that increasing taxes was an issue which was likely to get the community "most aroused." Comparable percentages for middle- and low-social-ranking communities are 66 and 79 percent. The value of providing industrial growth and a resultant low tax rate as opposed to a sacrifice in amenities was nicely juxtaposed in another question which asked, "Would you favor more industrial growth and more jobs for your local community even if it meant an increase in noise and traffic and industrial type buildings? Among residents from high-social-ranking communities, 18 percent favored the proposal and 82 percent opposed it. From the middle-social-ranking group 46 percent favored it and 54 percent opposed it. Among lower-social-ranking communities 78 percent favored it and 22 percent opposed it.

The value or role of maintaining the community's social characteristics and composition was ascertained by asking respondents whether they thought the goal of keeping undesirables out and the goal of maintaining the "quality" of residents were very important for local government.

High- and low-social-ranking communities do not express clear-cut differences with respect to this goal. The direction of response is different for the two questions. Sixty-two percent of the residents of high-social-ranking communities thought that keeping undesirables out was very important. Seventy-five percent of low-social-ranking community residents thought so as well. Comparable percentages for public officials were 70 and 86 percent. However, whereas 69 percent of residents from high-social-ranking communities thought that maintaining the "quality" of residents was a very important goal for local government, only 43 percent of residents from low-social-ranking communities thought so. Among public officials the percentage differences were much closer, 61 and 57 percent.

Table VIII–4

Percentage of Residents and Public Officials Who Judged It
Very Important for Government to Maintain the
Social Characteristics of the Community

	Social-rank Grouping of Municipality		
	Upper	Middle	Lower
Residents			
Keep undesirables out	62.0	79.5	75.0
Maintain "quality" of residents	69.0	47.0	43.0
Public Officials			
Keep undesirables out	69.6	73.2	85.5
Maintain "quality" of residents	60.8	66.6	57.0

The differences in the direction of the response to the two questions, maintaining quality of residents and keeping undesirables out, raises a problem; but before suggesting a solution, the overall impact of the response should be clear. Respondents from both high- and low-social-ranking communities thought that keeping undesirables out was a very important goal. Further, more residents from all types of communities thought that undesirables moving in was more likely to get their community very aroused than any other issue including zoning, increasing taxes, poor public service, metropolitan government, and unequal tax burdens. One might expect that the goal of keeping undesirables out, and the goal of maintaining the quality of residents, are both directed at the image of government as a maintainer of the social structure and, therefore, that the direction of response to these two questions among high- and low-social-ranking communities would be the same. Assuming a consistency among respondents, the responses indicate however that the two questions were perceived as having different meanings. Residents of low-social-ranking communities may be relatively unconcerned about maintaining the "quality" of residents, but they are clearly concerned about an influx of certain persons viewed as "undesirables." Residents of high-social-ranking communities favor keeping undesirables out and maintaining the quality of residents, although they are less concerned about the threat of "undesirables" than lowered "quality" of residents.

In summary, respondents from high-social-ranking communities expect their municipality to provide better public services and public amenities as well as to maintain the social structure. Respondents from low-social-ranking communities expect their local government to keep taxes low, are less concerned with amenities, and expect government to keep certain types of potential residents out. The term "undesirable" is, of course, an ambiguous one. To the suburban residents of northern industrial cities, especially those in lower social rank areas, it probably means "Negro."

In addition to those discussed above, respondents also differed sharply by social rank with respect to several other goals and issues. Thus, 81 percent of the residents from high-social-ranking communities and 87 percent of the public officials from these areas thought that protecting property values was a very important goal for government, while only 54 percent of the residents and 50 percent of the public officials from low-social-ranking communities thought so. Only 31 percent of the residents from high-social-ranking areas thought that unequal tax burdens was an issue over which their communities would get "most aroused," but 54 percent of the residents from low-social-ranking communities thought so.

Attitudes, Opinions and Municipal Policy

Does municipal policy actually reflect the attitudes and opinions of residents? Do low social-ranking communities, in fact, de-emphasize amenities, opt for low taxes and practice discrimination? With proper operational definitions the question is answered in the affirmative. The municipal policy analysis generally showed a relationship between expenditures for amenities and social rank. Even in industrial centers, where rich tax bases could cushion the effect of tax burdens on householders, expenditures for amenities were not stressed.

When the extraordinary needs of Industrial and Commercial Centers were statistically controlled, low-social-ranking municipalities were found to spend less for municipal services than other Suburbs (Chapter IV). The differences in expenditures for public schools were most pronounced. That expenditure policies were in turn related to opinions about tax rates was verified in the analyses of tax effort and burden. Discounting the effect on tax rates of the school-aid subsidy, low-social-ranking municipalities were still inclined to maintain low tax rates at the expense of foregoing amenities, or perhaps, as in school expenditures, what higher-social-ranking municipalities might consider necessities.

Residents of low-social-ranking communities probably pay higher percentages of their income for less municipal service than do citizens living in places at the other end of the scale. Economic motivations may thus explain the former's predisposition toward maintaining low tax rates. For present purposes, however, it is sufficient to note that this preference as measured by their opinions has been effectively transformed into municipal policy.

Sufficient data have not been presented in earlier chapters to compare opinions with regard to maintaining the social structure of the community and municipal policies. To some extent, the zoning policies pursued by high-social-ranking municipalites are an attempt to prescribe the character of future residents along lines of income and social status. A more obvious manifestation of the attempt to "keep out undesirables" is the practice of racial exclusion. Municipal ordinances are of decidedly lesser importance than informal citizen, group and public-official actions in pursuing this policy.[4]

The opinion survey found citizens from low-social-ranking municipalities more concerned with "keeping out undesirables" than residents from high-social-ranking municipalities. If opinion and action are related, in this case one mght hypothesize that racial exclusion is practiced with more intensity by lower-social-ranking communities. But the practice and the effectiveness of policies of exclusion are not synonymous. A finding that there are more Negroes in lower- than higher-social-ranking Suburbs would not constitute a refutation of the hypothesis.

Earlier in the study we reported a .845 coefficient of correlation between social rank and the residential market value per household. Thus the largest stock of inexpensive housing is concentrated in the lower-social-ranking Suburbs. The demand for housing among Philadelphia area Negroes centers in the lower price range. The higher-social-ranking Suburbs are in a sense protected from racial change by this economic barrier of high priced homes. Based upon economic considerations alone, one would expect higher-social-ranking Suburbs to be virtually all white, while lower-social-ranking Suburbs should have larger percentages of Negroes. The fact that this expectation is not fulfilled indicates non-economic forces are operative.

The Suburban racial composition by social-rank quartile is shown, for 1950 and 1960, in Table VIII–5. The lowest quartile did indeed have the largest Negro population, numerically as well as proportionately, both in 1950 and 1960. It also experienced the largest increase in Negroes during the decade. This would support the view that the housing market is guiding the pattern of Negro migration. However, a closer examination of the pattern offers some qualifying indications.

The third-quartile Suburbs have a substantial supply of cheap housing too, yet they show a decline in Negro population despite the fact that they had the highest rate of increase in whites over the ten year period. But the fact remains that the lowest-social-ranking quartile did have the largest Negro influx.

Table VIII–6 shows the distribution of Suburbs by social-rank quartiles and percentage Negroes in the municipal population in 1960. Most of the Negro influx has been channeled into a few municipalities, while the rest of the fourth-quartile Suburbs remained virtually all-white. Two fourth-quartile Suburbs have no Negroes at all, 5 have under .1 percent, and 3 more have between .1 percent and 1 percent. On the other end of the scale, 3 lower-social-ranking Suburbs have 29.3 percent, and 76.1 percent Negroes respectively. While the over-all Suburban-Negro increase between 1950 and 1960 is concentrated in the fourth quartile, the fact is that Negroes were moving into rela-

Table VIII-5 Suburbs
Racial Distribution by Social-rank Quartile, 1950 and 1960

Social Rank Quartile	1950 White	1950 Negro	% Negro of total	1960 White	1960 Negro	% Negro of total	% increase 1950-1960 White	Negro	% of total increase White	Negro
High										
1st N=23	240,951	11,549	4.6	393,828	12,180	3.1	63.4	5.6	38.5	4.7
2nd N=22	166,995	2,665	1.6	253,557	3,854	1.5	51.8	44.6	21.8	8.8
3rd N=22	93,681	2,721	2.9	184,248	2,474	1.3	97.9	-9.2	22.9	-1.8
4th N=23 Low	201,229	27,903	13.9	268,924	39,818	14.9	33.2	42.7	16.8	88.3
TOTAL	702,256	44,838	6.4	1,099,657	58,336	5.3	56.6	30.1	100	100

Table VIII–6 Suburbs

Distribution of Percentage Population Negro
by Social-rank Quartiles, 1960

Percentage Population Negro

Social Rank	Under 1%	1 - 5%	5 - 10%	10 - 15%	Over 15%
High					
1st Quartile N=23	7	10	5	1	0
2nd Quartile N=22	15	3	1	2	1
3rd Quartile N=22	17	3	1	0	1
4th Quartile N=23 Low	10	6	2	2	3
Total Suburbs	44	32	9	5	5

tively few of these 23 lower-social-ranking Suburbs. Interestingly, the lower-social-ranking Suburbs that remain all, or virtually all-white, are the smaller municipalities. Perhaps here the maintenance of a community exclusion policy through informal means is most possible.

While the higher-social-ranking Suburbs have small Negro populations, the distribution among them compares favorably with the lower-social-ranking areas. The Negro population comprises approximately 5 percent of the Suburbs. There are as many higher social-ranking Suburbs (first-and second-quartile) with over 5 percent Negroes as there are lower social-ranking ones (third-and fourth-quartile). There are no first-quartile municipalities which practice total exclusion. The bulk of the first-quartile Suburbs approach the norm for all Suburbs in their Negro populations. There are some obvious factors which may explain this fact. There is a certain symbiosis between high-status local populations and a resident service class. In addition, a scattering of high-status Negroes does not represent the advance guard of many more potential residents of the high-status areas. Income factors safeguard against such an influx. Such speculation only serves to give some basis in social organization for the pattern observed.

In brief, the statistical evidence lends support to the hypothesis that there is effective exclusion of Negroes which is more operative in the low- than high-social-ranking areas. Given the income structure among Negroes and the presence of a large supply of inexpensive housing in the lower-social-ranking Suburbs, one would expect a wide dispersal of Negroes throughout these communities if market forces alone were operative. Instead, Negroes in the lower-social-ranking Suburbs are largely confined within a few communities. In the higher-social-ranking Suburbs with a more expensive housing stock, one would expect to find fewer Negroes. In fact, the Negro population in the first quartile is larger, constitutes a larger proportion of the population, and is more widely dispersed among municipalities than in quartiles farther down the social rank scale.

Suburban Residents and their Leadership

The proposition that leadership is situational, that it is not posited upon the existence of a peculiar trait possessed by an individual, but is dependent upon a continuing relationship between individuals in a particular social context, is the product of a long history of social research.[5] We have already described social differentiation among subareas as an important and distinguishing characteristic of urban areas. Since variation in the social composition of communities represents variation in the situational context of leadership, can we expect this variation to be reflected in differing social backgrounds of the leadership in these communities? Are local political leaders representative of their constituency in the sense of being typical?

To answer this question, we relied upon the responses to our survey of elected public officials. This was done with the full realization that the political leadership of a community is only one segment of a community's social leadership. We recognize that important public decisions in a community may often, or even regularly, be made by groups outside of the formal governmental structure. However, the official leadership of a community is the instrument through which important community decisions are formalized, regardless of where the decisions originate. Local government must be employed to give formal and authoritative expression to these decisions. The degree to which "informal" leadership can bring decisive influence to bear upon local government activity is in part a function of the composition of official leadership.

Table VIII–7

Social Characteristics of Suburban Political Leaders

| | Social-rank Grouping of Municipality | | |
| | Upper | Middle | Lower |
	N=23	N=14	N=15
Occupation:			
Percent "white-collar"	91.3	57.2	06.5
Percent attending college			
(one year or more)	78.4	28.6	0
Religion:			
Percent Protestant	91.3	63.5	66.6
Percent Catholic	8.7	28.9	33.3
Percent Jewish	0	7.5	0
Place of Work:			
Percent home community	21.7	21.4	46.7
Percent nearby suburb	13.1	21.4	46.7
Percent central city	65.2	57.2	6.5
Social Participation:			
Mean organization memberships	4.1	2.8	1.8
Mean active memberships	2.7	1.9	1.6
Mean offices held	1.2	.7	.5

Donald Matthews has shown that decision-makers at the state and national levels do not appear to be representative of their constituencies in the general population with regard to occupational and educational levels.[6] According to Matthews 90 percent of state and national office-holders are college graduates drawn from the top 15 percent of the labor force. But uniformity in the social backgrounds of decision-makers does not appear to be the case in local government. Table VIII–7 indicates that metropolitan political leadership is representative of its constituency in terms of both occupation and education. If anything, the social characteristics of local office-holders accentuate social differences among communities. For example, census data indicated that 13 percent of the employed males of our lower-ranking communities were engaged in "white-collar" occupations, and 58.5 percent of employed males in upper-social-ranking communities were so employed (an absolute difference of 42.5 percent). However, 91 percent of the leadership in upper-social-ranking communities listed "white-collar" occupations, while only 6.5 percent of officials from lower-ranking communities did so (an absolute difference of 84.5 percent). This same contrast is apparent in educational data: none of the office-holders responding from lower-social-ranking municipalities had any college experience, while 78 percent of the officials in upper-social-ranking communities had some college background. On the other hand, census data revealed that 5 percent of the population of lower-ranking communities possessed college experience while 37 percent of the population of upper-ranking communities did so. Thus official leadership not only reflected differences in the social composition of communities but even accentuated these differences.

Originally it was hypothesized that local leaders would tend to be chosen from among those who not only lived in the community but worked there as well. Since their commitment to the community and dependency upon its welfare would tend to be greater than the commuter's, it was thought that these residents would take a more active role in community affairs which in turn would lead to public office. As Table VIII–7 shows, the hypothesis is not confirmed. Instead, the representativeness of local leadership expresses itself again. Due to changes in its economic function, the central city's work force is becoming more "white-collar." This means that the core city is drawing its commuters from "white-collar" suburbs while residents of working-class communities tend to find employment in nearby industrial suburbs. Among resident respondents, 50 percent of those from upper-social-ranking communities and 56 percent from middle-ranking communities worked in the central city while only 7 percent of the residents from lower-social-ranking communities did so. The composition of official leadership reflected constituency differences in this regard.

Our data on residents also confirm the work of sociologists Bell and Force to the effect that the extent of social participation varies directly with community social rank.[7] As expected, political leadership in each type of municipality appeared significantly more active in social affairs—formal group membership, participation, and officeholding—than their constituents as represented in our resident response. But it was further observed that differences among social areas in patterns of social participation are also reflected in the social participation patterns of officials from these areas (see Table VIII–7). It was clear from our returns that this difference was not only quantitative but qualitative as well. In the upper-ranking communities the associations mentioned most often were the civic associations, garden clubs, Lions, Rotary, Kiwanis, swim clubs and country clubs. In the lower-ranking communities the organizations most often cited were the volunteer fire companies, Boy Scouts, the American Legion, V.F.W., and fraternal orders.

These findings indicate that the social character of political leadership in suburban communities varies rather consistently with the social composition of these communities. Decision-makers in different social types of communities are recruited from separate status levels and consequently bring to their respective roles diverse previous experiences. Separate sets of internalized values suggest that decision-makers in different types of communities will perceive, experience, and behave toward social and political issues in separate fashions. The accessibility of these decision-makers to various interests and diverse sources of information can also be expected to vary in a consistent manner. As a consequence, one can expect that a product of the correlation between community social structure and leadership will be variation in the policy choices of local government. The representative character of local leadership will reinforce the propensity of separate social types of communities to respond to metropolitan issues in diverse fashions.

Business and Professional Leaders: Opinions About Metropolitan Cooperation

In relating differences in municipal behavior to differences in social rank, we have repeatedly skirted one question. Do communities of a given social rank show a preference for particular policies because large proportions of their residents share a certain occupational and educational status which is accompanied by one set of preferences; or are preferences the socialized choices of those groups of individuals with similar occupational and educational status *who flock together in a given community?* If the former, then municipal policy is nothing more than the expression of collective differences in the social status of individuals. If the latter, then the community becomes a truly meaningful unit for metropolitan analysis; for it is the community and people defined in terms of their choice of environment, and not merely different demographic categories of individuals, that impart distinctions to styles of local political life.

We have seen that low-status individuals living in high-social-ranking municipalities tend to adopt the outlook of the predominant high-status groups in the community. It appears that the opinions of these individuals are shaped as much or more by their environment as by their personal status. Some additional evidence of environment's influence was obtained from another preliminary survey that was designed with a different question in mind. The object of this survey was to test the opinions on metropolitan issues of business elites residing in Philadelphia and its suburbs. In effect, the survey controlled for differences in social status, for all the respondents had high-social-ranking characteristics.

The sample from which opinions were elicited is composed exclusively of business and professional leaders who work in Philadelphia's central business district. Twenty-three of the respondents live in Philadelphia, the remaining 118 live in the suburbs. All but four of the suburban respondents live in high-social-ranking communities.

Respondents were asked who they felt was right in a conflict between Montgomery County and Philadelphia where the county objected to joining with Philadelphia for an area-wide transportation system under Philadelphia's terms. This particular issue had made the front pages of the metropolitan press at the time the questionnaires were mailed. Sixty-one percent of Philadelphia residents thought Philadelphia was right whereas only 30 percent of the Suburbanites thought so. Suburban responses in turn correlated with whether or not respondents commuted by train. Those commuting by train tended to think Philadelphia was right. Those commuting by car favored the Montgomery County position which at that time really meant no area-wide transit agreement. A different question getting at reactions to mass transit was also posed in the Delaware County sample. Citizens were asked if they favored their county or local government spending tax money to improve mass transit in the area. Whereas 45 percent of the respondents from high-social-ranking communities favored the proposal only 32 percent of respondents from low-social-ranking communities favored it. In this case as well, commutation was a decisive factor. Those who commuted tended to favor the proposal. Since more high-social-ranking individuals than low-social-ranking individuals are commuters (blue collar workers tending to be employed in the community in which they reside or in adjacent Suburban communities rather than in the central city), the response may reflect self-interest or involvement more than social rank.

Respondents were asked whether they would favor area-wide government, assuming it would save money and help keep taxes down. Sixty-one percent of the Philadelphians favored the proposal, whereas only 18 percent of the Suburbanites did.

There was less of a division by place of residence on two other questions. Asked for their opinions on a regional authority for air-pollution control, 78 percent of central city residents responded favorably as compared to 64 percent of the suburbanites. Eighty-three percent of the Philadelphians and 70 percent of the suburbanites thought that non-residents who work in Philadelphia should pay for Philadelphia services through such devices as a wage tax.

The last specific issue raised was the desirability of a regional park authority to maintain large parks open only to residents of the local areas. Fifty-six percent of Philadelphians favored regional parks and only 33 percent of the suburbanites did so.

Finally two general questions were posed. Respondents were asked whether they thought the Suburbs ought to cooperate more for the purpose of protecting themselves against the possibility of Philadelphia taking them over. Whereas 71 percent of the Philadelphians said no or thought there was no need for it, only 40 percent of the Suburbanites replied in the negative.

The last question asked whether, with respect to the present state of inter-governmental cooperation in the Philadelphia metropolitan area, respondents thought that Philadelphia and the suburbs should be merged, should cooperate more, that present cooperation was good enough, or that more cooperation might solve some problems but would lead to loss of suburban independence and consequently was not worth it. Seventy percent of the Philadelphians favored merger or more cooperation, and 30 percent favored the status quo. Among Suburbanites, 52 percent favored merger or more cooperation and 31 percent favored the status quo. The results indicate a surprisingly strong level of agreement among respondents when the referrent is a general attitude rather than a specific proposal. In other words, the general question of more cooperation elicits a uniformly favorable response, although, as might be expected, Philadelphians are more favorable to it. An almost identical proportion of residents in both Philadelphia and the Suburbs are opposed to more cooperation. However, as was evident from prior questions, it is the nature of the cooperative activity which provokes major differences of opinion. With respect to the specific issues, all respondents favor cooperation where the services provided do not necessarily bring residents of the metropolitan area in closer contact with one another.

One may suggest that the differences in city and suburban responses are not at all surprising, that status does not eliminate self-interest, that there are substantive policy differences between Philadelphia and its suburbs, and that city and suburban elites interpret these differences in terms of a conception of self-interest that centers around place of residence. One could suggest that metropolitan areas provide a replica, in miniature, of the international field in which theories of "national interest" apply. Of course, then, place of residence would serve to distinguish opinions about metropolitan issues.

On the other hand, one may argue that opinions are not really formulated through rational calculations of self-interest, not even in the case of high-status business and professional leaders. What may be involved are deeper attitudinal differences that are perhaps only coincidentally related to place of residence. Philadelphians may just be more cosmopolitan than Suburbanites and so, in turn, may be more disposed toward a regional outlook. To test this possibility, business and professional leaders were given a local-cosmopolitan battery. While the results were interesting and in the expected direction, the need for categorizing and sub-classifying responses reduced the sample to dangerously few numbers. Accordingly, these results must be interpreted cautiously.

More of the Philadelphians were judged cosmopolitan than local and, conversely, more of the Suburbanites were judged local than cosmopolitan. While Suburban cosmopolitans were more regionally oriented than Suburban locals, when Philadelphia and Suburban cosmopolitans were compared, the former were still more predisposed toward regional action.

The significance of this survey lies in the repeated emphasis upon place of residence as a factor contributing to differences of opinion. Opinion differences are related to differences in attitude. Whether localism and cosmopolitanism enter into locational decisions, or are rather a product of location, city and Suburban residents of similar status do differ in attitude. The degree to which opinion differences also stem from rational calculations of self-interest is problematic, but to whatever extent they do, place of residence is certainly a factor in this calculation.

Rational self-interest is the basis for many of the proposals for metropolitan cooperation, if not reorganization. In many places, this appeal is directed toward business and professional elites through leadership programs and seminars that sometimes appear to be more an attempt to create a metropolitan elite or power structure than a recognition of existing leadership patterns. The assumption behind these efforts is often that reason can be effectively employed with elite groups, and that they will, by virtue of their status, appreciate appeals to regional rather than local self-interest. Our data suggest that high-status is not equivalent to regional consciousness and that, whether or not there is, or should be, a regional interest that appeals to all metropolitan elites, their opinions about general as well as specific aspects of metropolitan issues are significantly affected by place of residence.

Place of Residence as an Independent Variable

Why might we expect residents of particular communities in a metropolitan area to possess differing attitudes or opinions? We have already seen that social status, an important determinant of the norms and values internalized by individuals, is spatially distributed in a consistent fashion. Persons of an equivalent position on a status scale occupy clustered places of residence. Persons of similar rank also tend to possess similar attitudinal attributes. Consequently, we may expect that the attitudes and opinions associated with class or status will also be spatially distributed in a consistent fashion. When a decentralized government structure is superimposed upon this distribution of attitudes, we can expect that the individual political units will reflect the dominant attitudinal characteristics of the constituency which they encompass.

However, the analysis of opinion differences by place of residence demonstrates that even holding constant for factors such as social rank, income, and place of work, respondents are still sharply divided by place of residence in many opinions about the metropolitan area. This suggests that place of residence is a causal factor in producing differences in opinions about governmental activity, and/or the choice of residence is intimately related to differences in attitude and political conviction. Although our evidence is not conclusive with respect to these possibilities, it is significant that choice of residence is not made randomly. The business and professional leaders were asked in what other municipalities they had considered residing before making their present choice. Only 19 percent of the Philadelphia residents and 26 percent of the Suburban respondents reported that they considered moving to any part of the metropolitan area other than the part in which they presently lived. Their range of choice was limited at the outset, although, given the high social rank of the respondents, the limitations must be thought of as self-imposed. We might expect, therefore, that residence in particular suburbs carries certain uniform value connotations and choice is made on this basis.[8]

Apparently, individuals in attempting to relate themselves to a specific social environment are likely to engage attitudes similar to those of the inhabitants of that environment. Identification with a particular community is achieved by adopting the dominant values of the community as one's own. This has the effect of reinforcing attitudinal differences among communities. Of course, there can be many forces operating to achieve and maintain homogeneity of opinion in any community. Conformity is enforced by various and subtle social mechanisms involving the acceptance or withholding of approval by one's neighbors. Homogenous attitudes are furnished social support which helps to reassure one of the wisdom of his views. Deviant opinions incite discord and deprive one of the self-confidence needed to face and overcome the possibility that one's neighbors consider his opinions foolish. The more important one's neighborhood social life is to him, the more dependent he is upon the acceptance and approval of persons living in proximity to him and the more the dominant attitudes of the community impinge upon his own.

Thus, in order to complete the description of the community as a force in shaping attitudes and opinions, we must move from social-area analysis into the study of social organization. Our data suggest the relevance of the community but cannot describe the process through which outlook is influenced by unique areal circumstances.

Notes

1. A more complete description of the two samples and the responses is found in Thomas R. Dye, *Certain Political Correlates of Social and Economic Differentiation Among Suburban Communities* (University of Pennsylvania, Unpublished doctoral dissertation, 1961). The sixteen municipalities grouped by social rank were: upper—Swarthmore, Lansdowne, Springfield, Haverford, Radnor, Nether Providence, middle—Yeadon, Folcroft, East Lansdowne, Norwood, Sharon Hill, lower—Chichester, Upper Chichester, Marcus Hool, Eddystone, Tinicum.

2. A more complete description of this sample and the results is found in; Charles S. Liebman, *Some Opinions of Business and Professional Leaders About Governmental Cooperation in the Philadelphia Metropolitan Area* (University of Pennsylvania, Fels Institute of Local and State Government, ditto, 1961).

3. While the social-class bias in the resident sample was largely controlled by grouping respondents, another very important variable influencing returns to mailed questionnaires, that of interest in the topic under investigation, continues to bias the resident response. Consequently in interpreting the material presented here, one must keep in mind that the resident respondents are probably more interested in, and concerned with, politics in general than the subpopulations they represent.

4. The nationally publicized entry of the first Negro family into a

development in Folcroft dramatizes the often more subtle means of community response. Bathed in the light of publicity, the community eventually formally accepted the newcomers. However, the initial response indicated the predisposition of many, including some municipal employees, to affirm a policy of exclusion. And subsequent neighborhood pressures on merchants and others indicate that the issue is far from final resolution.

5. Jennings summarizes this view of leadership in the following manner: "Both leadership and isolation appear as phenomena which arise out of individual differences in inter-personal capacity for participation and as phenomena which are indigenous to the specific social milieu in which they are produced. Individuals who in this community appear as leaders may or may not be found as leaders in another community of which they later become a part. . . . Helen H. Jennings, *Leadership and Isolation* (New York: 1943); for an excellent review of the literature on leadership see Cecil A. Gibb, "Leadership," in Gardner Lindzey (ed.), *A Handbook of Social Psychology,* Vol. II (Reading, Mass.: Addison-Wesley, 1954).

6. Donald R. Matthews, *The Social Background of Political Decision-Makers* (New York: Doubleday, 1954).

7. Wendell Bell and Maryann I. Force, "Urban Neighborhood Types and Participation in Formal Associations," *American Sociological Review,* Vol. 21 (February, 1956), pp. 25–34.

8. For a development of this idea in specific economic terms see Charles M. Tiebout, "A Pure Theory of Local Expenditures," *Journal of Political Economy,* Vol. 64 (October, 1956), pp. 416–424.

IX

Inter-local Cooperation

Differentiation within the metropolitan area is institutionalized in the variety of public policies pursued by municipalities. This situation can be expected to lead to, and has led to, an absence of policy coordination, separatism, and outright antagonism. Nevertheless, the very profusion of governments in the area stimulates demands for interlocal cooperation.

The small specialized Suburb's inability to provide certain services has been stressed repeatedly in the literature of metropolitan affairs. While the preceding chapters have demonstrated that service levels are related as much to values and preferences as to "ability," there are, nevertheless, some physical and economic limits to a municipality's ability to "go it alone." It is difficult to sustain high schools or libraries in communities of several hundred or even several thousand inhabitants. Many municipalities are unable to provide utility systems because of either size or geographic location. Metropolitan interdependence is recognized sufficiently to require no further elaboration here. It is enough to note that there are pressures for, and resulting examples of, cooperation between municipalities and assumptions of previously local services by higher levels of

239

government in the five-county area. This chapter is directed at inter-municipal arrangements. The one to follow concentrates on functional transfers through the reorganization of governmental responsibilities as exemplified by two proposals for county assumption of health services.

Cooperation as a Policy Decision

The decision by two or more municipalities to band together for the conduct of a specific activity, or the decision to create a county department are as significant policy choices as are decisions regarding public expenditures or the selection of local officials. Actually, the decision to enlarge service areas involves two distinct, yet related judgements. First is the question of whether to "go it alone"; second, what partners to select. In the case of a proposal for adding new responsibilities to the county government, the "partners" are really all municipalities within the county. In the more common inter-local agreement, to which we now turn, partners usually refer to contiguous or, at least, nearby municipalities. The process of choosing a partner often settles the question of whether to cooperate at all, for the availability of a "suitable" partner can be crucial. Standards for determining the suitability of partners, as is the question of whether or not to cooperate, are affected not only by preferences, but also by physical and fiscal imperatives.

Analysis of inter-local cooperation must take into account numerous factors that influence the possibility and/or necessity of cooperation. One that sometimes deters cooperation elsewhere, is absent in this sector. There are no significant legal obstacles to interlocal cooperation in Pennsylvania. State legislation permits, and, at times, encourages cooperation in a large number of local activities.

Cooperative arrangements vary in structure, formality, permanancy, and scope. We consider here only formal agreements negotiated between governmental units, thus excluding a most confusing complex of private-public-private agreements for fire-protection services. Similarly, we do not include the many informal working contacts among professional employees and elected officials of neighboring municipalities. Another widespread type of cooperation, tuition arrangements whereby most schools accept pupils resident in another district are also excluded as they are largely accomodations for families who live closer to a school in another district than the one in their own.

Formal cooperative arrangements are primarily of two kinds. The first is some form of contractual relationship whereby participants negotiate and apportion shares of costs and responsibilities for providing a particular service. The second is the single-purpose authority. In essence, it is a special district, and while it also involves a contract and cost apportionments, the service is conducted by a legally independent entity, in which the participants are represented. School-district mergers and jointures are slightly modified counterparts of the intermunicipal contract and authority. The contract accomplishes the goal of extending service areas with the least sacrifice of policy control by participants. It is, understandably, the most frequently used device for interlocal cooperation. But the independent authorities are not as removed from municipal control as their name would imply.

Who Cooperates for What?

The number of municipalities that participate in the many cooperative arrangements in the five-county sector are listed in Table IX-1. The high incidence of Suburban participation re-

242 Suburban Differences and Metropolitan Policies

flects the fact that they are most active in providing services. Townships offer comparatively few services and consequently have little opportunity to cooperate. Towns are often physically unable to cooperate since they are surrounded by rural areas of only limited activity.

Table IX–1

Formal Intermunicipal Agreements in the Five-county Sector

| Service | Total=226* | Number of Municipalities Participating with One or More Others | | |
		Suburbs 90	Towns 41	Townships 94
Police:				
Police Radio	108	76	18	14
Mutual Assistance	25	7	7	11
School	193	58	41	94
Sewage Disposal	84	70	11	3
Planning	46	12	11	23
Libraries	37	20	10	7
Water	36	26	5	5
Refuse Disposal	33	8	6	19
Roads and Bridges	24	10	6	8
Health (Milk Control)	5	5	0	0

* The total number of municipalities includes Philadelphia, but excludes the twelve municipalities not treated in this volume. This table is adapted from George S. Blair, *Interjurisdictional Agreements in Southeastern Pennsylvania* (Philadelphia: Fels Institute of Local and State Government, 1961).

Even in the Suburbs, where most, if not all urban services are performed, external forces condition the number of agreements in effect as much as do local preferences or values. Several examples may be given. Because populous Delaware County has assumed the normally municipal function of refuse disposal, the need for intermunicipal agreements for that activity has been greatly diminished in that portion of the sector. Throughout the area, cooperation in roads, bridges and water supply is similarly slight as a result of the activities of counties, the state, and several large private-water utility companies. Thus Table IX–1 cannot be construed as indicating what services generate the greatest demand for cooperation. Service areas are enlarged through more than just interlocal cooperation.

The number of Suburban agreements does prompt us to ask if some types of Suburbs cooperate more than others. The business and professional leaders surveyed in Chapter VIII were found to be more disposed toward metropolitan cooperation the more cosmopolitan were their attitudes. Residents and public officials from high-social-ranking municipalities were found to be more cosmopolitan than those from low-social-ranking municipalities. Earlier, we saw that high-social-ranking communities generally favored higher levels of service. If cooperation results in raising service levels, one might expect to find an atmosphere favorable to cooperation in high-social-ranking municipalities.

Is there in fact a larger incidence of cooperation in high-social-ranking communities? This question is tested in Table IX–2 where Suburban cooperation is examined by the social rank of cooperating units. While the hypothesis is given some support, the pattern is so uneven as to raise as many questions as are answered. Social rank is somewhat related to the size of Suburbs. The low-social-ranking municipalities tend to be small, old, river communities. Their need to cooperate in order to initiate a service or to raise standards is probably greater than that of the larger high-social-ranking municipalities. But even though the low-social-ranking municipalities are small, they cooperate less, thus supporting the validity of the hypothesis that high-social-ranking communities are more prone to cooperate.

Table IX–2

Number of Suburbs Participating in Selected
Cooperative Agreements by Social Rank

Social Rank	Health	Refuse Dis- posal	Plan- ning	Librar- ies	Water	Schools	Sewage	Police Radio	Total Agree- ments
First Quartile	3	8		10	5	13	20	16	75
Second Quartile	2		5	6	8	16	18	20	75
Third Quartile			5	2	7	20	16	21	71
Fourth Quartile			2	2	6	9	16	19	54

Ideally one should control for size and possibly develop some "objective" standards of necessity for cooperation prior to examining propensities to cooperate. But size is not the only consideration pertinent to this question. Let us assume that high-social-ranking communities are more interested in high service levels and that they will enter into joint arrangements to the extent that services are thereby enhanced. Cooperation is not necessarily a means to increased services. In schools, it is the small, high-social-ranking communities that have vehemently opposed state efforts to force mergers. They champion the position that quality is not related to size of district. For them, merger may mean a dilution of service levels by requiring them to compromise with districts of low social rank. Thus for school cooperation, the geographic proximity of a *suitable* partner may be the determinative variable.

Planning affords another illustration of the dubious relationship between service levels and cooperation. Most of the higher-social-ranking municipalities have long engaged in planning.

Their comprehensive plans have been formulated and implementing ordinances have long been in effect. Some of the newer (and often lower-social-ranking) Suburbs have only recently initiated planning services. Some do so cooperatively, but since federal-701 money is now available for those who plan in a cooperative fashion, agreement is really brought about by the federal "carrot." Parenthetically, we might add that efforts to encourage several groups of Suburbs that include a number of high-social-ranking units and others of lower social rank to plan jointly have not been successful. Once again the concept of "quality" takes on a controversial meaning in contrasting independent or cooperative action.

The distinction being drawn is one that relates to the character of services, roughly those that affect the life-style of a community and those that do not. Schools and planning fall into the first category; sewers, water, refuse disposal and police radios in the second. Just where libraries and health measures fall is difficult to determine without examination of specific circumstances. This distinction will be treated in greater detail in the remainder of this chapter.

But what of the question: who is willing to cooperate? Bearing in mind all the foregoing qualifications, size, assumption of services in some areas by non-local governments, and the differences in the character of the services in question, we suggest that high-social-ranking communities are predisposed to cooperate insofar as cooperation will raise service standards and does not affect life-style. Low-social-ranking municipalities are less disposed to enter into agreements despite the fact that many are so small as to be unable to provide some services independently.

The careful reader may well feel uncomfortable with the foregoing paragraph, for it does hasten to a generalization on the basis of a rather broad survey. It is evident that when the question of willingness to cooperate is raised, its reply leads to a second question—cooperation with whom? The latter lends itself to more precise measurement and testing.

Who Cooperates with Whom?

Given the necessity and/or predisposition to cooperate, who will a municipality choose for its partner? Why will a municipality cooperate with one but not another of its neighbors? Is the selection of partners random, based on cost calculation; or is it the product of social and economic differentiation, and, as such, related to the incidence of cooperation?

Agreements for schools, sewage disposal, and police-radio systems provide enough examples of cooperation to examine these questions. Furthermore, the three represent distinct kinds of activities with varying impact upon and presumably importance to residents. Of the three, only schools relate directly to the lift-style of a community. The education of children is an extension of parental care. No other local activity has as direct an affect on the lives of parents and their offspring.

A sewage-disposal system can affect the amenities of daily life, but is scarcely comparable to schools in its social significance. Once installed and in proper operation, it is taken for granted and forgotten. A sewage-disposal system is, however, like the schools, a large capital investment.

Police-radio agreements affect the amenities of life very little and represent small investments of resources. It is a rare citizen who will know or care to know whether his local government is involved in such an agreement.

Respondents in the survey of business and professional leaders were overwhelmingly in favor of cooperation in the abstract, or where the object of cooperation, air pollution, for example, involved neither life-style nor large financial outlays. When questioned about cooperation for regional parks, facilities very much affecting life-styles by bringing heterogenous populations together, suburban respondents were opposed. Of course, the questions were addressed to the idea of cooperation between Suburbs and Philadelphia, not between one set of Suburbs and another. Insofar as Philadelphia represents an image of a lower-class, low-status population, we suspect that an unwillingness to cooperate with the city in activities significant to life-style values is accompanied by similar reluctance to cooperate with Suburbs of dffering status.

As a preliminary hypothesis, we would expect to find that for functions affecting life-style, Suburbs will seek to cooperate with other communities of similar social status as opposed to those of different status. Where life-style is not affected, social differences may not relate to patterns of cooperation, but, especially where large capital investments are involved, economic differences may be of prime importance.

To assess the relationships between social and economic differences and intermunicipal cooperation or non-cooperation, several definitions and measures must first be established. *Co-operation* is defined as the joint financing and participation in the management of a service or facility in which long term obligations are binding upon the participants. In order for a relationship between municipalities to be styled one of *non-co-operation*, the possibility of agreement has to be present. Therefore, the following conditions must be met for a choice between cooperation and non-cooperation to be possible. (1) Both municipalities must be engaged in providing the services in question. (2) The municipalities must be contiguous for cooperation to be feasible. Although contiguity is not essential to cooperation, in practice it is generally the case. Moreover, for operational purposes, contiguity was a necessary condition for testing the hypothesis.[1]

By map inspection, 534 pairs of contiguous municipalities were located in the five-county sector.[2] Using the Suburban and semi-urban classifications, 198 pairs were found in the Suburbs, 294 in the semi-urban area (Towns and Townships), and 42 pairs crossing the line dividing the two and comprised of one Suburb and one Town or Township. (This last group will hereafter be called urban-rural).

We wish to measure the social and economic distances between each of these contiguous pairs and relate these differences to cooperation or non-cooperation. Two social and economic indices are available for each municipality: social rank and market value per capita. The social and economic distance between municipalities in a pair is defined as the absolute difference in their social rank and market value per capita. The smaller the difference in any index for a pair of municipalities, the less social or economic distance exists between them and the more similar they are to each other. The greater the differences in index scores between paired municipalities, the more dissimilar they are. The central hypothesis may now be stated operationally: *If intermunicipal cooperation in a metropolitan area is a function of social and economic distance between communities, the mean of the differences in index values will be smaller for cooperating than for non-cooperating municipalities.*

School Agreements. Table IX–3 compares pairs of municipalities that cooperate and do not cooperate for public schools. For the hypothesis to be borne out, the mean of differences in indices for cooperating pairs must be less than for non-cooperating pairs. The table indicates this to be true in the urban-rural pairs, those comprised of Suburban and semi-urban municipalities. For each group, however, social distances, as measured by social rank, are statistically more significantly related to the presence or absence of cooperation than the market value index.

Table IX–3

Mean Differences Among Pairs of Cooperating and Non-cooperating
Municipalities for School Agreements

	Suburban			Urban-rural			Semi-rural		
	Cooperating	Non-cooperating	Total*	Cooperating	Non-cooperating	Total†	Cooperating	Non-cooperating	Total
Social Rank	10.4	16.9	16.0	8.6	14.1	12.8	7.3	7.8	7.5
Market Value Per Capita (Dollars)	1,131	1,467	1,424	1,685	1,437	1,515	927	994	974
Number of Pairs	26	172	198	13	29	42	162	132	294

*Differences between cooperating and non-cooperating pairs of municipalities are significant at the .01 level of significance.
†Differences between cooperating and non-cooperating pairs of municipalities are significant at the .05 level of significance.

One of the major incentives for cooperative school arrangements is the pooling of pupils and resources for the construction and operation of high schools. Central schools and school-district consolidation originated in rural areas. Indeed, as previously indicated, the incidence of school cooperation is greater in the semi-urban than the Suburban portion of the metropolitan area. But this apparent difference in behavior cannot be explained merely by reference to the larger populations of Suburban school districts.

In recent years, school-district consolidation has been urged upon suburban districts as well as rural communities. Pennsylvania's current recommended standards of school-district size are considerably higher than the 2500-pupil standard previously employed. Nevertheless, even with regard to the 2500 standard, there are only 21 Suburbs and one semi-urban district that can be considered large enough to maintain independent school systems. There are in fact 32 Surburban districts operating independently, but *none* in the semi-urban area.

Our hypothesis suggests that the more extensive use of cooperative school arrangements in the semi-urban area is a function, in part, of the lesser social distance among pairs there than is found in the Suburbs. Note that in the "Total" column of Table IX–3, the mean of the differences is larger for each index value in the Suburbs. Urban specialization tends to create sharp social breaks which follow municipal boundaries. Inter-municipal social distances influence not only the pattern of co-operation, but also its extent. Only 26 out of 198 Suburban pairs had agreements, while 162 out of 294 semi-urban pairs did. The urban-rural pairs lie in between with 13 out of 29 cooperating. The 26 Suburban pairs that did cooperate were atypical for the group. The mean difference in social rank for all suburban pairs is 16.0, but only 10.4 for the cooperating communities. A similar pattern holds for the taxable resources, although not always at a high level of statistical significance.

In the urban-rural area the mean differences in market value per capita between cooperating and non-cooperating pairs are in the opposite direction from that expected. Since none of the differences in market value per capita in any of the three groups are at a .10 level of significance, the difference in the urban-rural area might have arisen solely due to chance. It may also re-sult from the fact that the market-value index does not always coincide with the year in which an agreement took place. Vari-ances of as much as ten years between index and agreement year are included.[3] Most communities do not experience rapid demographic changes. However, along the fringes of the urban area the most rapid shifts do take place. Fringe-area industriali-zation and large housing developments are the most common form which these changes take. It is likely that some disparities in market value per capita have taken place subsequent to the development of joint school systems. The hypothesis is sup-ported even in this changing area with regard to social rank, however. Either populations channeling into fringe areas are not upsetting the social balance of agreeing pairs, or changes in social composition occur at a slower rate than changes in municipal resources. Our observation is that both these propositions are true.

In the semi-urban pairs, the differences in means are both in the expected direction, but at less than a .05 level of statistical significance. We suspect that social rank is not as determinative an influence on the public policies of semi-urban municipalities as on the behavior of Suburbs, where the closeness, size, and more frequent interactions of populations evoke greater consciousness of differences in community social status.

Further evidence of the inhibiting effect on cooperation of differences in status and resources is provided by the current controversy over school redistricting in Pennsylvania. In 1961, the state enacted a redistricting law requiring the formulation of districts having minimum enrollments of 4,000 pupils. The law stemmed from the studies of the Governor's Committee on Education which had recommended districts with no less than 5,000, and preferably 10,000 pupils. Even before the Committee's report, the Delaware County Board of School Directors had authorized the County Superintendent of Schools to consolidate the county's 43 districts into a smaller number of administrative units. But the County Superintendent had made no headway and was reported to have felt that reorganization could be achieved only if ordered by Harrisburg—the state capitol.[4]

The act of 1961 did, in effect, order reorganization throughout the state, requiring the new districts to be activated by January 1, 1965. Local reaction was immediate, and, as might have been expected, bitter. (More surprising than the reaction is the fact that the state legislature passed a *mandatory* redisricting law.) In their statements in opposition to consolidation plans, local officials have, with more or less frankness and tact, identified those factors that are here statistically described as inhibiting cooperation.

One of Delaware County's planned consolidations combines the school district of Springfield with that of Morton, a
poor borough with a large Negro population. In a statement regarding the prospective merger, the president of Springfield's
school board told the County Board of School Directors that
"the differences in wealth, tax rate, and other economic factors
will tend to downgrade our ability to support the type of program Springfield has heretofore sustained." [5] Although opposition was here expressed solely in economic terms, others have
cited less tangible considerations of quality of education *and
students,* and community expectations. Wealthy Nether Providence is slated to be merged with several communities including the equally distinguished Swarthmore. Nether Providence's
position before the County Board was that "we believe a district
can become so large that children lose their identity and individuality," but if there has to be a merger ". . . the merger
which you have proposed would be acceptable." [6]

Opposition to redistricting has not been confined to metropolitan Philadelphia. One of Governor Scranton's first acts after
his election in 1962 was to suspend the timetable for consolidation, while consideration was given to exempting quality
schools or districts with divergent community characteristics
from the merger requirement. In a feature story on Thaddeus
Stevens of Reconstructionist fame that appeared soon after the
Governor's action, one Harrisburg journalist gave vent to his
strong sentiments (and perhaps those of his newspaper as well)
with the following comment:

> There is good reason to believe that Stevens, a fanatic in his time
> on education and civil rights, would be excoriating the so-called
> "quality of education" yardstick and the "community characteristics"
> criteria, now being proposed, as favoring the rich over the poor
> and as discriminatory, where so many well-to-do suburban school
> districts throughout the State are involved, against the Negro. The

hypocrisy involved in this phase of school district reorganization controversy is so thick you can cut it with a knife.[7]

Sewage Agreements. School cooperation brings people of several jurisdictions together and seriously affects life-styles. It takes place, but tends to be between communities of similar social-status and fiscal resources. The disposal of sewage is essential to urban living, but has little to do with life-style. Analysis of sewage agreements might be expected to emphasize the importance of financial and technical considerations over differences in social status. Table IX–4 repeats the analysis of co-operating and non-cooperating pairs for sewage disposal.

One of the conditions for pairing municipalities is that both potential parties to the agreement must provide the service in question; thus only sewered communities are included. The condition, in effect, confined the analysis to the suburban portion of the sector. The "total" column in Table IX–4 indicates that there is little difference between cooperating and non-cooperating pairs with respect to social rank, but there are significant differences with respect to community wealth. The conclusion might be drawn that municipalities do not mind negotiating with neighbors of differing social rank over matters of as little social significance as sewage, but are concerned about their neighbors wealth because the maintenance and future expansion of the joint system will be influenced by the tax situation of the members. However, as the remaining portions of the Table show, this is only partially true.

The municipalities along the Delaware River are old industrial locations. They frequently have substantial tax bases, but low-social-ranking populations. As one goes up the tributary streams from the river, the social rank rises. Since sewage "runs down hill," the low-status communities have had a monopoly of the access points for sewer trunks to the river. For the higher-

Table IX–4

Mean Differences Among Pairs of Cooperating
and Non-cooperating Municipalities for Sewer Agreements

	Total			Delaware River Outlet			Other Outlets		
	Cooperating	Non-cooperating	Total	Cooperating	Non-cooperating	Total	Cooperating	Non-cooperating	Total
Social Rank	15.9	15.3	15.6	17.4	11.9	16.1	11.2	18.0	15.0†
Market Value Per Capita (Dollars)	1,223	1,829	1,440†	1,278	2,194	1,506†	1,057	1,537	1,324
Number of Pairs	113	63	176	85	28	113	28	35	63

†Differences between cooperating and non-cooperating parts of municipalities are significant at the .05 level of significance.

status upstream communities to dispose of their sewage, they must deal with the lower-status downstream communities. Table IX–4 lists all sewered communities with systems emptying directly into the Delaware River from the Delaware-Pennsylvania state boundary to Bensalem Township, which represents the strip of pre-war river-front development. These are labeled "Delaware River Outlet."

Here, pairs of municipalities with sewer agreements actually have a higher mean social-rank difference (though not significantly higher) than the pairs of municipalities without sewer agreements. However, with regard to taxable wealth, the agreeing municipalities in the Delaware River Outlet area have a significantly smaller mean difference than the pairs of municipalities without sewer agreements. Joint sewer systems are rarely financed by uniform tax rates applying to all participating municipalities. Rather the shares to be paid by each municipality are worked out at the time of the agreement. Nevertheless, as indicated above, the economic well-being of cooperating municipalities is a matter of vital concern to the partners. High-status municipalities using Delaware River outlets had no choice but to negotiate agreements with low-status communities, but it would appear that they sought to cooperate with those low-status communities that were on a par in taxable resources.

The remainder of the sewered communities not in the Delaware River outlet group are shown in Table IX–4 under the heading "Other Outlets." These municipalities are located further up the streams from the Delaware River and along the Schuylkill and its tributaries. In these areas, municipalities freqently have a range of choice in deciding with which other communities, if any, they will join in building sewerage systems. Here there is no solidly built-up, riparian industrial strip monopolizing river access.

Agreements among these communities occur between those of similar status (social rank). It is interesting that although the agreeing communities also resemble each other more closely than do the non-agreeing communities with respect to taxable wealth, the difference in wealth between agreeing and non-agreeing communities is not statistically significant, even at the .10 level. It would appear that where a range of choice does exist, status is a more important concomitant of agreement than is taxable resources.

Police-radio Agreements. School and sewerage systems have far differing social and cultural connotations, but both involve expensive capital facilities. In each case, cooperation usually requires protracted negotiations among municipal officials, although, perhaps, with regard to sewers, little general public involvement. Police-radio agreements do not affect life-styles, involve modest financial outlays and are of concern primarily to technicians. Are they also influenced by the social and economic distance between municipalities?

Table IX–5 applies the paired analysis to police-radio agreements for those municipalities having police radios. Again the analysis must be confined to the Suburbs. For this rather minor service, social and economic distances apparently do not affect patterns of cooperation. There is no evidence of a preference for cooperation between similar municipalities.

Table IX–5

Mean Differences Among Cooperating and Non-cooperating
Municipalities for Police-radio Agreements *

	Cooperating	Non-cooperating	Total
Social Rank	14.2	17.1	15.9
Market Value per Capita	$1,645	$1,304	$1,445
Number of Pairs	80	114	194

* None of the differences were significant at the .05 or even .10 level.

The Prospects for Cooperation

The preceding suggests the prime importance of similarities in social rank as a precondition for some kinds of cooperation and an importance, albeit of a secondary nature, of equality of tax resources. Certainly, the data demonstrate that, at least among Suburban municipalities, even if equality of tax resources is a necessary condition for cooperation, it is not a sufficient one.

If social rank and community wealth are both important determinants of cooperation, it is to their combined trends that we must look to assess prospects for future cooperation. Before doing so, one *caveat* must be entered. We have, in a sense, proposed the outlines of a theory of cooperation. Utilizing the theory necessitates the assumption that a great many variables not considered will remain equal. This assumption is particularly risky with regard to at least three factors. One is the extent of physical needs; the second, the public's perception of those needs; and the third, the activities of participants located outside of the metropolitan area.

If the sewage disposal problem worsens, pressure for agreements within municipalities may overcome objections to cooperation, and technical considerations may outweigh social values. As more and more individuals and groups interest themselves in metropolitan problems and push for more cooperation, their effect may be to arouse an area-wide constituency that perceives problems and solutions in metropolitan terms and serves as a stimulent to further cooperation. Furthermore, if the constituency is able to capture the allegiance of the dominant political party, the influence of intermunicipal difference may be lessened. Finally, if the state completes the mandatory merger of school districts, and if it or the federal government prods the development of additional types of action that disregard differences in social status or tax resources, local opposition to cooperation may have to give way.

Bearing this *caveat* in mind, and returning to the more static elements of our model, let us look at trends in the Suburban distribution of tax resources. Between 1950 and 1960, there was increasing homogeneity in fiscal resources among the 90 suburbs. Jesse Burkhead finds a similar trend toward fiscal homogeneity in the Cleveland metropolitan area.[8] However, in discussing change in Chapter II, it was necessary to distinguish between those 65 municipalities that were Suburbs in 1950 and the 25 that first reached urban density or were engulfed by the expanding urban area between 1950 and 1960. The newer Suburbs, it was noted, generally attract a younger, higher-social-ranking population, and enjoy greater market value per capita as land values increase faster than population. This same point is noted by John Riew in commenting on Burkhead's findings. He suggests the possibility that increasing uniformity in tax resources is accounted for "by those outlying jurisdictions which had grown rapidly during the forties, some emerging from rural or semi-urban to more urbanized areas."[9]

For our analysis, then, we have distinguished between the

65 old and 25 new Suburbs. In Table IX–6, using Burkhead's measure of variation $V = \dfrac{Q_3 - Q_1}{Q_2}$ and defining fiscal resources as market value per capita, we find, for the 25 new Suburbs, only a slight increase in homogeneity.

Table IX–6

Variation in Market Value per Capita of Old and New Suburbs, 1950 and 1960

	Coefficient of Variation	
	1950	1960
Old Suburbs N = 65	65.0	44.2
New Suburbs N = 25	47,6	44.9

Alone, these results are of limited utility; for resources are a significant determinant of cooperation only in conjunction with social rank. Even if we assume the importance of resources, we must still ask what changes are taking place in the tax resources of municipalities grouped according to their social rank?

Changes in Tax resources. The two Suburban groups were ordered by their 1960 social rank and divided into quartiles. Table IX–7 reports the mean market value per capita in 1950 and 1960 for municipalities in each quartile.

Table IX–7

Mean Market Value of Suburbs by Social Rank Quartile, 1950 and 1960

	Low			High
	4th Quartile	3rd Quartile	2nd Quartile	1st Quartile
Old Suburbs: N=65 1950	$3459	$2448	$2778	$3968
1960	4145	3188	3630	4828
Absolute Increase	686	740	852	860
1960 Values as % of 1950	119.8%	130.2%	130.7%	121.7%
New Suburbs: N=25 1950	$2570	$3378	$3076	$5280
1960	3820	5064	4034	6263
Absolute Increase	1250	1686	958	983
1960 Values as % of 1950	148.9%	149.9%	131.1%	118.6%

The pattern is different for the two types of communities. Among the newly urbanized, rapidly growing communities those low in social rank are increasing their market value per capita much more rapidly than those of high social rank. To project this trend further into the future, however, may be unjustified. All these communities were very sparsely settled in 1950. As their farm land was converted to residential and industrial property, market value rose sharply. Changes in population composition occur more slowly. One might expect that by 1970 these communities will be substantially reordered by social rank and that, at that time, their pattern will approximate that of the older communities.

In the older suburbs, the low-social-ranking municipalities did not keep pace with the higher-social-ranking communities' increase in resources. This would be more strikingly portrayed if we were to omit one municipality from the lowest quartile. It experienced a tremendous growth in per capita market value, largely due to a 14 percent population decline.

The old, low-social-ranking communities include a substantial number of highly industrialized municipalities with very high market values. This accounts for the fact that mean market value in the lowest-social-ranking quartile exceeds those of all but the highest quartile. One might anticipate that if the market values of the low-social-ranking communities rose substantially more rapidly than those of the high-social-ranking communities, it would be possible for this differential to offset status differences and engender cooperative arrangements. Whereas one partner to an agreement would be expected to contribute fiscal resources, the other would contribute status and prestige. Although this kind of outcome is by no means certain, it is a possibility. However, over time, the market values of the highest-social-ranking communities are increasing more than those of the lowest-social-ranking communities, at least among the older urbanized communities. The market values of many low-social-ranking communities was high to begin with. The fact that resources in high-social ranking communities are increasing very rapidly results in a portrait of the metropolitan area as a whole becoming more homogeneous. But this homogeneity, which was expressed in Table IX–6, where social rank was disregarded, is more likely than not to have an unfavorable impact on cooperation.

Given our method of comparing contiguous pairs, it is impossible to suggest what difference in market value per capita can compensate for a difference in social rank in the other direction, that is, where the lower-social-ranking of two municipalities is the wealthier, or *vice versa*. Most of the pairs with large social-rank differences are either similar in wealth (wealthy Industrial Centers paired with wealthy high-status residential Suburbs), or extremely different in wealth, but, the wealthier is also higher in social rank. But some indication of the offsetting contributions of social rank and resources can be gained from another look at Suburban pairs and school agreements. If we divide Suburban pairs into those with large and small differences in social rank and average the market value differences of those that cooperate and do not cooperate for schools the distribution is as follows:

Table IX–8

	Small Differences in Social Rank	Large Differences in Social Rank
Mean Market Value Differences of Cooperating Pairs	2,659	$1,505
Mean Market Differences of Non-cooperating Pairs	$954	$1,964

The numbers involved are admittedly small, but the distribution does point emphatically to the possibility of cooperation where extremely large differences in wealth exist, but where the participants are not too dissimilar in social rank. In fact, the largest resource differences are to be found among the cooperating pairs with the least social-rank difference. Unfortunately, there are too few cases where the wealthier of two school districts is the lower in social rank to test the possibility that differences in opposite directions compensate for one another. But another type of compensation is evident. The formula for distribution of state aid to public schools partially offsets differences in district wealth. It appears that this compensation is in part responsible for not discouraging cooperation among school districts of similar social rank but widely differing wealth.

State aid serves to increase social rank's influence on cooperation. A high-social-ranking school district may covet a wealthy low-social-ranking neighbor's tax base, but the attractiveness of cooperating with the latter is lessened as a result of the state's equalization policy. The high-status district may join a similar community of less wealth, secure in the knowledge that state aid will partially compensate for its lack of resources. This calculation of relative advantages is particularly applicable to jointures, where each of the partners set their own tax rates and receive their own shares of state aid. For mergers, the effect of a partner's wealth on the combined district tax role may be a more influential consideration.

Changes in Social Rank. Is there any evidence of increased homogeneity in social rank that might indicate a potential for future cooperation? Table IX–9 presents suburban social-rank means by quartile for 1950 and 1960, with the quartile ranking based on 1960 values. Since social rank is a standardized score, it is more valid to look at the absolute, rather than percentage changes in the scores.

Social-rank differences are increasing more among the newer than the older Suburbs. The newer Suburbs are still in the "shaking down" stage. Greatest increases in social rank appear

Table IX-9

Mean Values of Social-rank Quartiles, 1950 and 1960

		Low 4th Quartile	3rd Quartile	2nd Quartile	High 1st Quartile
Old Suburbs: N=65	1950	8.1	17.2	27.0	51.0
	1960	8.5	17.8	28.4	56.7
Absolute change		.4	.6	.5	5.7
New Suburbs: N=25	1950	20.2	20.4	31.3	43.1
	1960	21.6	30.0	43.0	58.5
Absolute change		1.4	9.6	11.7	15.4

in those that ranked highest in 1960. But changes in quartile distribution occurred between 1950 and 1960, and shifts were so erratic that one would be unjustified in predicting a continuation of this trend. The most rapid changes in social composition do occur among these newly developing Suburbs. As their population grows, we can expect more stability and a pattern more closely resembling the 65 older Suburbs.

Among the older Suburbs, the quartile rankings are relatively stable between 1950 and 1960. Of the 16 municipalities in the lowest quartile in 1960, all but 2 were in the lowest quartile in 1950. These 2 were then among the lowest of the second quartile. In the highest 1960 quartile, only one municipality had been in a lower quartile in 1950.

The mean social-rank increase between 1950 and 1960 was greatest in the highest-ranked municipalities whose 5.7 increase stands out above a remarkably stable pattern in the other 3 quartiles. Furthermore, change among the lower quartiles is virtually uniform and not merely one community's increase cancelling and averaging out a decrease in another. In contrast to the new Suburbs, those that showed the greatest change in social rank were not necessarily those with the largest population increases.

The stability in social rank of most older Suburbs is of greatest significance because of the possibility that cooperation may be less dependent upon the extent of social-rank differences among communities than their both being above, or below, some "critical point" of social rank. The analysis of pairs has viewed a social-rank difference of 20 as measuring the same social distance regardless of whether the difference was one of 60–40 or 30–10. The existence of a "critical point" cannot be verified, but it is possible that once a community reaches a position, let us say, where 40 percent of its adult population is employed in high-status occupations and has had college experience, the social distance between it and a neighbor with a social rank of 90 is relatively insignificant.

However, while high-social-ranking municipalities are substantially increasing their numbers of white-collar, college-educated adults, those in lower quartiles, despite national trends in occupation and education, are gaining few more than they had in 1950. Social distance is increasing between the two types of communities, not only in a relative sense, but also in terms of the lower-status communities' approaching any "critical point."

Summary

In a numerical sense, cooperation is likely to increase within the metropolitan area if only as a result of the increase in governmental activity that can be expected to accompany continued population growth. Cooperation is a product of many factors, among them the sheer physical necessities of proximity and activity. We originally hypothesized that high-social-ranking municipalities would be more predisposed toward cooperation than those of low social rank, only to find that their greater amount of activity, more than their attitudes, is probably responsible for their large number of cooperative agreements. Insofar as the high-social-ranking communities will probably continue to exhibit relatively greater concern for the number and quality of municipal services provided, their participation in cooperative activities can be expected to continue to exceed that of low-social-ranking municipalities.

Although not fully corroborated, a second hypothesis with respect to social rank appears to be relevant to the question of interlocal cooperation. Social and economic distance between municipalities influences cooperative activities involving lifestyles and large capital investments. However, differences in social rank appear to be more significant than inequalities of resources. There is some indication that the relative influence of the two factors can be manipulated by state policy. At least with regard to school agreements, state equalization policy has tended to minimize the consequences of discrepancies in district wealth. Generally, given a choice as to the selection of partners to an agreement, cooperation occurs among municipalities with similar social rank and tax resources, in that order. Where agreements are necessary for the performance of a particular function, and little choice with respect to social rank is available, the resources of prospective partners become the prime consideration. This scale of values is not operative for some minor cooperative activities with but slight social and financial impact.

Time can be expected to change the conditions and the relevance of factors influencing cooperation. In terms of the two here considered—status and resources—current trends suggest few changes in the pattern of cooperation depicted. Over time, there does seem to be greater homogeneity in the distribution of tax resources, but when trends in fiscal measures are related to social rank, this apparent homogeneity can be attributed primarily to the growth of new Suburbs. In the older Suburbs, there is some tendency for resources to increase faster in high-social-ranking municipalities.

The homogeneity thus displayed may in fact be disfunctional
to cooperation, since the resources of older low-social-ranking
Suburbs were higher in 1950 than many high-social-ranking
municipalities', but are increasing less rapidly than the latter's
resources. Increasing acommodation of industrial land uses within high-status communities promises further to reduce the fiscal
advantages of older Industrial and Commercial Centers. If, in
the past, the wealth of the Industrial and Commercial Center
has been able to balance or counteract the social distance between it and higher-social-ranking Suburbs, the trend toward
homogeneity in resources, unless accompanied by homogeneity
in social rank, promises to accentuate the status differences between municipalities. There is no evidence that social-rank differences are decreasing. Quite the contrary, social cleavages appear to have become more pronounced.

A final word about cooperation must take into account those
who are formally entrusted with the negotiations leading to cooperative agreements. Public officials, in the final analysis, ar-
range for and supervise joint activities. Much has been said
about the intransigence of local officials, their self-perpetuation
and unwillingness to legislate themselves out of jobs. Our study
suggests that public officials are indeed representative of their
constituencies, and that their behavior with regard to interlocal
cooperation is probably related more to the social and economic
differences in their constituencies than to their personal or
political differences.

We have attempted to measure political differences between
cooperating and non-cooperating municipalities elsewhere.[10]
But measuring political difference is difficult. A Republcan
councilman from one municipality may find it hard to negotiate
with a Democratic councilman from another, but most Suburban municipalities and their elected officials are Republican.
Are there gradations of Republicanism that affect the pattern of

cooperation? Measured by voting returns, there are degrees to which communities may be labelled Republican. Differences in degrees are related to cooperation and non-cooperation, but they are also so closely correlated with social rank that political difference cannot be regarded as itself influencing patterns of cooperation, but rather as representative of deeper social distinctions between communities.

The question of party affiliation as such is nowhere sharply identified in the foregoing analysis of pairs. However, in the next chapter, in regard to the county health-department votes, the political parties did take a stand. Here we have an opportunity to observe the cross pressures of social rank, partisanship, and service consideration as they pertained to a decision on the enlargement of a service area.

NOTES

1. Restricting the analysis to contiguous pairs also helps dispel the criticism that social distance is slight because similar communities tend to cluster and therefore cooperate more frequently because they are in geographic proximity. By looking at cooperating and non-cooperating contiguous pairs, we are, in effect, controlling for geography. Communities do tend to cluster, but we ask, for example, why one chooses to cooperate with its eastern, rather than its western neighbor.

2. Sixy-six pairs of contiguous municipalities were eliminated because each contained at least one of the twelve municipalities excluded from the study due to large institutional populations.

3. Methodically, data for indices of agreeing pairs shoud be gathered at the time agreements occur. Aside from nonavailability of data, there is a problem of selecting the proper year for an index of non-cooperating pairs.

4. *Philadelphia Bulletin* (April 4, 1961), p. 50.

5. *Philadelphia Bulletin* (November 27, 1962), p. 55.

6. *Ibid.*

7. George Draut, "The Ghost of Thad Stevens," *The Evening News* (Harrisburg, February 14, 1963), p. 26. To complete the story, we might add that the 1961 redistricting act was eventually repealed by the legislature.

8. Jesse Burkhead, "Uniformity in Governmental Expenditures and Resources in a Metropolitan Area: Cuyahoga County, *National Tax Journal,* Vol. 14 (December, 1961), p. 347.

9. John Riew, "Uniformity in Governmental Expenditures and Re cources in a Metropolitan Area: A Comment," *National Tax Journal,* Vol. 15, (June 1962), p. 219.

10. See the authors, "Differentiation and Cooperation in a Metropolitan Area," *Midwest Journal of Political Science,* Vol. 7 (May, 1963), pp. 145–155.

X

Functional Transfers: Two Cases

Transferring an urban municipal function to a higher level of government, whether it be a county, the state, or a new regional government, is a form of cooperation of a different order than the intermunicipal agreement. It strikes at the very foundation of urban differentiation, altering the process of intergroup compromise as well as its scope. Although a county health unit, for example, may be viewed as an agreement between all municipalities in a county, the variety of interests accommodated in this unit is far greater than that of any intermunicipal agreement. As important, is the change in patterns of access to decision-making that accompanies such a transfer.

Any cooperative agreement must be founded upon at least minimal consensus as to goals and objectives. Consensus implies a process of compromise involving great or small concessions by the agreeing parties. Where the participants in an agreement are few, the concessions are likely to be minor. Where the participants are many and varied in outlook, the concessions perforce must be greater. Consent to county assumption of previously municipal services is in the latter category. In the counties involved in this study, representatives were elected at large. Thus the possibility was real that county decisions might be at variance with the wishes of some municipal governments.

In an intermunicipal agreement, the activity continues to be managed by the political representatives of participating localities. While centralization of functions involves a transfer of responsibility from one set of political representatives to another, it also often implies a change in the relative influence of political and professional leaders. In public health, as well as in numerous other activities, professionals are among those most actively championing transfers of functions.

Interlocal agreements and functional transfers have the common objective of enlarging service areas. The former does so with the least damage to the political and structural integrity of the system of urban differentiation. The latter poses a real threat to the system and to the political mechanisms that help perpetuate differentiation. The issues surrounding decisions regarding agreements and functional transfers are sufficiently different to attract diverse participants in debate and to involve different levels of argument.

The question of a functional transfer has twice been raised in metropolitan Phiadelphia, and both times has been settled through the direct participation of the electorate. Separate referenda have been held on the formation of a county health department in Bucks and in Montgomery Counties. While the referenda concerned a single function and a limited form of metropolitan reorganization, the issues were relevant to the questions of differentiation and integration central to this volume. Indeed, the metropolitan problem in its entirety was identified with the county health department movement by those responsible for its emergence in Pennsylvania. They suggested that "a by-product of such cooperation in health matters may be a broadening of cooperation in other governmental functions best handled on a regional basis." [1]

The County Health Department Movement

A 1948 report of the American Public Health Association culminated in the passage of legislation in 1951 permitting the creation of county health departments. Act 315 of that year introduced this, and a second innovation, into Pennsylvania's public health policy. For the first time, state health grants were offered localities meeting certain performance standards. To date, none but county departments have been deemed eligible for state aid.

The county health department movement has been far from successful in Pennsylvania. Only five departments have been formed to date, and one was abolished subsequent to several years of operation. The idea has been viewed suspiciously and, for the most part, unfavorably throughout the state, but our concern is with its reception in two of Philadelphia's suburban counties. The county health department proposal was approved by a two to one majority in Bucks County in 1953. Five years later, the voters of Montgomery County rejected the same proposal by an equal margin.

Care must be taken not to read too much into a referendum on a single issue. On the other hand, a vote for or against a county health department reflects attitudes and opinions about a host of issues relevant to metropolitan integration. At issue are fundamental attitudes toward personal and community health, judgments as to the adequacy of existing service levels, opinions about the proper level of government activity, professionalism in the public service, and in Montgomery County, receptivity to the leadership of political parties and local officials. This last factor is crucial to an understanding of the difference in the Bucks and Montgomery votes.

Public health educators have identified those individuals and groups to whom their activities have the greatest appeal. Drawing upon our preceding chapters, we might predict a pattern of voting on a health issue to which they would probably agree. Included in such a prediction would be calculations of social rank, population size, density, growth, wealth, and electoral participation. A predictive model based on these characteristics would assume a condition fervently hoped for by public health practitioners—the neutrality of political parties. Party neutrality did accompany the Bucks referendum but in Montgomery County, the activities of political parties were such as to completely distinguish the nature, issues, and outcome of the two referenda.

The Referendum Campaigns

Public health is dominated by the interplay of public, private, semi-public and professional organizations. In no field of governmental activity has more attention been paid to community organization and group participation. Standard public health procedures of organizing citizen participation and utilizing the resources of health and welfare agencies were employed in both counties. Paradoxically, however, the better organized campaign was the less successful.

The Bucks Campaign. Bucks County is customarily divided into three regions—Lower, Middle and Upper Bucks. Lower Bucks contains all of the County's Suburbs and in the early 1950's was in the midst of rapid development. Upper Bucks is still largely rural today. The middle portion of the County is slowly developing. In the early 1950's, Lower Bucks was straining under the pressure of its rapid growth. The pressures were not alone those applied to its roads by the parade of moving vans to and from Levittown and Fairless Hills. In particular, problems of waste and refuse disposal were being evidenced. In Middle Bucks as well, reassessments of community facilities were being undertaken. Most important, the entire County was conscious of, and often uneasy about, the changes that were occurring. Significantly, the health reorganization movement gained its first foothold and rudiments of organization in relatively stable Middle Bucks.

The initiative for the referendum can be traced to the county Medical Society and the stimulus it received from the state health department. Interest in the proposal spread to the leaders of the TB and Health Society, the Federation of Women's Clubs and several Leagues of Women Voters. This initial alliance of professional, volunteer, social, and civic interest proved to be a winning combination.

In the summer of 1952 the County Commissioners were asked to form a county health department, an alternative available under Act 315. The Commissioners replied to the TB and Health Society's request by suggesting that the proposal warranted a referendum.

Going into 1953, the course before the plan's proponents was clear. A petition and referendum campaign would have to be organized, and interest in the proposal generated. A two-year campaign culminating in a 1954 referendum was envisioned by the professional community organizers. The mere details of organizing a county-wide campaign seemed to call for moving at a slow, sure pace. The county's three regions were matched with even finer gradations among the County's social, civic and service organizations. Moreover, in Lower Bucks, established channels of communication had been disrupted by its rapid population growth. The campaign leaders would have to develop their own means of communication.

In the spring of 1953, the timetable was shortened in favor of a referendum that fall. Some of the early supporters were impatient and anxious to bring their activities into the open. Their impatience threatened to disrupt the semblance of organization already achieved. State officials were also pressing for speed. They preferred holding the referendum during the off-year election rather than having the proposal overshadowed by the gubernatorial campaign of 1954. And there was a growing belief that the iron was hot, particularly in Lower Bucks where more issues were arising that could divert future attention from the health campaign.

Shortening the timetable reduced the possibility of forming an effective, broadly representative, county-wide organization to direct the campaign. A Bucks County Citizens' Health Council was in fact organized, but played a minor role in managing the campaign. It did little, but its very inefficiency may have been well suited to the decentralization typical of the County's community organizations.

A number of groups and individuals lent their endorsements to the proposal, but for the most part, promotional efforts were limited to small meetings and personal appeals by women's organizations, civic and professional groups, and, in Lower Bucks, the labor unions. Except for the personal efforts of several doctors, little activity penetrated into Upper Bucks.

The campaign received editorial support from several of the county's newspapers, but far from intensive news coverage. A radio debate between a member of the Medical Society and a representative of the statewide Association of Second Class Township Supervisors provided the sole instance of vocal opposition to the proposal. The Association's criticisms were not picked up by others and were not even widely publicized in township circles.

Up to election day, campaign leaders were wary of attack from either of the political parties or from local officials, but opposition did not develop. In Bristol Township, all Democratic candidates endorsed the proposal; but elsewhere the referendum was successfully "kept out of politics." On November

3, 1953, more than 47,000 Bucks voters went to the polls. The health department proposal was approved by a vote of 19,408 to 9,885.

The Montgomery Campaign. Initiation of the health department proposal in Montgomery County can also be traced to the efforts of that county's medical society. In 1956, the Medical Society joined with a number of health and welfare agencies in sponsoring a health survey of the county. The survey was undertaken by an *ad hoc* group, the Citizens' Public Health Survey Committee. Its membership and the talents it called upon for preparation of the report numbered several hundred prominent individuals. Their product was worthy of the effort. The survey is regarded as one of the finest prepared in the State. Chief among its recommendations was the call for a county health department.

After presenting their report in 1957, Committee leaders approached the County Commissioners and the Republican County Chairman with the health department recommendation. They received a less cordial welcome than had their Bucks predecessors. The political leaders would take no action, but did not conceal their opposition to the proposal. They doubted the need for a department, especially since it would require raising the extremely low county tax rate of which they were so proud.

The course before the Committee was then similar to that faced five years earlier in Bucks. But Montgomery leaders had an organization with extensive community contacts ready and willing to procede with a referendum campaign. The survey committee was reconstituted as the Citizens' Committee for a Montgomery County Health Department. Since its report had attracted some attention, it decided to hold the referendum at the 1958 gubernatorial election rather than chance a loss of interest that might accompany delay.

The Citizens' Committee stressed organization, preparation,

expertise, and central leadership. Its campaign moved into high gear in the summer of 1958, gaining in intensity as the election neared. However, there was another difference in the background of the Bucks and Montgomery campaigns in addition to campaign organization. Under the Public Health Law, only cities, boroughs, and first-class townships are authorized to engage in public health activities. At the time of the Montgomery referendum, there was 32 local health boards in the county, serving 75 percent of its population. In Bucks, only 35 percent of the population had been served by local health units, and most of its growth was occurring in second-class townships. In Montgomery, Lower Merion's was the only health board that offered a semblance of complete local health service. It employed a full-time staff of 7 persons and spent $1.14 per capita on health services, while most other communities spent less than $.20.[2]

Montgomery County did not experience rapid, disruptive growth. Few dramatic examples such as had existed in Lower Bucks could be pointed to in support of a county department. Consequently, health department proponents waged a low-keyed and generalized campaign. Moreover, despite the low level of municipal performance, they could not pose a county department as an alternative to few or no services. They would have to challenge the adequacy and ability of existing local units, chancing arousing resentment and stimulating counterattack.

Stimulate it they did. Shortly after the opening of the campaign, organized opposition emerged from four fronts: local government officials, the Republican Party, the newspapers, and one small, but vocal organization, Montgomery County for America that might today be labelled a "super patriot" group. Singly and in combination these were formidable opponents.

Each of the County's associations of local officials, the boroughs, first-class and second-class township organizations, and even the volunteer fire companies, voiced their opposition to the proposal. The associations' positions were affirmed by resolutions of many individual municipalities and in some cases by their health boards. The Lower Merion Board of Health was the only official body to favor the department despite the fact that, if adopted, Lower Merion residents would probably have ended up paying for the support of two departments. The Lower Merion commissioners did not go as far as their health board, but did not join with other first-class townships in denouncing the proposal.

The Republican county organization announced a position of neutrality, but soon indicated where its sentiments lay. Most of its leaders were municipal officers, whose positions were well known. Moreover, party machinery was used for disseminating opposition literature.

If the Republican organization could hide behind a cloak of neutrality, no similar mantle was available to cover the Democratic Party's embarrassment. In September, the Democratic County Committee pledged its support of the proposal, possibly hoping to capitalize on a Republican inconsistency uncovered when the Republican gubernatorial candidate announced his support of county health departments in principle. But most of the few local Democratic officeholders joined in the municipal resolutions opposing the department. In fact, the Party was shaken when its minority member of the County Commissioners joined with his Republican colleagues in urging rejection of the proposal and actively campaigned against it in his home territory. For this he was commended by the newspapers as having placed principle above party, something he had apparently done on a number of previous occasions. The party took a different view of the matter, refusing to renominate him the following year.

Only one newspaper supported the proposal. The others, for

the most part neglected to distinguish between reporting and editorializing. Much of their information and arguments were supplied by the County Commissioners and Montgomery County for America. The latter group was frequently represented in the newspapers. The proposal was viewed as an ill-disguised attempt at wrecking local government. If this movement for socialized medicine was not directly communist inspired, its proponents were at least dupes who were inadvertantly aiding the communist cause.

The less extreme opposition centered around three assertions: the department was not needed since local officials were doing a good job; the department would necessitate an exorbitant tax increase; its establishment would further the trend toward the abolition of home rule and increasing governmental centralization with its odious controls over the individual.

Several days prior to the election, the Republican County Chairman reviewed his party's activities. Among other accomplishments, the party had:

. . . cautioned the voters against being hypnotized into going for an expensive, duplicating health board because we know that the health of our citizens could not be in better hands, so why waste thousands of dollars [sic] for a duplicate. Intelligent voters will see through this smoke screen and vote against the county health board.[3]

A quarter of a million Montgomery County residents voted for governor on November 6, 1958. They defeated the health department proposal 75,834 to 40,752.

The Bucks and Montgomery Votes

Our analysis of the referenda is concerned with two questions, intensity of interest in the issues, and their outcome. We suspect that both were influenced by urban differentiation and the unique political circumstances surrounding the Montgomery referendum. Unfortunately there were so many cross-pressures at work in the referenda that the votes do not lend themselves readily to correlation analysis. A matrix consisting of 12 varia-ables was calculated for both counties. The results, while often statistically significant, required such qualification that simpler methods of rank ordering and descriptive analysis were decided upon.

Referendum Participation. In both counties, campaign leaders were wary of presenting their proposals at the gubernatorial election, although the gubernatorial year was selected in Montgomery. Their reluctance stems from the following reasoning. A general election stimulates large turnouts. The greater the turnout, the larger the number of voters who are indifferent to the proposal will be in a position to vote against it. Indifference will generally result in low rates of participation in the referendum (percentage of turnout voting for or against the proposal), but it is also likely to produce a large number of negative votes.

Related to the above, are the positive motivations for presenting the proposal at an off-year election. Interest in a municipal election is not as great as in a state-wide or national contest. The former may be expected to produce larger turnouts from among high-status than low-status groups. (Although status is associated with cosmopolitanism, high-status individuals nevertheless participate more extensively in all elections). High-status groups are thought to be most receptive to proposals for the betterment of health services. Moreover, the smaller the turnout, the more important becomes the votes of those who have been stimulated into voting by the promotional campaign.

In Bucks County, turnout and participation followed expected patterns. The county-wide rate of participation was a rather high 62 percent of voter turnout. Greater turnout and participation were recorded in the higher-social-ranking municipalities, although there was some tendency for rates of participation to decline in some areas of largest turnout. Turnout, participation, and yes-voting on the referendum all increased with social rank. None were influenced, however, by party voting. There is no evidence that the referendum itself influenced turnout, rather it appears that participation was a consequence of turnout.

Participation in Montgomery County was an extremely large 70 percent of turnout. Voters were not at all indifferent to the referendum. High turnout, high participation, and extreme opposition to the proposal were all related. Even with social rank held constant, participation increased with turnout. This suggests the presence of a stimulus generating interest in the proposal independently of the social status of voters. With social rank held constant, participation and disapproval of the proposal are associated with Republicanism (the Republican percentage of those voting for governor at the same election in which the referendum was held). One must conclude that the Republican Party influenced both participation and the outcome of the referendum.

Urbanism and Cooperation. Service needs are most pressing in the urban portion of the metropolitan area. To the extent that a county health department can provide more service than local health boards, and to the extent that public health problems are more likely to arise and be perceived in urban places, one might anticipate greater support of the proposal in the Suburbs than in Towns and Townships. In Bucks County, the mean Suburban vote for the referendum was 74.8 percent compared to a semi-urban mean of 55.8 percent. In Montgomery County, 31.4 percent of the Suburban vote and only 28.7 percent of the semi-urban vote favored the proposal.

A regional basis of support is evident in Bucks County. Lower Bucks voted most favorably, Upper Bucks least. The seven municipalities that rejected the proposal were all located in Upper Bucks. In this gross sense, urbanism was the most influential determinate of voting. Even within the Suburbs, however, the support given to the department varied consistently with urbanism.

Throughout this study, population density has been used to measure urbanism. But in examining the effect of urbanism on service needs, it is not destiny alone, but density and rate of population growth that is most important. An area that slowly moves from a rural to urban density presumably has time to make the changes necessary to adjust to its new environment with a minimum of friction and disruption of past intra-community relationships, leadership, and methods of operation. When increases in density are accompanied by rapid population growth, problems both associated with, and apart from, the changing physical environment arise. The process of urbanization is reflected in both density and rate of growth.

When density and population growth are each correlated with the referendum votes, no significant relationships appear. But if growth and density are combined by simply ranking Suburbs by both density and rate of growth and averaging the two rankings, a measure of the urbanization process is obtained that correlates with support for the referendum in both counties. The rank-order correlation is .761 in Bucks and .589 in Montgomery. Thus, it was in the municipalities that were absorbing a large influx of population that the local consensus was most favorable toward increased and/or improved health services.

Party Affiliation, Social Rank and Cooperation. In Bucks County, the political parties took no position on the referendum. Not unexpectedly, there is no relationship between party affiliation and the referendum vote. There is, however, a positive relationship between support of the proposal and social rank when density and population growth are held constant. Ten of Bucks 14 Towns were quite similar in density and rate of growth in 1953. For these 10 the rank-order correlation of yes-voting and social rank is .654. The 24 Townships were uniformly low in density and growth, and for all 24 the rank-order correlation is .735. The 14 Suburbs were too dissimilar in density and growth to enable controls to be exercised.

Generally, we conclude that social rank was a factor contributing to support of the county health department, but that it was decidedly secondary in importance to the influence of urbanism.

Montgomery County experienced no such dramatic increase in population as did Bucks. This may, in part, account for the lack of support given the proposal. However, in Montgomery, the referendum was more favorably received in the more urban communities. But party affiliation exerted the most influence on participation, and on the outcome of the referendum.

Both political parties in Montgomery adopted positions on the proposal. Montgomery County is overwhelmingly Republican. The opposition of that party was disastrous to the supporters of the health department plan. The product-moment correlation of yes-voting and Republicanism for the 60 Montgomery municipalities is −.304. The more Republican their vote for governor, the more opposed they were to the proposal. Although statistically significant, this correlation is slight, due to the independent effect of social rank. Social rank and Republicanism correlate quite highly. At the same time that Republicanism was influencing opposition to the proposal, social rank was operating in the opposite direction to support. The interplay of social rank and party affiliation can be seen more clearly with the introduction of a few controls.

The Democratic Party supported the proposal. There were

eleven municipalities in Montgomery County that gave the Democratic candidate for governor 50 percent or more of their votes. In two of these, however, the local Democratic organization led by the minority County Commissioner opposed the proposal. In the remaining 9, the vote for the referendum was 44.4 percent, compared to 29.2 percent in the 49 Republican municipalities. This evidence of greater support in the Democratic municipalities is the more significant when it is noted that they were almost all low in social rank. Even within this group, there is a .762 rank-order correlation between yes-voting and social rank.

Before leaving the Democratic communities, it is worth emphasizing that despite the impact of social rank with party affiliation held constant, where the local party leadership opposed the referendum, social rank did not appear to influence the vote. Both Democratic communities in which local leadership opposed the proposal were, as Democratic areas generally go, relatively high in social rank. Yet both gave less support to the proposal than any other Democratic municipality. Only 17 and 22 percent respectively of those voting on the proposal supported it.

Increasing Republicanism in Montgomery County was accompanied by increasing opposition to the proposal. Controlling for social rank, this relationship is most obvious. Of the ten municipalities with social rank of 20 to 30, the rank-order correlaton between yes-voting on the proposal and Republican vote for governor is −.616. In the 9 communities with social rank of 30 to 45, the correlation is −.808 and among the 12 communities with social rank above 45, the correlation is −.717. Only among the 18 communities with social rank of 10 to 20 is there no significant correlation.

As social rank increases, both Republicanism and support of the proposal increase. But in any category of social rank, in-

Table X–1

Percent GOP and Percent Favoring the County
Health Department by Social Rank in Montgomery
County Republican Municipalities

	Social Rank 10-20 N=18	Social Rank 20-30 N=10	Social Rank 30-45 N=9	Social Rank Over 45 N=12
Percent GOP	62.4	64.4	68.0	71.6
Percent Voting Yes	26.5	26.8	32.6	32.8
Rank-order Correlation Republicanism and Yes-vote	−.168	−.616	−,808	−.717

creasing Republicanism is accompanied by greater opposition
to the proposal. If Republicanism is held constant, the countervailing influence of social rank becomes most evident. In the
3 categories of Republicanism, 50 to 60, 60 to 70, and 70 to
80 percent, the rank-order correlations of yes-voting and social
rank are .696, .624 and .586 respectively.

Table X–2

Social Rank and Percent Favoring the County
Health Department in the Republican Municipalities
of Montgomery County

	Percent GOP 50-60 N=16	Percent GOP 60-70 N=14	Percent GOP 70-80 N=18*
Social Rank	25.1	29.6	37.5
Percent Voting Yes	32.0	30.5	26.0
Rank Order Correlation Social Rank and Yes-vote	.696	.624	.586

* Bryn Athyn is excluded as it must be from so many tabulations.
It was the most Republican of all municipalities and extremely opposed to the proposal while being relatively high in social rank.

People, Politics and Public Health

Leaders of the Montgomery campaign exhibit more than a
trace of envy when they speak of the Bucks referendum. To

them, Bucks typified rational community decision-making un-marred by the tainted touch of politics. Indeed, the outcome of the Bucks referendum would hearten the most ardent public health educator for it was most clearly a victory for the profes-sionals engaged in community education.

The Bucks referendum supports the hypotheses developed in this and the preceding chapter. Urbanization contributed heavily to the proposal's support. The objective criterion of need, therefore, independent of status or life-style, appears to be a major determinant of responses to proposals for coopera-tion or transfers of functions. Moreover, in their more favor-able reaction, the higher-social-ranking municipalities evidenced a greater perception of need and a more positive predisposi-tion toward cooperation and the betterment of governmental services.

Urbanization and social rank were related to the support given the Montgomery proposal as well. But perceptions of need were conditioned by the less dramatic urbanization that took place in Montgomery County. Furthermore an additional factor influenced perceptions and attitudes in Montgomery County. Political leadership set the context in which the refer-endum campaign was conducted. The difference in the Bucks and Montgomery votes is not so much in the reactions of mu-nicipalities of varying social rank and urbanism as in the politi-cal contexts in which they occurred.

This difference is resented by the Montgomery proponents, for they feel that extraneous issues were injected into the refer-endum. Specifically, they resent the politician's unwillingness to confine himself to the professional questions uppermost in their minds. In essence, the difference in context between Bucks and Montgomery is that, in the former, the referendum cen-tered on the issue of public health service, while in the latter, services were viewed in the broader context of the politics of municipal autonomy and self-identification. The Montgomery contest was not between health and no health, but between competing leaderships and values, one stressing service goals, the other appealing to divergent values. Its outcome was both a reflection of the priorities assigned values by the public and an affirmation of traditional political sources of community leadership.

The Bucks and Montgomery votes indicate, by contrast, the importance of leadership in addition to those characteristics that have been identified as influencing cooperation in the metropolitan area. But the question still remains as to why political leadership emerged to oppose the referendum in Montgomery and not in Bucks. Here we leave the realm of analysis for that of conjecture.

Several reasons have already been suggested. One is that the rapid growth of Bucks County had left its political leaders confused and somewhat unsure of their following. Certainly they had as much personal stake in home rule as did local representatives in Montgomery County. But their constituents were newer, less molded to the traditions and differences in their communities and consequently, possibly less receptive to a depiction of county government as a far-off menace working with the state to deprive them of their freedom.

A related factor was the absence of active leagues of municipalities in Bucks and a corresponding inability to mount an opposition. Although the municipal associations in Montgomery County did not manufacture the conflict that defeated the proposal, their leadership served to highlight the issues at stake and to arouse public perception of the conflict. Certainly some political leaders in Bucks were equally aware of the full implications of the proposal, but they lacked the organization and initiative supplied by the key leaders of Montgomery County's associated municipalities.

Summary

The story of the Bucks and Montgomery County health votes in some ways illustrates the difference between the politics of a substantive and a symbolic issue. In Bucks County, the voters responded to a health issue. The issue in Montgomery was not health, but consolidation; moreover, the symbol of consolidation more than its substance.

One of the key differences in the two was timing. Not only in the sense of the internal development of the two counties, but also in terms of the national attention that has been focused on metropolitan areas and their problems. By 1958, Montgomery County had been made aware, as had the rest of America, that it faced a "metropolitan problem." And it had learned, too, that some of the problem's solutions were perhaps more to be feared than the problem itself.

Not that many Montgomery voters were aware of Toronto, but it is more than a coincidence that the Bucks referendum took place prior to, and the Montgomery referendum subsequent to Toronto's experiment in metropolitan government. By 1958, the metropolitan problem had become an everyday term. Few proposals for governmental reorganization would thereafter escape involvement in the totality of suspicions and conflicts within metropolitan areas.

Significantly, the major criticism of the health department proposal in Montgomery County was its contribution to the *further* loss of home rule. By 1958, having become more conscious of the differences between their communities, political leaders and the public were hypersensitive to any hint of centralization. Although the health department proponents would have preferred it, the proposal could not be kept out of the social and economic "politics" of the metropolitan area.

In Bucks County, specialization expressed itself through the pattern of pro and con voting on the issue. High-social-ranking, densely populated, and growing areas were most favorably inclined toward the new and increased services being offered. This response is completely consistent with our earlier findings regarding municipal expenditures.

In Montgomery County the voter response was as if the very system of specialization was in question. The county was cast in the role of a villainous metropolitan government that would, with the aid of the state, obliterate all distincions among localities. While the fears raised were often bizarre, one cannot say that they were without any foundation. Centralization does indeed change patterns of access to decision-making, the character of majorities, and the values that prevail.

The reaction of specialized subareas to a proposal for integrating or consolidating a single function may depend less on its substance than the way in which it is perceived. Perception, in turn, is likely to depend upon the character of the leadership brought to bear on the issue. These comments are relevant to proposals for functional reorganization as well as to more general proposals for governmental reform.

Lest the reader question whether we have generalized too far from too selective a source, we reproduce, without comment, most of the conclusions of a study of the 1959 referendum at which the proposed plan for a Greater St. Louis City-County District was rejected.

1. Voter turnout on issues of metropolitan reorganization is correlated with social rank, but this relationship is an uneasy one and subject to alterations by other factors such as partisan activity.
2. The direction of the vote is also correlated with social rank: individuals high on the scale are more apt to support area-wide reform than those of lower rank.

3. No clear relationship has yet been established between extent of voter turnout and direction of the vote.
4. Extent of voter participation increases with intensity of partisan activity.
5. The most effective opposition arguments in reorganization campaigns are tax increases and "super government" or loss of local autonomy.
6. Apartment dwellers and renters are less susceptible than homeowners to the usual opposition arguments. [The Bucks and Montgomery votes shed no light on this proposition when the crude measure of single-family dwelling units was correlated with the outcome.]
7. The most important factor in determining the direction of the vote is political support or opposition. No metropolitan plan *can* pass over the active opposition of the political parties. No such plan is likely to pass without active partisan support.[4]

NOTES

1. *Keystones of Public Health for Pennsylvania* (Prepared by the Survey Staff of the Committee on Administrative Practices of the American Public Health Association, 1948), p. 9.
2. Montgomery County Health Survey Committee, *Health Survey Report,* February 1957, p. 14.
3. *The Times Chronicle,* October 30, 1958.
4. Henry J. Schmandt, Paul G. Steinbicker, George P. Wendel, *Metropolitan Reform in St. Louis: A Case Study* (New York: Holt, Rinehart and Winston, 1961), p. 59.

XI

Urban Differentiation and the Future of Metropolitan Government

The central proposition of this study has been that differentiation and specialization in metropolitan areas results not only in interdependence among local units of government, and consequently in pressures for governmental integration, but also in divergent local interests and policies that perpetuate demands for autonomy. Most metropolitan studies have focused upon interdependence and the most clearly needed governmental integrative mechanisms. Approached in this manner, the metropolitan area is easily viewed as a patchwork of local governments that "ought not" to be so fractionated. Our emphasis upon divisiveness in metropolitan areas is not meant to ignore interdependence, nor is it intended to express a judgment on the merits of integration or autonomy. Rather, it stems from a belief that the divisiveness implied in urban differentiation must be fully explored in order to gauge the prospects for policy coordination in metropolitan areas.

Our exploraton into areal differentiation has been a quest for suburban corporate personalities. Although our investigation has extended to traditional small towns and almost rural communities, our emphasis has necessarily been upon those municipalities that we have labeled "Suburbs;" for they are currently participating in the process of urbanization.

Starting from ecology's depiction of spatial specialization as a distinctive urban trait, we have attempted to trace the relationship of ecological patterns to the public life of the metropolis. Our quest has been limited by the methods employed. Our tools have stressed measurable qualities, though no quantitative dogma has guided our work. A study of social and political organizations and their relationship to both ecology and local policies would be a fitting and needed companion to this study. Nevertheless, we have been able to sketch some shadowy suburban personalities, albeit with the blunt strokes of demography.

In our investigation, we have not asked how the present pattern of specialization developed. The legacy of the past has been accepted as a given independent variable, and we have examined how that legacy is related to present policy choices. In approaching the question of choice, a studious effort has been made to avoid the intellectual snares encountered in the use of such concepts as individual will or circumstance. We have divided the legacy into three categories—needs, resources, and preferences. Needs have been represented by the physical and functional development of the community, measured by the types of economic activity carried on in a municipality and the intensity of its deployment of space (density). Resources have been measured by individual and municipal wealth. The term "preferences" has referred to the kinds of people resident in the specialized territories. While all of these categories are related, they do single out aspects of a human settlement susceptible to separate analyses.

In the term corporate personalities, we are referring both to the physical and social characteristics of a municipality and to the behavior it exhibits. It is relatively easy to document and describe differences in the characteristics of Suburbs; it is more difficult and more enlightening to ask if those elements of personality are related to behavioral aspects of corporate existence. If they are, and if, as we suspect, municipal policies and the nature of the activities and persons that locate in particular municipalities reinforce one another, we are well on our way toward answering what might be the popular way of phrasing our guiding question: What does local control mean to suburban municipalities?

Areal Differentiation and Policy Variation

Municipal policies were found in the first instance to be a function of need. The Suburb's role in the metropolitan economic system has a profound effect on its service structure. Industrial and commercial enterprises give rise to municipal costs, as do densely developed residential patterns. But in arriving at this conclusion, the static character of our analysis must be stressed; for there is some indication that this situation may pass. As we contrast old and new industrial and commercial centers, it is apparent that we are witnessing one of the rare instances of privatization of hitherto public services. Industrial parks and shopping centers have spacious grounds with private governing arrangements. As long as they are new and modern, they represent tax-base windfalls and add relatively little to the costs of municipal government. A later generation may have to reckon with vacancies and changing tenants, but for now, industrial parks and shopping centers add to municipal tax rolls while servicing themselves, not out of taxes, but from prices charged consumers.

Equating both older industrial and commercial centers and

densely populated residential areas with higher municipal costs
has said nothing about the ratio of costs added to resources, nor
has it questioned the distribution of costs between classes of
taxpayers. Some, but not all, of the older commercial and industrial centers have gained more in resources than they have
lost in increased costs. But one thing they have all had in common—a tendency toward blight and concentrations of inexpensive housing occupied by populations of low social rank.

The most significant characteristic of modern industrial and
commercial developments is their ability to be designed so as to
impose little blight on an otherwise pleasing residential environment. Increasingly, high-social-ranking, once exclusively residential Suburbs are welcoming them. The tax-base lottery which
formerly consigned industry and inexpensive homes to the same
place may no longer operate in that fashion. Economic distances
and inequities among suburbs may increase as wealthy residential places continue to attract modern industrial and commercial
installations.

Privatization of costs that are public in densely populated
communities is also a characteristic of low-density residential
areas where, as examples of residential amenities absorbed by
home-owners, private sewer systems, garbage disposals, and
backyard jungle gyms are in order. Other things being equal—
and they never are—the range of services provided by municipalities increases with population density and per capita municipal expenditures increase accordingly. One of the "non-
equal" factors is the tendency for low-density residential developments to attract high-social-ranking populations who have
service preferences and expectations that exert a countervailing
pressure on service levels.

While the needs of a community circumscribe its service
responses, its resources have a surprisingly slight effect. There
is little evidence that municipal spending is guided by the

availability of resources. Statistical controls suggest that factors associated with wealth rather than wealth itself explain variations in municipal and school support. Both the poor and rich older industrial communities spend considerably for municipal services. But while high-social-ranking municipalities, most of which are wealthy, spend a great deal for public schools and for services that may be considered residential amenities, industrially wealthy, low-social-ranking municipalities concentrate their expenditures on demand generated by industry, despite the opportunity to milk an industrial tax base for residential services. Expenditures are not merely a matter of "those that have spend."

If municipal resources and personal wealth only slightly serve to stimulate expenditures, they do determine the ease with which communities can fulfill their service demands. Obviously the tax base's effect on tax effort and the distribution of tax burden are reflected in a community's evaluation of service needs. But once again our data suggest that the outcome of this evaluation is influenced more by differences in the tax consciousness and attitudes toward government of varying social groups than by the actual amount of resources available and effort required to support high service levels. The distribution of resources in the metropolitan area is important for the advantages and disadvantages it gives to communities, even if it is not determinative of their actions.

The formula employed for the distribution of state aid to public schools is deliberately designed to equalize resource advantages, at least to the point of a minimum, if inadequate, expenditure per pupil. Beyond this minimum, resource advantages continue to be enjoyed by many municipalities; but these advantages are reflected in tax rates, not in levels of public school expenditure. In public education, even more than in municipal programs, it is the character of the inhabitants, not the resources of a community that defines its style of public life. One population characteristic, social rank, is clearly most directly related to differences in public school expenditures.

Preferences are secondary to needs in influencing municipal expenditure patterns, but still more important than municipal resources. The two population attributes that structure municipal preferences are social rank and the age distribution of adult population. A preference for municipal amenities accompanies rising social rank. The de-emphasis of public services accompanies colonization by young families.

The preferences and life-styles of differing types of communities are related to their unique environments and are expressed in the makeup of their expenditure package. Industrial communities emphasize property protection and traffic movement, while residential areas evince more concern for less economically oriented services; those high in social rank stressing libraries as well as schools. Densely populated municipalities respond with the highest expenditures for police, fire, and waste disposal. Sparsely populated communities focus on planning to protect and guide values still to be realized in a developing pattern of land use. Corporate personalities, evidenced by policy as well as descriptive characteristics, emerge from detailed analysis of community finance.

Policy Variation and the Process of Differentiation

What does local control mean to suburban municipalities? It means the ability—perhaps limited, but nevertheless available —to exercise preferences and enjoy resource advantages in the expression of a public personality, albeit within the confines of a physical environment largely determined by past decisions. But to what extent can municipal policy itself be an instrument for determining environment? Can it influence the process of social and economic differentiation and thereby reinforce the construction of coroprate personalities?

One set of municipal policies is obviously an attempt to seize the municipal future by the forelock and to assert the continuing character of a community. Land-use policies, particularly zoning, have a poor record of success in resisting the blandishments and open purses of artful developers, yet they are a major tool in the assertion of municipal values. Although there is an evident trend toward more uniform zoning patterns (based primarily on economic advantages attributed to certain types and densities of land use), the current status of Suburban zoning appears entirely consistent with the present system of economic and social specialization. Whether or not the zoning ordinances will hold is perhaps dependent upon the continued recruitment of residents who share the values of those who passed the zoning ordinances.

The zoning ordinance is a recruiting advertisement, but equally important, each municipal ordinance and budget is, in a fashion, an announcement to the world of a particular attitude toward amenities, public education, and neighborhood development. Some school systems enjoy metropolitan and indeed national reputations for excellence. Some communities are known to be good places to retire. That such reputations are built and influence locational decisions is evidenced by the clustering of certain population groups in particular municipalities. Educated, white-collar workers and professionals choose to locate in communities whose life-styles appeal to their middle-class values. Official land-use policies appear to have little influence over this process of selection, for a wide range of housing prices is available in most municipalities.

For one low-status group, Negroes, exclusion from high-social-ranking areas is not a matter of choice. But to what extent low-status whites are prevented from inundating high-status areas by social or other types of controls is not known. What is known is that the system of status segregation is far from perfect. It would appear, particularly in view of the opinions expressed by residents of low-status communities, that a major portion of the segregation of low-status whites is self-imposed and that the values shared in, and expressed through, the policies of high-status municipalities have little appeal to them.

But the social structure of the metropolis is not that rigid. Corporate personalities change, perhaps because the process of developing and publicizing a corporate identity is not always understood, nor is it often officially pursued with tact or intelligence. It is difficult for a community to raise its hand high and announce, "Those with our views and our wealth come join us in building *our* community." Yet some system of communication must exist to serve the process.

One system of social communication is evident, at least at the highest status levels, when business and professional leaders new to the region report that their housing alternatives were known to them and confined to a small portion of the metropolis prior to their coming here. For the most part, however, the major civic chroniclers are the builders, subdividers, and realtors. Their Sunday newspaper ads are a not always accurate means of publicizing community identities. Although they are often committed to the retention of local values, as outsiders and businessmen (in the case of builders, businessmen often concerned only with immediate or short-run profits), they are subjected to stimuli that sometimes run counter to the desire to preserve community identities. Perhaps if the metropolitan communication system was better organized, the pattern of differentiation and social segregation would be even more sharply defined.

Suburbs change, whether because of changing societal values, or because of their inability to achieve and maintain lasting corporate personalities. Ecologists have long been fascinated by changes in core city neighborhoods. While the cities were still growing, neighborhoods changed as ethnic blocs invaded and succeeded each other and as status ladders were climbed. The new metropolitan pattern is far from clear. The post-war exodus to the suburbs has had a profound effect on the character and occupancy of core city neighborhoods. It is probably too soon to tell whether it will also lead to life cycle changes in suburban municipalities.

An effort was made to gauge Suburban changes between 1950 and 1960. Changes there were. Some Suburbs were slipping down the social-rank scale; in many the adult population grew older, indicating a tendency for joint aging of people and place. Our attempts to relate these changes to policy shifts bore no fruit. Perhaps ten years is too short a time in which to re-orient the public life of a community.

We were struck by the fact that no Suburb underwent the radical changes that occurred in some center-city neighborhoods. Since the Suburb is a corporate entity, it has powers never completely available to city neighborhoods which enable it to erect barriers to change. While the Suburban municipality may be likened to a center-city neighborhood, its corporate character affords it the opportunity to engage in a politics of protection and preservation of values that, if previously available to city neighborhoods, would seriously have altered the nature of their change. There is no doubt that local control does have meaning for suburban municipalities.

Areal Differentiation and Policy Integration

Specialization introduces problems of coordination, for it is founded upon interdependence. Specialized communities can exist only by being accesible to complementary specialized places. The need for accessibility derives from the fact that specialized activities are in turn related to a common system, largely economic in character. Both the well paid and the poorly paid derive their sustenance from a common economic enterprise. For the rich to live separately from the poor, both must have accessibility to the enterprise. In larger terms, if specialization is motivated by the desire to excel in production, commerce, creativity, or some other single form of economic or social endeavor, the fulfillment of this desire is dependent upon the remaining activities being performed by others, thus permitting a concentration of energy in one direction.

Economic interdependence is one essential attribute of metropolitan areas. Indeed, most definitions of the metropolis employ economic concepts. Moreover, the system of economic interdependence is usually viewed, in definitions and studies of metropolitan areas, as centering around the relationship of a core city to its environs. Thus McKenzie described the metropolitan area as "a functional entity extending as far as the city exerts a dominant influence."

There is no doubt that the social and economic organization of the City of Philadelphia exerts an organizing influence on the Suburban and more rural hinterlands on which we concentrate in this study. But it is also apparent that much of the new, spreading, low-density urban development occuring in metropolitan Philadelphia and elsewhere is, to an extent, independent of the core city. In a sense we might say that the Suburbs represent a new and different form of urbanism. If the traditional city organized specialized activities to serve an extensive hinterland, the modern metropolis organizes activities to serve a broader regional or national economy. Suburban factories, shops and houses are not necessarily oriented to the core city: they represent the replacement of older urban forms and functions. The interdependence of the new urban form and the integrative demands which it provokes are not merely a matter of center city-suburban relations. Rather, with a continuing decline in importance of the center city, one might suggest that the major problems yet to be faced in metropolitan areas are those stemming from intra-suburban relations. In part, this has motivated our study's concentration on suburban behavior.

Metropolitan Problems

The term "metropolitan problem" has often been affixed to any situation requiring cooperation or interaction between adjacent units of government in urban areas. Problems are usually identified on a service basis, and there is hardly any governmental activity which has not been identified as constituting a metropolitan problem.[1] The advocacy of metropolitan government is, for some, based merely on the belief that almost every activity has an intergovernmental aspect.

Some writers have distinguished between *metropolitan problems* and *problems in a metropolitan area*.[2] This observation contains a very sound insight, but it lacks specificity. The following classification attempts to make explicit the crucial distinction between the two. The distinction is based on the recognition that the major characteristic of metropolitan areas is the coincidence of spatial specialization and autonomous local governing units. A metropolitan problem is one that, unlike other intergovernmental problems, results from this coincidence.

Problem One: Maintaining the System. If people want to work in one community, sleep in another, shop in a third, and play in a fourth; if high-status persons want to reside apart from those of low status; if smoky factories are to be separated from homes; in short, if spatial specialization is to exist within a metropolitan economy—then basic services necessary for the development of each subarea and means through which they may be accessible to one another, must be provided.

Transportation and communication are the primary avenues

of maintaining accessibility. The latter is provided primarily through the private sector of our economy, the former is shared by private and public management, with government playing an increasingly important role. But transportation is not the only service through which government makes the system feasible. Certain basic utilities, such as water and sewage disposal, are often requisites for urban development. If they cannot be locally provided, and if a larger service area is a technical or financial necessity for continued development, then autonomy in policy formulation must give way to integrated mechanisms if the component units are to survive. Thus we characterize as a truly metropolitan problem the *maintenance of services providing the supports necessary for the continued existence of areal specialization.*

Problem Two: Unequal Distribution of Resources and Services. In every metropolitan area, there are "have" and "have not" communities, with the core city often being the most advertised of the "have nots." Such disparities are largely a by-product of the system of areal specialization. Of course there always have been, and probably always will be, differences in individual and community wealth. In a metropolitan context, such differences are aggravated by the efficiency with which the system of differentiation is maintained. Moreover, the multiplicity of local governing units, when imposed upon specialized populations, affects their ability to reconcile differences between groups. It is in this sense that we take exception to views such as that of Banfield and Grodzins who argue that housing is not a metropolitan problem. We agree that the structure of metropolitan government is not the *cause* of slums or blight; we agree that the mere existence of different housing standards does not constitute a problem; but we disagree with their belief that alterations in governmental structure will not alter housing policies. Such alteration can distribute the burden of housing costs over wider areas, it can impose higher minimum standards, it can organize leadership that is lacking in those areas where housing is poorest, it can attack the roots of the social and economic differences that segregate the poor and dictate their housing. It can do all this if one recognizes the extent to which urban differentiation affects the distribution of the supply of housing and the costs of remedying its inadequacies, and if one holds government responsible for producing change.

Our disagreement with Banfield and Grodzins is similar to that between the professionals and local politicians. As we have seen, some Suburbs may choose to deemphasize or do without some services. Although we did not specifically probe this question, we suspect that some working-class Suburbs would willingly forgo basic health services, for example, if commensurate tax savings would accrue. Thus the existence of different service standards reflect both differences in burdens associated with supplying financial support and differences in the preferences of specialized populations. Whether or not the local people approve of the differentials, disparities in services result. Professionals will identify such disparities as metropolitan problems when local officials and residents will not.

There is still another basis for labelling inequities in resources and services a metropolitan problem. When upper-middle-class suburbs draw off leadership, and, more particularly, wealth from the rest of the system, the remaining areas are impoverished thereby. As a result the cost and burden of providing services vary throughout the metropolitan area. The attainment of a recognized minimum standard becomes excessively costly to some communities and so an acceptable standard of service is not always provided throughout the area.

Thus we characterize as a metropolitan problem *the unequal distribution of resources and services that result from the process of specialization.*

Problem Three: Border Relationships. Contiguous units of government must engage in many reciprocal relations merely as a result of their proximity to one another. This is as true for rural as urban areas. The fleeing criminal crossing municipal boundaries is a clear example. Such fugitive pursuit problems are common to all governments; yet we frequently refer to this situation as metropolitan when it occurs in an urban environment, but not when it occurs in rural areas. River pollution evokes upstream-downstream conflicts regardless of whether the jurisdictions involved are urban or rural. Factories in rural areas may poison animals and plants with discharges of noxious fluids or fumes. That such discharges affect more than one political jurisdiction does not make the problem metropolitan.

The politics of mere propinquity does not constitute a truly metropolitan problem, since it is unrelated to the fundamental metropolitan characteristic—areal specialization. For this reason, cooperative demands that emanate simply from border relationships represent pseudo-metropolitan issues. Success in initiating and maintaining cooperation on matters such as fugitive-search systems, police-radio networks, common streets, minor utility exchanges, etc., should not be viewed as symbols of metropolitan fraternalism which are precursors of true union.

It should be added, however, that the density and greater activity of urban governments increases the number of border contacts between municipalities in metropolitan areas. While urbanism may thus generate a high level of municipal interaction, the qualitative nature of border policies is not thereby changed. These policies deal with problems that are distinct from those of system maintenance and resource and service inequities. Generally, border problems are easily solved until money is required. At that time, the nature of the problem changes, as questions of the proration of costs and obligations arise.

The three classes of problems described above are not mutually exclusive. It is difficult to conceive of any governmental policy or service without some overtones that would qualify it for inclusion in all three categories. Moreover, the importance of the three, and the degree to which they are popularly recognized at any one time, differ. Proposals offered as solutions to metropolitan problems are received and judged in accordance with how problems are perceived and what interest they evoke. A proposal for a joint sewer authority may at the same time be perceived as relating to (1) maintenance of the system (2) service and resource inequities or (3) a border problem of contiguous urbanized communities. How individual municipalities will react to the proposal is conditioned largely by what problem they view it as solving and what problems they feel may result from the proposal. Nevertheless, some policy areas tend to fall in one category more frequently than in another.

Transportation would undoubtedly head any list of policies related to the maintenance of the system of metropolitan specialization. While some integrated means of planning and managing transportation systems are increasingly being employed, their consequences are such as to profoundly influence the manner in which communities specialize, their relationships to other communities and area-wide distributions of wealth. Thus while municipalities depend upon a more-or-less integrated transportation system for their accessibility to complementary municipalities, it is with the greatest reluctance that they relinquished control over transportation policy. But they have relinquished it.

In nearly every metropolitan area, state highway departments have always supplied a modicum of coordination over the highway network. In the Philadelphia area, transportation planning and operation is sufficiently recognized as metropolitan in character that the county and state governments have assumed jurisdiction over it. The creation of a regional transportation-planning agency sustained mostly by federal funds, and the signing of intercounty and interstate agreements on transit development reflect recognition of the essential integrative role of transportation. Municipal activity is becoming confined to lobbying before these higher units of government.

Water and sewage disposal systems are second only to transportation in providing support to the metropolitan system. It has been possible to secure cooperation from very diverse Suburbs for the provision of both these utilities. Cooperative arrangements between Philadelphia and the Suburbs are also common. Indeed, the only firm cooperative arrangements involving financial obligations between the Suburbs and the central city have concerned transportation, sewage disposal, or water.

In considering metropolitan problems which result from inequities, it must be recognized that the seeking of specialized areas by home-owners or businesses is the very cause of the "problem." To attempt to redress inequities on a voluntary basis is laregly unrealistic. Wealth-sharing plans have never achieved great popularity among those who enjoy favored positions. Furthermore, in most areas, resolving inequities is not essential to maintaining the system. The fact that older industrial centers may, in the process of social segregation, end up with indigent populations for whom they cannot provide is, if of any interest to Main Line residents, perhaps welcomed by them. The very existence of inequities testifies to the success of specialization. Redistributions of resources and services are the most difficult area in which to achieve metropolitan agreement, in part because they are closely related to social inequalities.

The redistribution achieved by the state's school-subsidy program is the result of pressures applied from the outside. Hard-pressed Suburbs can find many other hard-pressed districts with which to ally in the state legislature, and the resulting redistribution encompasses not only metropolitan areas but the entire state. Service inequities peculiar to urban areas have found less favorable reception in state capitols; hence grants-in-aid for municipal services are a rarity in comparison with school grants.

The Basic Conflict of Metropolitan Government

The question of structuring metropolitan government reflects the basic dualism characteristic of metropolitan areas: the existence of specialization and the need for integrative mechanisms. Most metropolitan proposals are caught between these centrifugal and centripetal elements of the system. The fact that one cannot have specialization without integration does not furnish a basis for agreement. It only assures that questions touching on these two facets of the system will continually be raised and not permanently ignored. Thus the metropolis furnishes an inexhaustible political agenda for discussion by political leaders, political scientists, and urbanists.

The underlying normative question implicit in any proposal for structuring government in a metropolitan area is whether the proposed government is designed to maintain or to modify the system. In the past, those who have advocated consolidation as the ultimate "solution to the metropolitan problem" have, in effect, sought a comprehensive modification of the existing system of areal specialization. So, too, have some of the "Garden City" planners, who, although they would not consolidate, would decentralize the metropolis into economically though not socially, specialized subareas. On the other hand, the narrowly designed, single-purpose special district or authority and the intermunicipal contract concepts have been conceived so as to have as small a disturbing effect on the status quo as possible.

Of the two extreme suggestions for structuring government in metropolitan areas, proposals closer to the latter have been most successful. Metropolitan politics in the United States, as well as in Philadelphia, have never really encompassed a radical revamping of the metropolis as a system of specialization. Why should it? It is unrealistic to expect citizens to acquiesce voluntarily in giving up the prized values of urban dfferentiation. Thus, while the general-purpose, consolidated metropolitan government has had little acceptance, the special-purpose government has been used frequently. The criticism directed toward this latter development has been that we are in danger of assembling such a complex of special-purpose governments that the problem of policy coordination will be intensified rather than reduced. Such fears are well grounded.

Frequently, the quest for a solution to metropolitan problems is a quest for a governmental structure as politically acceptable as the special district and yet as comprehensive as consolidation. Such solutions do not exist. Moreover, the quest is perhaps misguided. While centralization or decentralization do affect such questions as economy, efficiency, and speed of action, the true test of the adequacy of a metropolitan governmental system is whether it can so structure the political process of negotiation and compromise as to deal effectively and adequately with metropolitan problems.

In the absence of a local political arena in which the demands for integrative services and the claims for greater equities can be arbitrated, such issues are often taken to the state capital and increasingly to Washington. The integrative demands take the form of requests for special regional agencies. Redressing inequities occurs through grants-in-aid. To achieve either goal, parties in the metropolitan area must gain allies or at least still opposition from parties outside the immediate region. The strategy with regard to the state capitol or Washington is much the same—the use of political party organizations to form a coalition of urban interests with their nominally affiliated partisan colleagues from non-urban territories. While the procedure varies from state to state, most of the essential metropolitan decisions are made outside the metropolitan area.

In part, this locus for decision-making is an outgrowth of the legal foundations upon which our federal system rests. In part, it is the inevitable outcome of the search for outside coalitions that has been fostered by the inability to gain consensus within the area.

Prospects for Metropolitan Government

Metropolitan problems are not being overlooked entirely. Yet there are cogent arguments to suggest that the most effective and perhaps the only way to handle these problems adequately is to create *one* forum within the area to which *all* problems can be brought for negotiation and compromise—in short to create *one metropolitan government*. But to posit metropolitan government as a desirable goal and to view it as attainable are separate matters. Our analysis offers little encouragement to those who are working for metropolitan government. Our outlook is pessimistic, not because of the record of failures, but because of the underlying bases for the failure of metropolitan government proposals.

The attainment of metropolitan government is unlikely either through direct approaches or through the expansion of single-purpose agencies into general-purpose units. Single-purpose metropolitan agencies, whether special districts or new county departments, tend to concentrate on those activities that supply the integrative supports for subarea specialization. These are the services most widely recognized as essential to the well-being of the entire area and each of its parts. It is unrealistic to expect officials and supporters of such programs to endanger their agencies by expanding operations to include issues over which there is less agreement. Although county and regional planners often speak as if they would like to have it, would there be county planning agencies if it were seriously proposed that they be given zoning authority?

The creation of single-purpose agencies to provide integrative supports has an additional and even more important effect on the prospects for metropolitan government. By isolating these services in separate agencies, the political incentives for a general forum are removed; for the "piecemeal" approach to governing the metropolis first siphons off those issues for which there is little choice but cooperation between have and have nots, suburbs and core cities. Left are those problems for which there is the least incentive to negotiate and the least amount of flexibility in bargaining—those which most divide the metropolis. Will the stimulus for metropolitan government come from these?

Most metropolitan areas have developed governmental mechanisms for providing some integrative services. In so doing, the thornier problems of regional agreement on minimum service standards and equitable distributions of costs have been left in the cold. Denied the ability to attach their issues to the bargaining around integrative services, those who are concerned with problems of resource and service inequities have little leverage in their favor. No metropolitan area is likely to obtain voluntary cooperation among all its municipalities in pooling resources to furnish hospital care for the indigent. Such an issue will not even be accepted as a "legitimate" metropolitan responsibility. Dozens of other unevenly distributed services will be similarly dismissed. These questions cannot be raised as metropolitan problems if there is no metropolitan government to appeal to. There can be no metropolitan government if those activities which bind the region are handled on an item by item basis.

A pattern of government for metropolitan areas is emerging. Those services which maintain the system are increasingly being supplied by area-wide agencies of one type of another. Problems of inequities are ignored or shunted to the state and federal level. Border incidents are left to an intermunicipal ambassadorial system.

Thus ways are found to handle metropolitan problems. They are often slow, uneven, awkward, uncoordinated and incomplete, but there are ways. The case for a metropolitan government is not based on the lack of alternatives, but in the belief that the alternatives do not work well enough. Does the pattern of government we have described provide a process of negotiation and compromise that deals effectively and adequately with metropolitan problems?

The question may be moot; for by now we may have built in so many provisional remedies that it may be too late to try to restructure the process. In most major metropolitan areas, regional organizations which are not limited to single purposes, but which also have no operating responsibility are being superimposed on the pattern of metropolitan government. The RCEO in Philadelphia, the MRC in New York, the COG in Washington, the ABAG in San Francisco, are examples of general-purpose metropolitan forums. Most are straining to keep going. Not the least of their difficulties is finding an agenda with which to occupy themselves; for existing single-purpose agencies have skimmed off those issues for which there is agreement on the necessity for regional action. The new metropolitan councils do not promise to alter the emerging governmental pattern. In those jurisdictions where activities necessary to maintenance of the system have not yet been organized, the councils may fix their agenda on one or more such issues and sponsor or become themselves single-purpose agencies. Elsewhere they will become fraternal, no-purpose organizations.

A change in the pattern of government coming from within

the metropolitan area is hard to imagine. An alternative is the vision of pressure from outside the region producing change, and the possibility of federal and/or state action seems the more probable. Federal programs in urban areas have, for some time, been stressing regional planning and cooperation. Indeed, federal stimulus can be blamed for some of the single-purpose agencies that now exist. If the federal government can tie its programs together, a more comprehensive approach to metropolitan areas might be reflected in local reorganization of thought and action. An even greater "if" in the prospects for change is the actions of state governments. As yet, state governments have been reticent to use grants as enticements toward regional compromises. Will the stimulus to change federal and state policy be forthcoming?

An even greater "if" in the metropolitan future is the impact of technological change. So important is this "if" that it may remove the conditions relevant to discussion of metropolitan government. Earlier, we described the automobile's effect on the structure of the metropolis. There is every reason to believe that new technology will have even more radical effects. Already there are indications that transportation and communication technology are reshaping the urban structure into a new mold. The automobile ended the rail-centered form. The perfected auto and improved communications may be ending the early automotive form. Improved highways and truck transport are enabling industrial plants to sever their connections with metropolitan centers. Increased automation will undoubtedly affect both the process of production and the nature and location of labor markets. Air transport and closed circuit television have already diminished the need for proximity in communications and supervision.

We do not wish to draw a picture of a completely automated society in which each person manipulates electronic impulses from a cell that can be located anywhere. Nevertheless, one should recognize that we are entering an era in which a new type of national system whose economic, social, and political consequences have yet to be felt, is being superimposed on the metropolitan system.

New forms of specialization are beginning to emerge. We already have national recreation and retirement towns, socially graded and related to the entire nation. More important, specific industrial activities that promise to represent a greater proportion of total economic activity in the future are already showing their independence from the urban complex. Some large research institutions can locate practically anywhere that their prized employees want to live.

The new interstate highway system raises the prospect of industrial centers scattered in small or large clusters around the intersections of major routes. The increased household and industrial appetite for space encourages a new form of development utilizing low-cost land in order to maintain a reasonable balance of land to total development costs. Conceivably, new widely scattered employment centers may separate into high- and low-wage places fostering a new form of areal specialization.

While we might speculate further on the specific possibilities of a new urban form, it would serve little useful purpose to do so here. We must emphasize, however, that there is no present indication that technology will be a servant helping to reknit the urban society into an integrated unit. Instead all the forces of technology are encouraging and enabling further areal specialization. Future technology will enable high- and low-social-status communities to have even greater physical distances between them. Whether this in fact happens will depend upon national policies affecting the distribution of income and opportunities as well as on compromise in metropolitan and regional bargaining agencies. But those who are concerned about metropolitan government as a form of local control over local problems should not look to technology for any comfort. If we confine our discussion to present conditions and technology, then we must reiterate that the governing of the metropolitan area is a matter of living with differences. The premise for action can never be leveling those differences, but only one of trading advantages or disadvantages.

NOTES

1. In a recent national study, even the universal governmental function of personnel management has been given the metropolitan label. See: *Governmental Manpower for Tomorrow's Cities,* a report of the Municipal Manpower Commission (New York: McGraw Hill Book Co., 1962).

2. Edward C. Banfield and Morton Grodzins, *Government and Housing in Metropolitan Areas* (New York: McGraw Hill Book Co., 1958).

Appendices

APPENDIX A

Table I

Population, Density, and Age, 1950 and 1960,
for the Pennsylvania Sector of
The Philadelphia Metropolitan Area

Municipality	Total Population 1950	Total Population 1960	Population Density 1950	Population Density 1960	Persons 25–34 Years as % of Persons Over 21 1950	Persons 25–34 Years as % of Persons Over 21 1960
Core City						
Philadelphia	2,071,605	2,002,512	16,312	15,768	23.8	19.3
Suburbs						
Bucks County						
Bensalem	11,365	23,478	565	1,168	25.4	23.5
Bistol Boro.	12,710	12,364	9,777	6,869	27.8	19.2
Bristol Twp.	12,184	59,298	743	3,706	32.8	35.4
Falls	3,540	29,082	145	1,217	29.3	33.2
Hulmville	860	968	2,150	2,420	23.0	24.0
Ivyland	358	425	1,193	1,417	25.0	19.4

Table I (cont'd)

Municipality	Total Population		Population Density		Persons 25–34 Years as % of Persons Over 21	
	1950	1960	1950	1960	1950	1960
Langhorne	1,579	1,461	3,158	3,848	22.2	16.4
Lower Southampton	3,562	12,619	524	1,856	27.3	23.9
Middletown	4,987	26,894	258	1,395	25.6	36.9
Morrisville	6,787	7,790	5,221	4,100	25.0	14.3
Penndel	1,100	2,158	2,750	5,395	24.8	22.5
Tullytown	648	2,452	324	1,226	19.2	28.1
Upper Southampton	2,027	7,941	317	1,240	24.0	22.5
Warminster	7,127	15,994	699	1,599	44.4	36.1
Chester County						
Malvern	1,764	2,268	1,470	1,890	23.6	22.9
Tredyffrin	7,836	16,004	396	808	24.8	20.3
Delaware County						
Aldan	3,430	4,324	5,717	7,205	20.2	14.9
Aston	5,576	10,595	996	1,796	34.6	32.9
Brookhaven	1,042	5,280	613	3,106	30.9	28.5
Chester City	66,039	63,658	13,758	13,261	26.9	19.8
Chester Twp.	3,547	3,602	2,086	2,572	38.4	26.0
Clifton Heights	7,549	8,005	12,582	13,342	34.9	23.5
Collingdale	8,443	10,268	9,381	11,409	24.3	21.3
Colwyn	2,143	3,074	7,143	10,246	23.8	28.5

Darby Boro	13,154	14,059	16,443	17,574	29.0	20.6
Darby Twp.	3,454	12,598	2,159	7,874	24.8	37.6
East Lansdowne	3,527	3,224	17,635	16,120	22.3	15.5
Eddystone	3,014	3,006	3,014	3,006	23.4	15.1
Folcroft	1,909	7,013	1,364	5,009	21.6	41.0
Glenolden	6,450	7,249	7,167	8,054	26.1	19.2
Haverford	39,641	54,019	3,964	5,402	20.9	16.5
Lansdowne	12,169	12,601	10,141	10,501	18.3	15.5
Lower Chichester	2,938	4,460	2,671	4,054	26.2	30.4
Marcus Hook	3,843	3,299	3,494	2,999	24.4	19.4
Marple	4,779	19,722	460	1,896	26.0	24.7
Media	5,726	5,803	7,158	7,254	22.4	18.3
Millbourne	901	793	9,010	7,930	23.4	14.9
Morton	1,352	2,207	3,380	5,518	21.7	21.4
Nether Providence	6,173	10,380	1,342	2,257	24.1	14.4
Newtown Twp.	3,518	9,270	348	918	24.2	23.3
Norwood	5,246	6,729	6,558	8,411	27.3	25.3
Parkside	1,637	2,426	8,185	12,130	19.9	20.4
Pospect Park	5,834	6,596	8,334	9,422	23.3	20.8
Radnor	14,709	21,697	1,066	1,572	22.1	17.9
Ridley Park	4,921	7,387	4,921	7,387	20.7	22.4
Ridley Twp.	17,212	35,738	3,310	7,065	33.6	30.1
Rose Valley	498	626	710	894	23.8	16.6
Rutledge	919	947	4,595	4,735	25.8	12.7
Sharon Hill	5,464	7,123	6,830	8,904	25.6	23.1
Springfield	10,917	26,733	1,733	4,243	25.2	19.3
Swarthmore	4,825	5,753	3,446	4,109	16.1	12.6

Table I (cont'd)

Municipality	Total Population		Population Density		Persons 25–34 Years as % of Persons Over 21	
	1950	1960	1950	1960	1950	1960
Tinicum	5,314	4,375	966	795	30.0	17.9
Trainer	2,001	2,358	2,001	2,358	27.3	20.3
Upland	4,081	4,343	5,830	6,204	32.4	21.2
Upper Chichester	6,997	9,682	1,029	1,424	28.6	26.3
Upper Darby	84,951	93,158	11,178	12,258	26.4	18.1
Upper Providence	3,598	6,059	610	1,026	28.3	21.9
Yeadon	11,068	11,610	6,918	7,256	20.2	14.1
Montgomery County						
Abington	28,988	55,831	1,946	3,746	17.8	19.6
Ambler	4,565	6,765	5,072	7,516	22.4	24.8
Bridgeport	5,827	5,306	8,324	7,580	26.5	21.6
Bryn Athyn	913	1,057	481	556	24.4	19.2
Cheltenham	22,854	35,990	2,597	4,089	19.0	15.7
Collegeville	1,900	2,254	1,188	1,408	23.1	17.2
Conshohocken	10,922	10,259	10,922	10,259	23.2	7.8
East Norriton	2,987	7,773	490	1,273	18.6	28.4
Hatboro	4,788	7,315	2,993	4,572	28.9	22.5
Hatfield Boro.	1,624	1,941	2,707	3,235	29.1	21.8
Hatfield Twp.	3,101	5,759	304	565	26.7	25.8
Horsham	3,663	8,933	219	534	22.9	24.2
Jenkintown	5,130	5,017	8,550	8,362	14.7	12.6

Lansdale	9,762	12,612	3,905	4,204	22.0	20.6
Lower Gwynedd	2,475	4,546	272	500	20.3	18.4
Lower Merion	48,745	59,420	2,092	2,545	16.9	9.2
Lower Moreland	2,245	5,731	330	843	23.5	16.1
Lower Providence	5,887	9,955	398	673	28.5	23.8
Narberth	5,407	5,109	10,814	10,218	19.6	15.2
Norristown	38,126	38,925	10,304	10,520	22.5	18.8
North Wales	2,998	3,673	4,283	5,247	24.0	19.9
Plymouth	5,118	11,430	609	1,364	29.6	30.4
Rockledge	2,261	2,587	5,653	6,467	21.6	17.1
Springfield	11,403	20,652	1,839	3,338	27.6	18.9
Trappe	773	1,264	336	550	26.2	27.9
Upper Dublin	6,637	10,184	511	783	23.0	20.2
Upper Gwynedd	2,164	4,661	267	576	25.1	19.8
Upper Merion	6,404	17,096	381	1,017	27.8	33.7
Upper Moreland	8,936	21,032	1,176	2,769	31.7	27.1
West Conshohocken	2,482	2,254	2,758	2,504	28.4	19.7
Whitemarsh	5,977	12,286	412	847	25.1	20.6
Whitpain	3,063	7,331	239	572	23.0	24.5

Townships

Bucks County

Bedminster	2,268	2,740	71	86	23.6	20.2
Bridgeton	944	948	124	146	21.7	23.3
Buckingham	3,007	4,018	93	127	23.0	18.9
Doylestown Twp.	2,364	3,795	147	243	21.3	19.0

Table I (cont'd)

Municipality	Total Population		Population Density		Persons 25–34 Years as % of Persons Over 21	
	1950	1960	1950	1960	1950	1960
Durham	668	735	68	75	24.2	20.8
East Rockhill	1,626	1,990	125	153	25.0	22.9
Haycock	1,084	1,273	52	69	21.4	18.8
Hilltown	3,688	5,549	136	204	21.2	22.7
Lower Makefield	3,211	8,604	176	473	22.3	17.8
Milford	2,865	3,524	103	128	20.2	23.1
New Britain Twp.	1,367	3,090	85	197	23.0	30.3
Newtown Twp.	1,013	1,468	84	121	24.0	20.2
Nockamixon	1,305	1,785	59	81	23.5	17.5
Northampton	2,248	6,006	85	228	23.4	22.0
Plumstead	2,353	3,354	86	121	21.5	20.9
Richland	3,050	3,783	147	182	24.5	21.5
Solebury	2,208	2,972	81	109	19.2	16.2
Springfield	2,668	3,085	82	95	25.1	19.1
Tinicum	1,552	1,746	52	58	22.6	16.5
Upper Makefield	1,410	1,991	66	94	24.3	18.8
Warrington	2,336	4,148	168	299	28.4	21.4
Warwick	906	1,810	81	161	22.1	25.6
West Rockhill	2,020	2,484	120	149	22.6	21.4
Wrightstown	909	1,734	91	171	21.8	23.9

Chester County

Birmingham	429	453	66	70	23.4	21.0
Charlestown	854	1,931	68	153	26.1	24.4
East Bradford	1,187	1,713	77	111	23.6	21.6
East Brandywine	1,108	1,618	98	143	22.9	20.4
East Caln	403	758	101	211	24.4	31.9
East Coventry	1,499	2,183	148	216	21.1	22.9
East Fallowfield	1,795	2,745	117	178	28.0	20.3
East Goshen	1,039	1,694	99	161	25.9	22.0
East Marlborough	1,868	2,417	117	152	23.8	12.7
East Nantmeal	665	730	41	44	27.4	18.9
East Nottingham	1,748	2,298	87	114	23.5	22.9
East Pikeland	1,395	2,817	157	316	27.6	25.8
East Whiteland	1,740	5,078	158	462	21.1	31.5
Elk	462	539	54	63	22.0	17.8
Elverson	370	472	370	472	26.9	19.7
Franklin	666	817	45	54	21.1	23.9
Highland	904	1,029	51	58	24.4	23.2
Honeybrook Twp.	1,261	1,584	50	63	24.6	24.8
Kennett	2,145	3,026	137	192	26.3	21.7
London Britain	559	686	56	68	23.3	23.7
London Grove	1,844	2,734	104	154	25.2	24.4
Londonderry	595	718	52	62	37.7	26.1
Lower Oxford	1,657	2,007	88	106	25.9	21.5
New Garden	3,027	3,718	186	228	28.2	29.4
New London	660	845	55	71	27.2	22.8
North Coventry	3,242	4,367	230	310	25.3	21.8

Table I (cont'd)

Municipality	Total Population		Population Density		Persons 25–34 Years as % of Persons Over 21	
	1950	1960	1950	1960	1950	1960
Penn	705	1,097	75	116	27.3	23.6
Pennsbury	686	936	67	91	22.4	17.4
Pocopson	475	1,315	57	156	22.1	17.6
Sadsbury	1,502	2,066	231	318	26.5	29.8
Schuylkill	3,835	3,461	376	356	33.0	22.5
South Coventry	863	1,212	108	151	27.8	24.5
Upper Oxford	903	997	51	57	24.0	25.5
Upper Uwchlan	761	909	64	77	25.1	22.8
Uwchlan	761	995	73	94	21.1	23.2
Wallace	771	1,065	63	87	24.2	24.5
Warwick	1,144	1,436	60	75	21.3	21.7
West Bradford	1,530	1,894	81	101	21.1	24.8
West Brandywine	1,122	1,675	85	126	29.1	24.1
West Caln	1,485	2,140	67	96	26.0	25.4
West Fallowfield	1,069	1,425	58	78	23.5	25.4
West Marlborough	786	901	45	52	23.5	23.2
West Nantmeal	806	968	58	69	25.4	27.3
West Nottingham	881	1,137	62	80	24.4	20.6
West Pikeland	683	782	67	76	24.3	18.9
West Sadsbury	802	1,102	74	102	20.9	25.1
West Vincent	1,116	1,431	62	79	23.6	22.1

West Whiteland	1,573	4,412	121	339	32.1	29.2
Westtown	994	1,947	114	223	27.7	20.6
Willistown	2,709	6,492	146	351	23.7	24.0
Delaware County						
Bethel	1,283	1,834	238	340	22.8	20.3
Birmingham	836	1,093	95	126	18.2	18.8
Concord	1,945	3,149	141	228	23.0	23.3
Montgomery County						
Douglas	2,046	3,083	129	195	26.8	23.6
Franconia	2,774	3,910	195	275	25.7	18.9
Limerick	3,290	5,110	147	228	27.6	25.9
Lower Frederick	1,620	2,108	195	254	28.0	23.8
Lower Salford	2,290	3,389	160	237	24.8	25.3
Marlborough	1,432	1,875	114	149	25.4	20.4
Montgomery	1,566	2,700	139	250	25.5	20.8
New Hanover	1,745	3,218	79	146	26.4	27.1
Perkiomen	1,211	1,992	258	426	26.1	28.8
Salford	794	1,068	83	111	24.1	22.7
Towamencin	1,604	3,724	165	385	24.7	30.2
Upper Frederick	891	1,157	87	112	22.6	18.1
Upper Hanover	1,762	2,293	84	109	24.2	16.5
Upper Pottsgrove	1,173	1,987	230	388	30.3	22.0
Upper Providence	4,486	5,607	296	308	24.1	18.8
Upper Salford	1,119	1,273	126	243	23.4	20.6
Worcester	1,939	3,250	121	203	23.4	22.9

Table I (cont'd)

Municipality	Total Population		Population Density		Persons 25–34 Years as % of Persons Over 21	
	1950	1960	1950	1960	1950	1960
Towns						
Bucks County						
Chalfont	828	1,410	591	881	21.9	22.2
Doylestown Boro.	5,262	5,917	3,289	2,573	20.4	15.9
Dublin	400	517	800	862	20.8	20.5
New Britain Boro.	581	1,109	484	924	21.7	28.0
New Hope	1,066	958	888	798	21.8	12.4
Newtown Boro.	2,095	2,323	5,238	5,162	21.6	17.3
Perkasie	4,358	4,650	1,743	1,860	24.7	18.5
Quakertown	5,673	6,305	3,546	3,709	23.9	16.2
Richlandtown	762	741	2,540	2,470	27.3	17.1
Riegelsville	871	953	2,178	2,376	25.5	20.7
Sellersville	2,373	2,497	1,978	1,920	23.3	20.6
Silverdale	384	489	960	1,225	27.7	24.6
Trumbauersville	838	785	2,095	1,962	24.6	19.5
Yardley	1,916	2,271	2,737	3,225	27.3	21.1
Chester County						
Atglen	668	721	835	901	18.6	22.6
Avondale	941	1,016	1,882	2,032	24.9	21.2
Coatesville	13,826	12,971	9,875	7,631	24.2	17.5

Downingtown	4,948	5,598	2,910	2,799	26.3	21.4
Honeybrook Boro.	864	1,023	2,160	2,558	24.5	21.5
Kennett Square	3,699	4,355	3,699	4,355	22.7	19.6
Modena	824	859	2,000	2,148	30.2	28.1
Oxford	3,091	3,376	2,208	2,411	22.2	20.0
Parkesburg	2,611	2,759	2,611	2,759	25.5	19.7
Phoenixville	12,932	13,797	5,388	4,758	26.6	11.0
South Coatesville	1,996	2,032	1,109	1,128	30.5	22.3
Spring City	3,258	3,162	4,073	3,952	22.2	19.4
Valley	3,148	3,101	500	516	28.8	15.1
West Chester	15,168	15,705	8,427	8,725	22.0	17.6
West Goshen	3,542	8,214	293	679	26.1	25.6
West Grove	1,521	1,607	3,042	3,214	21.8	18.0
Montgomery County						
East Greenville	1,945	1,931	3,242	3,218	22.0	16.1
Green Lane	550	582	1,833	1,940	24.4	20.0
Lower Pottsgrove	3,389	3,824	452	512	37.9	22.4
Pennsburg	1,625	1,698	1,806	1,887	20.3	15.9
Pottstown	22,589	26,144	4,610	5,335	24.1	20.7
Red Hill	914	1,086	1,143	1,357	23.5	20.9
Royersford	3,862	3,969	4,291	4,410	21.5	18.6
Schwenksville	563	620	1,408	1,550	22.3	21.4
Souderton	4,521	5,381	3,478	4,139	23.8	21.3
Telford	2,042	2,763	3,403	4,605	21.6	18.4
West Pottsgrove	3,007	3,501	1,074	1,250	30.2	20.9

Table II

Social Rank and Residential Market Value per
Household, 1950 and 1960 for Pennsylvania Sector
of the Philadelphia Metropolitan Area

Municipality	Social Rank Index		Education Percentage		Occupation Percentage		Residential Market Value per Household	
	1950	1960	1950	1960	1950	1960	1950	1960
Core City								
Philadelphia	15.9	17.2	8.7	10.2	26.0	24.4	$ 5,005	$ 5,397
Suburbs								
Bucks County								
Bensalem	16.0	14.5	9.4	8.9	22.9	21.1	4,761	8,835
Bristol Boro.	11.8	14.0	6.7	2.6	19.0	27.3	4,816	5,686
Bristol Twp.	12.4	10.0	8.4	7.7	18.1	14.9	4,263	8,698
Falls	18.1	25.8	13.1	18.4	22.1	28.5	2,976	9,602
Hulmville	20.5	18.7	15.8	12.1	22.8	24.2	3,921	7,025
Ivyland	24.6	39.0	8.9	27.0	37.8	41.0	6,377	9,540
Langhorne	33.2	32.3	22.3	21.3	36.1	35.8	6,077	9,266
Lower Southampton	20.1	24.7	11.9	12.3	26.7	33.8	6,866	12,053
Middletown	20.7	46.0	11.9	29.5	27.7	48.8	4,447	11,584
Morrisville	24.3	18.9	15.6	13.6	29.3	22.8	6,174	9,660
Penndel	14.7	16.3	7.6	9.1	23.0	23.7	5,847	9,731
Tullytown	12.5	30.5	11.0	20.0	16.9	34.7	2,854	8,664
Upper Southampton	40.1	37.7	23.7	22.2	45.9	43.7	6,703	12,954

	17.5	22.7	10.2	14.7	24.4	27.8	1,706	10,067
Warminster	17.5	22.7	10.2	14.7	24.4	27.8	1,706	10,067
Chester County								
Malvern	23.8	26.0	17.0	15.8	26.8	31.7	5,800	7,366
Tredyffrin	36.2	67.5	23.7	47.0	39.5	63.7	7,399	16,288
Delaware County								
Aldan	37.6	32.3	20.9	22.0	45.1	34.9	9,398	11,118
Aston	14.2	20.7	10.4	12.7	18.7	26.7	4,867	8,660
Brookhaven	14.6	21.8	10.1	13.2	19.8	28.1	6,308	11,428
Chester City	8.7	10.6	4.6	6.5	17.7	17.3	3,963	5,839
Chester Twp.	3.0	1.0	3.5	2.5	8.4	6.3	2,023	6,424
Clifton Heights	15.6	16.7	8.4	8.9	23.4	24.7	6,819	9,000
Collingdale	13.3	14.0	6.4	9.1	22.0	24.0	5,723	7,890
Colwyn	10.9	10.3	6.4	6.5	18.1	17.0	6,241	7,263
Darby Boro.	13.7	13.0	7.8	7.7	21.1	19.9	5,457	6,637
Darby Twp.	6.3	17.5	4.9	9.7	12.1	25.0	3,584	8,473
East Lansdowne	20.4	23.5	7.1	13.1	33.0	31.0	6,653	7,966
Eddystone	8.3	5.9	5.3	4.2	15.0	12.3	4,845	10,955
Folcroft	21.4	14.5	6.6	6.9	35.2	23.4	5,500	9,255
Glenolden	21.5	19.1	12.3	11.7	28.6	25.3	6,734	9,218
Haverford	50.4	51.6	29.0	31.3	56.6	56.0	12,608	14,243
Lansdowne	52.9	46.9	33.0	30.9	56.1	48.6	8,537	9,611
Lower Chichester	7.2	7.0	6.5	5.5	11.8	12.6	5,262	7,622
Marcus Hook	6.1	6.2	3.0	2.8	14.1	14.4	2,599	5,368
Marple	43.6	53.0	25.0	31.2	50.2	58.3	10,185	14,848
Media	35.8	36.5	23.5	22.9	38.9	40.8	6,072	8,193
Millbourne	46.7	28.7	26.9	15.1	53.0	34.9	6,811	7,956

Table II (cont'd)

Municipality	Social Rank Index		Education Percentage		Occupation Percentage		Residential Market Value per Household	
	1950	1960	1950	1960	1950	1960	1950	1960
Morton	15.8	25.9	12.7	17.3	18.6	29.9	5,562	9,659
Nether Providence	45.4	57.4	30.9	36.7	46.9	56.7	12,291	16,601
Newtown Twp.	37.2	50.5	24.0	30.3	40.8	55.3	8,319	15,175
Norwood	28.3	23.3	16.7	15.0	34.7	28.3	6,828	8,647
Parkside	13.0	18.2	4.4	11.4	23.8	24.1	7,558	9,388
Prospect Park	25.2	20.9	14.9	13.4	31.6	26.2	7,161	8,791
Radnor	48.8	58.4	29.9	40.9	53.0	55.8	10,801	16,632
Ridley Park	35.0	33.7	20.3	21.8	41.5	37.6	8,453	9,377
Ridley Twp.	21.2	19.6	12.8	12.2	27.5	28.1	6,735	9,317
Rose Valley	86.4	87.8	51.9	59.9	89.2	84.0	13,800	24,311
Rutledge	36.7	24.2	29.5	17.7	33.3	26.7	8,387	8,774
Sharon Hill	25.4	21.2	13.9	14.4	33.1	25.6	7,842	8,792
Springfield	53.9	55.7	31.9	34.0	59.0	59.6	11,871	14,041
Swarthmore	88.5	90.6	63.4	70.8	79.0	73.7	14,680	16,371
Tinicum	5.1	5.5	3.6	5.6	11.8	10.8	3,273	7,380
Trainer	4.3	7.1	2.3	4.5	11.9	14.0	4,385	5,719
Upland	11.5	12.9	7.8	8.2	17.4	19.2	3,242	5,849
Upper Chichester	5.2	8.2	3.5	4.3	11.9	16.1	4,689	8,916
Upper Darby	40.8	36.9	21.6	21.0	49.5	43.7	9,032	10,163
Upper Providence	44.4	52.1	27.8	36.2	48.1	50.9	9,279	14,858
Yeadon	36.5	32.5	18.0	17.6	46.7	41.4	9,381	10,316

Montgomery County								
Abington	44.5	48.4	27.6	29.4	48.5	52.8	12,032	13,577
Ambler	23.6	25.7	12.7	15.2	31.6	32.0	6,858	8,047
Bridgeport	6.2	8.5	4.2	4.0	12.8	16.8	5,670	7,547
Bryn Athyn	70.8	74.7	51.0	57.3	64.3	63.3	9,432	10,917
Cheltenham	53.7	64.0	30.6	37.0	60.2	68.6	12,771	13,383
Collegeville	42.6	38.4	32.7	28.2	39.4	37.6	7,614	8,587
Conshohocken	9.7	9.7	6.3	6.3	16.1	16.1	5,434	6,557
East Norriton	35.4	45.0	21.7	22.3	42.1	55.6	8,621	11,195
Hatboro	35.0	33.5	20.8	19.6	40.9	39.7	8,276	9,547
Hatfield Boro.	14.7	18.2	8.0	9.7	22.5	26.1	8,730	7,978
Hatfield Twp.	18.5	19.0	11.3	10.2	24.8	26.9	4,086	8,602
Horsham	22.8	28.3	13.1	17.9	29.8	33.1	5,179	10,651
Jenkintown	37.6	50.8	17.5	31.5	51.1	54.2	10,115	10,550
Lansdale	21.0	29.2	11.8	14.4	28.2	38.8	8,214	8,858
Lower Gwynedd	37.5	52.0	21.6	34.3	43.2	52.9	8,746	15,004
Lower Merion	59.3	68.8	36.4	44.0	62.7	69.1	17,346	18,824
	47.5	59.0	33.9	31.5	46.1	59.5	10,038	18,615
Lower Providence	12.4	26.0	6.1	12.8	20.8	35.5	6,350	8,793
Narberth	54.5	51.2	35.0	31.9	56.4	54.5	8,248	8,829
Norristown	13.8	14.6	7.6	8.6	21.5	21.5	6,376	6,299
North Wales	22.1	21.6	15.3	15.3	26.0	24.0	6,971	8,115
Plymouth	19.9	17.9	12.2	15.0	26.0	17.3	8,180	12,262
Rockledge	14.6	19.8	5.4	11.8	25.2	26.3	8,343	8,625
Springfield	50.9	57.2	27.9	34.7	58.8	61.1	12,762	14,893
Trappe	32.0	31.2	20.0	20.1	36.8	35.3	7,286	11,092
Upper Dublin	34.0	47.4	19.1	28.5	41.3	51.0	9,043	16,046

Table II (cont'd)

Municipality	Social Rank Index		Education Percentage		Occupation Percentage		Residential Market Value per Household	
	1950	1960	1950	1960	1950	1960	1950	1960
Upper Gwynedd	21.5	35.1	11.5	23.8	29.6	37.5	7,937	12,568
Upper Merion	17.8	41.8	3.6	28.9	32.2	46.9	6,188	12,443
Upper Moreland	20.3	32.7	13.5	23.8	33.5	43.4	6,826	11,474
West Conshohocken	3.4	5.9	2.4	3.2	10.3	13.4	3,920	6,726
Whitemarsh	29.2	52.9	15.7	33.5	37.3	55.4	8,889	13,672
Whitpain	31.0	49.4	17.0	30.8	38.7	52.8	6,171	13,485
Townships								
Bucks County								
Bedminster	28.5	20.9	10.6	10.5	42.1	29.8	1,373	6,410
Bridgeton	10.5	15.4	7.4	9.4	16.6	22.0	3,525	7,357
Buckingham	33.2	48.5	15.9	29.8	43.7	52.5	3,962	10,350
Doylestown Twp.	31.1	38.0	19.8	25.6	35.7	40.1	3,107	12,138
Durham	24.8	24.2	11.0	12.0	35.6	33.3	1,695	5,964
East Rockhill	12.2	14.5	5.5	8.6	21.3	21.3	1,846	7,444
Haycock	26.0	21.7	14.6	15.2	33.3	25.6	1,216	6,769
Hilltown	23.4	22.1	9.2	12.2	35.3	29.7	2,639	10,465
Lower Makefield	56.4	63.6	32.0	41.6	63.1	63.7	10,308	8,097
Milford	19.5	15.6	7.1	7.7	31.4	24.2	1,770	6,386
New Britain Twp.	33.6	33.9	17.3	20.5	42.6	39.5	1,177	10,264
Newtown Twp.	41.9	50.1	30.4	35.9	41.0	48.0	3,710	10,506
Nockamixon	24.3	14.2	10.8	10.6	35.0	18.4	2,209	7,665

Northampton	36.8	37.3	19.8	24.2	45.1	40.7	4,014	12,247
Plumstead	26.8	27.8	11.6	13.0	38.1	38.1	3,039	7,921
Richland	15.4	15.3	7.3	9.7	24.5	21.3	2,870	7,679
Solebury	46.7	49.5	30.4	37.3	48.9	45.4	4,122	13,678
Springfield	16.5	20.4	5.6	14.3	28.2	24.5	2,800	6,153
Tinicum	24.4	28.0	10.4	18.2	35.7	32.4	3,142	9,193
Upper Makefield	41.3	43.5	25.0	34.4	46.4	38.8	3,127	11,883
Warrington	30.6	25.3	19.5	15.6	35.1	31.0	5,905	11,389
Warwick	37.8	30.2	23.6	19.4	42.1	40.4	4,347	12,242
West Rockhill	14.9	17.2	5.9	9.6	25.3	25.6	2,056	7,148
Wrightstown	33.5	39.1	14.6	25.6	45.7	42.0	1,778	9,545
Chester County								
Birmingham	35.4	53.0	20.9	43.9	41.5	43.2	1,446	7,879
Charleston	35.9	43.9	21.5	34.6	41.5	38.5	4,118	8,419
East Bradford	41.7	40.5	26.6	30.0	45.1	39.0	2,838	9,358
East Brandywine	30.9	26.5	23.2	19.2	31.2	28.5	2,247	6,538
East Caln	27.2	26.0	16.3	26.1	33.3	20.0	3,626	7,416
East Coventry	24.8	24.5	15.5	13.6	30.3	31.9	2,523	6,598
East Fallowfield	15.0	19.2	10.1	13.4	20.6	23.5	4,627	7,002
East Goshen	30.9	31.7	21.4	23.2	33.4	32.5	3,262	8,920
East Marlborough	29.3	39.3	21.4	31.2	31.5	35.6	2,315	11,543
East Nantmeal	37.2	37.4	26.5	18.8	37.8	47.2	845	3,336
East Nottingham	23.2	17.3	7.0	7.3	37.8	27.6	1,163	2,715
East Pikeland	22.1	26.8	12.4	17.3	29.5	31.4	4,586	8,685
East Whiteland	22.3	40.3	14.7	28.9	27.1	40.0	3,963	9,192
Elk	24.8	26.9	3.9	15.7	44.0	33.5	958	2,452

Table II (cont'd)

Municipality	Social Rank Index		Education Percentage		Occupation Percentage		Residential Market Value per Household	
	1950	1960	1950	1960	1950	1960	1950	1960
Elverson	26.1	12.3	19.5	13.6	27.6	11.8	4,298	5,585
Franklin	32.1	32.4	17.6	19.3	39.9	38.4	876	3,484
Highland	26.0	29.7	12.1	12.0	36.3	42.6	984	2,754
Honeybrook Twp.	21.0	13.3	8.8	6.6	31.9	21.8	973	3,185
Kennett	30.7	42.8	17.1	27.2	38.1	46.2	1,721	8,825
London Britain	36.9	39.5	19.0	18.2	46.1	51.4	998	5,782
London Grove	20.0	23.4	12.3	15.2	26.1	28.3	2,781	4,743
Londonderry	29.6	23.6	16.1	12.1	37.5	32.3	1,186	3,147
Lower Oxford	32.5	30.1	22.6	21.0	34.6	32.5	1,501	4,307
New Garden	23.4	26.7	10.5	14.4	33.8	33.9	2,174	4,132
New London	30.6	30.3	12.5	19.7	43.4	34.3	1,338	3,467
North Coventry	12.0	15.1	5.6	9.8	20.8	21.0	4,976	8,383
Penn	28.2	25.9	16.3	17.2	34.9	30.1	1,802	4,417
Pennsbury	43.6	44.4	25.7	32.7	49.3	42.3	1,991	7,088
Pocopson	37.6	45.9	27.3	29.9	37.5	48.2	1,758	10,553
Sadsbury	16.0	17.9	9.0	10.7	23.4	24.4	4,797	6,736
Schuylkill	29.8	33.6	21.5	24.2	31.3	34.5	3,632	10,526
South Coventry	19.8	27.5	14.4	18.5	23.2	31.0	3,351	5,072
Upper Oxford	28.3	19.8	13.2	12.7	38.7	25.1	1,352	2,339
Upper Uwchlan	33.1	34.3	21.6	20.4	36.8	46.1	1,253	4,296
Uwchlan	26.9	39.8	14.9	28.6	34.4	39.8	1,887	5,938
Wallace	32.7	22.7	20.8	17.1	37.0	24.8	2,441	4,503

Warwick	19.6	20.7	9.6	12.3	28.7	27.2	1,975	6,610
West Bradford	24.7	30.5	16.2	22.6	30.2	31.2	2,113	5,492
West Brandywine	24.5	30.9	15.0	34.5	30.4	17.8	1,759	5,475
West Caln	14.9	14.1	4.3	6.5	27.1	23.1	2,114	5,543
West Fallowfield	33.6	27.5	18.0	9.9	41.7	41.2	1,645	3,924
West Marlborough	26.8	24.4	15.5	19.4	33.5	25.1	834	3,680
West Nantmeal	22.7	22.9	10.0	15.9	33.3	26.5	2,205	3,816
West Nottingham	25.3	16.9	12.0	6.8	35.2	27.5	1,354	2,734
Chester County								
West Pikeland	38.4	43.2	24.4	31.6	42.3	41.7	2,486	8,364
West Sadsbury	17.7	13.3	0	5.5	35.7	23.1	1,581	4,139
West Vincent	30.7	42.2	19.7	25.2	35.1	47.5	963	5,128
West Whiteland	24.6	36.0	14.6	25.6	30.9	36.9	3,745	8,915
Westtown	48.6	34.5	33.6	21.4	48.2	39.4	5,272	12,214
Willistown	32.7	51.4	19.0	34.9	39.1	51.3	6,222	12,465
Delaware County								
Bethel	16.0	45.4	8.6	29.0	23.8	48.4	4,100	12,370
Birmingham	37.0	33.8	27.6	29.2	36.2	28.9	3,156	15,588
Concord	33.2	27.2	24.4	18.5	33.7	30.6	2,943	13,263
Montgomery County								
Douglas	10.9	14.1	4.7	4.2	19.9	25.9	3,635	7,537
Franconia	19.7	18.1	5.0	7.2	33.8	28.9	4,013	9,654
Limerick	16.2	17.8	8.3	11.1	24.4	23.8	2,739	7,726
Lower Frederick	13.9	19.7	10.0	10.8	18.6	27.3	4,175	7,798
Lower Salford	17.0	20.5	3.3	8.8	31.8	30.9	4,460	7,928

Table II (cont'd)

Municipality	Social Rank Index		Education Percentage		Occupation Percentage		Residential Market Value per Household	
	1950	1960	1950	1960	1950	1960	1950	1960
Marlborough	11.8	14.2	5.8	8.9	20.2	20.5	1,220	5,596
Montgomery	28.8	34.3	13.5	22.3	39.3	37.9	4,643	15,205
New Hanover	12.5	21.2	2.9	13.0	24.9	27.2	1,790	5,995
Perkiomen	18.0	18.7	10.3	11.5	25.1	24.8	4,756	9,144
Salford	20.5	21.2	13.5	10.1	25.5	30.6	1,416	6,027
Towamencin	25.9	39.5	10.4	20.7	38.1	48.4	3,402	9,806
Upper Frederick	20.5	21.8	12.4	13.8	27.7	27.3	2,316	5,683
Upper Hanover	15.2	18.1	6.3	25.4	25.2	10.1	2,517	5,605
	7.4	16.5	3.8	9.5	15.3	23.5	2,826	7,445
Upper Pottsgrove	20.8	14.8	19.5	9.4	18.9	20.9	4,867	7,482
Upper Salford	18.0	15.8	4.7	13.2	36.0	26.3	2,877	6,172
Worcester	37.4	23.8	22.2	21.8	43.1	27.5	4,687	11,520

Towns

Bucks County

Municipality	Social Rank Index		Education Percentage		Occupation Percentage		Residential Market Value per Household	
	1950	1960	1950	1960	1950	1960	1950	1960
Chalfont	26.4	41.2	21.1	23.7	26.2	47.8	6,591	11,484
Doylestown Boro.	31.4	39.2	19.7	24.0	36.0	44.0	7,415	9,420
Dublin	12.8	13.1	5.5	6.1	22.3	22.1	4,377	8,344
New Britain Boro.	38.3	38.0	27.5	23.3	38.3	42.9	6,156	12,184
New Hope	38.0	38.4	26.2	32.2	39.5	33.0	6,203	9,422
Newtown Boro.	29.2	33.0	18.5	21.1	33.9	37.2	6,992	7,528
Perkasie	16.6	16.4	9.6	10.4	23.7	22.3	5,831	8,064

Quakertown	18.1	22.2	7.6	12.9	28.6	29.1	6,164	7,753
Richlandtown Boro.	11.2	5.9	5.6	3.7	19.4	12.9	3,633	8,655
Riegelsville	19.7	14.9	13.5	9.1	24.2	21.5	5,122	8,748
Sellersville	18.1	17.4	13.2	14.1	21.8	19.3	6,511	8,566
Silverdale	16.9	10.1	5.0	5.5	29.6	17.8	5,279	8,208
Trumbauersville	6.0	12.7	1.0	8.2	16.3	18.8	3,936	6,534
Yardley	32.1	35.2	20.4	26.2	36.6	34.8	6,796	8,615
Chester County								
Atglen	21.8	35.9	14.6	27.0	26.3	34.9	4,548	5,600
Avondale	18.7	10.7	11.4	7.3	25.0	16.5	4,431	5,880
Coatesville	16.8	14.1	11.1	9.4	22.2	19.7	5,525	6,151
Downingtown	17.2	19.1	12.2	13.5	21.6	23.1	5,990	7,986
Honeybrook Boro.	27.4	29.0	16.2	16.3	33.7	36.3	4,301	6,038
Kennett Square	25.2	30.3	13.9	19.9	32.8	34.1	6,929	8,825
Modena	3.9	6.5	2.7	1.5	10.9	16.5	3,182	5,060
Oxford	28.8	23.5	18.5	14.3	33.3	29.5	5,541	5,837
Parkesburg	15.4	17.5	11.0	12.2	20.1	22.1	3,590	5,228
Phoenixville	16.1	13.9	11.7	9.8	20.4	18.9	5,960	6,621
South Coatesville	7.5	6.0	5.7	8.9	13.2	15.1	3,026	4,194
Spring City	14.2	17.3	12.9	11.6	15.8	22.4	4,663	5,231
Valley	8.5	6.5	6.6	7.5	13.8	9.3	4,206	6,633
West Chester	30.8	27.1	22.0	21.7	32.5	26.9	6,498	6,781
West Goshen	35.7	26.1	24.7	32.9	37.4	15.1	6,515	11,592
West Grove	24.0	26.6	17.1	19.7	27.0	28.1	5,789	7,341

Table II (cont'd)

Municipality	Social Rank Index		Education Percentage		Occupation Percentage		Residential Market Value per Household	
	1950	1960	1950	1960	1950	1960	1950	1960
Montgomery County								
East Greenville	14.0	18.9	8.8	12.3	20.3	24.2	4,556	5,144
Green Lane	6.9	13.0	3.1	6.0	15.3	21.9	4,382	6,152
Lower Pottsgrove	7.5	19.9	3.4	12.8	16.0	25.3	3,653	7,849
Pennsburg	18.1	21.9	10.2	12.6	25.4	28.8	5,123	7,450
Pottstown	16.9	17.8	9.1	10.2	24.7	24.8	5,588	6,328
Red Hill	13.2	17.3	5.4	11.3	22.9	25.6	5,057	6,629
Royersford	14.3	17.0	9.9	11.8	19.4	21.7	4,931	6,682
Schwenksville	27.5	24.2	15.8	12.5	34.3	32.7	5,026	5,518
Souderton	15.6	17.2	6.5	9.8	25.7	24.3	6,566	8,671
Telford	15.0	15.3	7.7	9.2	23.3	21.8	4,679	7,690
West Pottsgrove	2.6	3.2	1.4	2.6	10.2	9.6	4,119	6,856

1. Standardized score based on education and occupation percentage.

2. Number of inhabitants with a year or more of college as a percent of total population 21 years or older.

3. Number of employed males in managerial, professional, and sales occupations as a percentage of all employed males.

4. 1950 Township data is of limited utility because all agricultural land was included in the value of residential property. In 1960, farm household values were separated out from other agricultural property in Bucks, Delaware and Montgomery, but not in Chester County. Hence 1960 resident market value data for Chester County Townships must be used with caution.

Table III
Market Value of Real Property, 1950 and 1960;
Land-use Composition 1960, for the Pennsylvania Sector
of the Philadelphia Metropolitan Area

Municipality	Market Value of Real Property in $000's		Market Value per Capita		Assessed Value in Res. Use 1960 %	Assessed Value, Ind. & Com. Use 1960 %
	1950	1960	1950	1960		
Core City						
Philadelphia	5,321,953	5,780,062	2,569	2,886	58	42
Suburbs						
Bucks County						
Bensalem	23,402	72,829	2,059	3,102	75	17
Bristol Boro	22,799	35,997	1,794	2,911	58	41
Bristol Twp.	25,455	157,255	2,090	2,652	81	17
Falls	10,327	184,241	2,917	6,335	39	60
Hulmville	1,335	2,626	1,552	2,713	78	19
Ivyland	816	1,297	2,280	3,052	90	8
Langhorne	3,401	5,300	2,154	2,755	86	13
Lower Southampton	9,346	47,789	2,624	3,787	87	10
Middletown	10,964	88,772	2,250	3,295	86	10

Table III (cont'd)

Municipality	Market Value of Real Property in $000's		Market Value per Capita		Assessed Value in Res. Use 1960 %	Assessed Value, Ind. & Com. Use 1960 %
	1950	1960	1950	1960		
Morrisville	16,167	29,029	2,382	3,726	80	19
Penndel	2,717	7,697	2,470	3,567	75	24
Tullytown	1,253	15,457	1,933	6,304	37	63
Upper Southampton	6,889	31,797	3,400	4,004	86	9
Warminster	6,090	45,084	855	2,819	84	11
Chester County						
Malvern	4,213	6,664	2,388	2,927	71	26
Tredyffrin	28,691	89,024	3,661	5,563	77	9
Delaware County						
Aldan	12,360	16,046	3,603	3,711	89	9
Aston	9,580	25,478	1,718	2,405	87	9
Brookhaven	2,324	16,747	2,230	3,172	92	6
Chester City	144,458	178,568	2,187	2,805	51	48
Chester Twp.	2,799	7,586	789	2,106	80	4
Clifton Heights	17,124	24,136	2,268	3,015	80	18
Collingdale	16,801	26,690	1,990	2,599	86	13
	4,596	7,536	2,145	2,452	85	15

Darby Boro.	24,989	30,459	1,900	2,166	83	15
Darby Twp.	4,025	29,113	1,165	2,311	90	6
East Lansdowne	7,652	8,629	2,170	2,677	89	11
Eddystone	29,301	25,967	9,722	8,638	37	62
Folcroft	4,139	18,341	2,168	2,615	91	8
Glenolden	15,221	20,307	2,360	2,801	87	12
Haverford	154,184	225,935	3,880	4,183	94	4
Lansdowne	37,132	47,180	3,051	3,744	84	15
Lower Chichester	10,331	14,612	3,516	3,276	62	36
Marcus Hook	30,270	40,336	7,877	12,226	13	87
Marple	19,145	85,249	4,006	4,323	91	5
Media	16,074	22,815	2,807	3,932	68	30
Millbourne	4,994	6,684	5,487	8,430	41	59
Morton	2,718	6,733	2,010	3,051	87	11
Nether Providence	22,586	51,071	3,659	4,920	93	5
Newtown Twp.	15,776	40,065	4,484	4,322	80	7
Norwood	11,978	17,853	2,283	2,653	92	7
Parkside	4,233	8,833	2,586	3,641	96	3
Prospect Park	16,332	20,402	2,780	3,093	88	11
Radnor	74,399	121,457	5,058	5,598	74	17
Ridley Park	16,057	24,740	3,263	3,350	84	16
Ridley Twp.	53,048	106,812	3,082	2,989	81	17
Rose Valley	2,562	4,485	5,145	7,165	95	.2
Rutledge	2,261	2,800	2,460	2,956	100	0
Sharon Hill	23,595	30,690	4,318	4,308	57	43
Springfield	42,037	114,645	3,851	4,288	85	14
Swarthmore	20,852	27,965	4,322	4,860	90	9

Table III (cont'd)

Municipality	Market Value of Real Property in $000's		Market Value per Capita		Assessed Value in Res. Use 1960 %	Assessed Value, Ind. & Com. Use 1960 %
	1950	1960	1950	1960		
Tinicum	39,190	33,107	7,375	7,567	22	72
Trainer	15,155	15,326	7,574	6,499	23	72
Upland	4,517	7,219	1,107	1,662	95	4
Upper Chichester	11,923	24,942	1,704	2,576	89	9
Upper Darby	289,823	353,287	3,412	3,793	78	21
Upper Providence	12,612	26,089	3,505	4,305	95	.1
Yeadon	33,132	40,674	2,993	3,503	83	16
Montgomery County						
Abington	116,031	269,306	4,000	4,824	81	16
Ambler	12,719	23,683	2,786	3,500	66	33
Bridgeport	14,434	18,794	2,477	3,542	57	42
Bryn Athyn	4,963	5,687	5,436	5,380	49	15
Cheltenham	105,238	191,415	4,605	5,319	78	21
Collegeville	3,901	6,589	2,053	2,923	62	31
Conshohocken	20,818	26,863	1,906	2,619	61	39
East Norriton	9,353	29,721	3,131	3,823	80	15
Hatboro	14,927	28,157	3,118	3,850	72	27
Hatfield Boro.	4,008	5,664	2,468	2,918	76	19

Hatfield Twp.	8,154	23,390	2,630	4,060	61	31
Horsham	11,527	34,699	3,147	3,885	75	11
Jenkintown	21,336	26,583	4,160	5,299	59	41
Lansdale	34,041	51,811	3,486	4,108	62	36
Lower Gwynedd	11,448	24,911	4,626	5,480	73	12
Lower Merion	301,311	434,198	6,181	7,308	76	20
Lower Moreland	10,725	39,430	4,777	6,880	77	14
Lower Providence	13,504	37,289	2,294	3,746	68	23
Narberth	16,979	19,632	3,140	3,892	77	23
Norristown	81,888	104,147	2,148	2,675	61	38
North Wales	7,899	11,043	2,635	3,007	81	17
Plymouth	20,289	60,989	3,964	5,348	63	32
Rockledge	6,659	9,126	2,945	3,528	84	15
Springfield	46,083	95,514	4,041	4,625	88	9
Trappe	2,396	4,495	3,100	3,556	83	9
Upper Dublin	21,094	49,804	3,178	4,890	85	10
Upper Dwynedd	13,658	40,965	6,311	8,788	39	54
Upper Merion	24,852	91,836	3,880	5,372	60	34
Upper Moreland	25,953	82,645	2,904	3,929	80	17
West Conshocken	4,953	6,621	2,000	2,937	62	36
Whitemarsh	28,053	69,182	4,694	5,631	64	26
Whitpain	11,461	34,744	3,742	4,740	76	8

Townships

Bucks County

Bedminster	6,161	11,406	2,716	4,163	42	5

Table III (cont'd)

Municipality	Market Value of Real Property in $000's		Market Value per Capita		Assessed Value in Res. Use 1960 %	Assessed Value, Ind. & Com. Use 1960 %
	1950	1960	1950	1960		
Bridgeton	1,635	2,789	1,732	2,940	76	20
Buckingham	10,174	22,212	3,383	5,528	55	8
Doylestown Twp.	7,358	15,948	3,113	4,202	70	10
Durham	1,389	3,282	2,019	4,465	39	25
East Rockhill	3,141	6,527	1,932	3,280	64	7
Haycock	2,044	4,567	1,886	3,588	53	7
Hilltown	9,116	22,393	2,529	4,035	69	9
Lower Makefield	14,141	48,537	4,404	5,641	87	2
Milford	5,271	10,994	1,840	3,120	56	4
New Britain Twp.	4,077	12,841	3,342	4,156	70	2
Newtown Twp.	5,131	8,373	5,065	5,703	49	8
Nockamixon	2,645	6,582	2,027	3,687	58	5
Northampton	8,483	28,010	3,774	4,664	73	9
Plumstead	7,956	14,404	3,381	4,294	52	10
Richland	6,038	13,064	1,980	3,453	63	12
Solebury	9,478	20,446	4,292	6,879	62	7
Springfield	5,904	10,329	2,213	3,348	53	4
Tinicum	4,765	8,644	3,070	4,951	34	6

Upper Makefield	4,476	11,557	3,174	5,804	58	2
Warrington	7,261	16,276	3,108	3,924	76	9
Warwick	3,600	9,086	3,973	5,020	62	8
West Rockhill	3,893	8,054	1,928	3,242	61	9
Wrightstown	3,758	7,430	4,134	4,285	64	5
Chester County					
Birmingham	1,554	3,080	3,622	6,799	32	8
Charleston	5,432	7,212	6,360	3,735	47	2
East Bradford	4,332	8,414	3,650	4,912	52	3
East Brandywine	2,051	5,260	2,257	3,251	53	5
East Caln	1,830	4,336	4,540	5,720	30	49
East Coventry	3,012	6,679	2,010	3,059	64	2
East Fallowfield	4,684	7,460	2,610	2,718	67	3
East Goshen	4,080	8,745	3,927	5,162	52	3
East Marlborough	7,144	11,546	3,825	4,777	67	7
East Nantmeal	2,182	3,330	3,281	4,562	21	2
East Nottingham	3,169	4,698	1,813	2,044	36	13
East Pikeland	3,760	9,928	2,695	3,524	72	10
East Whiteland	6,604	22,047	3,795	4,342	52	33
Elk	917	1,312	1,984	2,435	28	4
Elverson	648	1,075	1,754	2,278	73	17
Franklin	1,534	2,085	2,303	2,552	28	3
Highland	2,268	3,041	2,508	2,955	19	6
Honeybrook Twp.	2,882	2,940	2,285	1,856	27	2
Kennett	5,844	14,730	2,725	4,868	55	7
London Britain	931	2,094	1,665	3,052	50	1

Table III (cont'd)

Municipality	Market Value of Real Property in $000's		Market Value per Capita		Assessed Value in Res. Use 1960 %	Assessed Value, Ind. & Com. Use 1960 %
	1950	1960	1950	1960		
London Grove	4,308	8,325	2,374	3,045	40	18
Londonderry	1,626	2,250	2,735	3,134	23	1
Lower Oxford	2,452	5,116	1,480	2,549	38	7
New Garden	7,159	10,669	2,365	2,870	34	12
New London	1,507	2,427	2,283	2,872	29	67
North Coventry	6,917	14,477	2,133	2,329	74	6
Penn	1,924	2,765	2,728	2,521	39	10
Pennsbury	3,795	5,963	5,532	6,370	32	3
Pocopson	1,728	4,537	3,636	3,450	62	3
Sadsbury	3,017	5,393	2,008	1,711	77	6
Schuylkill	5,671	15,312	1,479	4,424	67	7
South Coventry	1,869	2,835	2,165	2,339	60	4
Upper Oxford	2,366	3,236	2,620	3,246	20	2
Upper Uwchlan	1,859	3,613	2,442	3,974	32	15
Uwchlan	2,089	3,162	2,744	3,178	49	1
Wallace	2,147	2,868	2,785	2,693	44	9
Warwick	2,482	4,047	2,170	2,818	53	2
West Bradford	3,001	5,998	1,962	3,167	48	3

West Brandywine	2,063	4,171	1,839	2,489	60	0
West Caln	2,565	5,554	1,727	2,595	56	4
West Fallowfield	2,218	3,741	2,075	2,625	38	6
West Marlborough	2,887	5,147	3,674	5,713	17	2
West Nantmeal	2,128	2,382	2,640	2,461	36	10
West Nottingham	1,284	2,278	1,458	2,004	33	11
West Pikeland	2,316	4,625	3,390	5,915	45	7
West Sadsbury	1,379	2,837	1,720	2,574	46	6
West Vincent	3,736	5,092	3,348	3,558	37	1
West Whiteland	4,907	17,685	3,120	4,008	61	22
Westtown	3,838	8,440	3,862	4,335	72	1
Willistown	12,842	30,690	4,740	4,727	72	2
Delaware County						
Bethel	3,244	6,643	2,528	3,622	88	9
Birmingham	2,755	5,589	3,295	5,113	85	8
Concord	4,775	12,059	2,455	3,830	85	3
Montgomery County						
Douglas	4,464	9,794	2,182	3,177	68	11
Franconia	5,795	15,616	2,090	3,993	63	16
Limerick	12,829	24,670	3,900	4,827	43	42
Lower Frederick	2,898	5,915	1,790	2,806	71	11
Lower Salford	6,425	12,735	2,805	3,758	57	13
Marlborough	2,413	4,258	1,685	2,271	59	5
Montgomery	4,681	17,597	2,989	6,517	71	11
New Hanover	3,884	9,534	2,225	2,963	57	0
Perkiomen	2,707	6,899	2,235	3,463	76	7

Table III (cont'd)

Municipality	Market Value of Real Property in $000's		Market Value per Capita		Assessed Value in Res. Use 1960 %	Assessed Value, Ind. & Com. Use 1960 %
	1950	1960	1950	1960		
Salford	1,785	3,391	2,248	3,175	42	5
Towamencin	4,030	14,393	2,512	3,865	68	12
Upper Frederick	2,034	3,251	2,283	2,810	57	6
Upper Hanover	3,464	7,564	1,966	3,299	47	3
Upper Pottsgrove	1,928	5,239	1,644	2,637	80	4
Upper Providence	13,909	28,222	3,100	5,033	39	49
Upper Salford	2,489	4,470	2,224	3,512	52	5
Worcester	6,850	14,225	3,548	4,376	76	4
Towns						
Bucks County						
Chalfont	2,386	5,923	2,882	4,201	77	18
Doylestown Boro.	15,980	27,161	3,037	4,590	68	30
Dublin	861	1,900	2,152	3,676	69	22
New Britain Boro.	1,842	4,412	3,170	3,979	87	9
New Hope	3,696	5,800	3,467	6,055	60	37
Newtown Boro.	5,916	7,742	2,824	3,333	74	26
Perkasie	10,773	15,935	2,472	3,427	77	19

Quakertown	15,063	23,198	2,655	3,679	70	29
Richlandtown	1,342	2,173	1,761	2,932	82	17
Riegelsville	1,716	3,074	1,970	3,225	86	11
Sellersville	6,282	10,100	2,647	4,045	66	31
Silverdale	916	1,388	2,386	2,838	80	14
Trumbauersville	1,274	1,875	1,520	2,388	83	0
Yardley	4,632	7,475	2,417	3,292	79	19
Chester County						
Atglen	1,275	1,648	1,908	2,285	76	18
Avondale	1,884	2,286	2,002	2,250	71	24
Coatesville	35,339	40,827	2,555	3,148	58	41
Downingtown	11,593	25,1100	2,343	4,484	52	46
Honeybrook Boro.	1,865	2,940	2,158	2,873	69	27
Kennett Square	10,882	17,531	2,941	4,025	66	34
Modena	2,243	1,865	2,722	2,171	54	44
Oxford	7,776	9,244	2,515	2,738	70	27
Parkesburg	3,598	5,298	1,378	1,920	81	15
Phoenixville	31,406	41,112	2,534	2,980	64	35
South Coatesville	5,812	6,449	2,912	3,174	35	60
Spring City	6,330	7,298	1,943	2,308	73	25
Valley	15,445	21,588	4,906	6,962	26	68
West Chester	35,182	45,832	2,319	2,918	65	33
West Goshen	10,468	32,275	2,955	2,727	79	11
West Grove	3,304	4,102	2,172	2,552	88	10
Montgomery County						
East Greenville	3,922	4,536	2,017	2,349	73	22

Table III (cont'd)

Municipality	Market Value of Real Property in $000's		Market Value per Capita		Assessed Value in Res. Use 1960 %	Assessed Value, Ind. & Com. Use 1960 %
	1950	1960	1950	1960		
Green Lane	904	1,423	1,644	2,444	79	20
Lower Pottsgrove	14,931	25,323	4,405	6,222	35	57
Pennsburg	3,943	4,940	2,427	2,909	88	8
Pottstown	66,812	90,244	2,958	3,452	54	44
Pottstown	1,924	2,917	2,105	2,686	72	24
Red Hill	9,523	14,401	2,465	3,629	58	40
Royersford	1,266	1,649	2,247	2,660	68	31
Schwenksville	1,849	18,093	2,620	4,521	76	22
Souderton	4,444	7,876	2,195	2,850	77	22
Telford	5,745	12,657	1,910	3,615	56	41

Table IV

Municipal Expenditures, School Revenues, School Attendance, 1960, for the Pennsylvania Sector of the Philadelphia Metropolitan Area

Municipality	Municipal Operating Expenditures per Capita 1959[1]	School Revenue per Pupil 1959-1960[2]	Percent School Revenue from State Aid	Resident Public School Population[3]	Public School Population as a Percent of Total Population	Enrollment Intentions, Parochial as a Percent of Parochial and Public[4]
Core City						
Philadelphia	$ 98.84	$ 423	32.8%	$236,436	11.8%	36.7%
Suburbs						
Bucks County						
Bensalem	14.81	622	32.4	3320	14.2	37.4
Bristol Boro.	32.35	425	37.5	1565	12.7	49.4
Bristol Twp.	18.10	468	34.4	8675	14.6	34.4
Falls	20.39	573	17.3	6419	22.1	30.3
Hulmville	10.21	424	46.9	178	18.4	23.8
Ivyland	10.66	440	49.7	92	21.6	12.8
	11.96	429	41.7	261	13.6	7.8
Lower Southampton	17.52	482	35.0	2399	19.0	30.1
Middletown	14.03	435	42.2	5275	19.6	32.0
Morrisville	30.05	618	29.9	1293	16.7	28.2
Penndel	17.73	466	32.5	321	14.9	48.6

Table IV (cont'd)

Municipality	Municipal Operating Expenditures per Capita 1959[1]	School Revenue per Pupil 1959-1960[2]	Percent School Revenue from State Aid	Resident Public School Population[3]	Public School Population as a Percent of Total Population	Enrollment Intentions, Parochial as a Percent of Parochial and Public[4]
Tullytown	41.84	632	17.1	483	19.7	29.8
Upper Southampton	15.09	445	36.2	1496	18.9	21.1
Warminster	12.43	448	56.5	2486	15.5	28.6
Chester County						
Malvern	24.02	641	43.7	305	10.8	31.7
Tredyffrin	20.94	512	26.3	3254	20.3	16.4
Delaware County						
Aldan	19.80	548	50.6	724	16.8	28.2
Aston	17.20	434	40.6	1723	16.2	33.0
Brookhaven	16.88	434	40.6	802	15.2	38.6
Chester City	33.23	434	39.8	9572	15.0	28.2
Chester Twp.	13.52	325	58.6	886	24.6	9.0
Clifton Heights	20.93	444	22.8	743	9.3	58.2
Collingdale	15.61	405	32.6	1336	13.0	88.7
Colwyn	16.95	396	28.7	316	10.3	48.8
Darby Boro.	18.18	396	36.8	1608	11.4	54.0
Darby Twp.	16.85	508	31.2	1197	9.5	57.2
East Lansdowne	22.03	507	18.4	290	9.0	57.0
Eddystone	41.00	477	10.6	440	14.6	34.2
Folcroft	19.49	398	56.5	701	10.0	49.4

Glenolden	19.73	528	33.3	908	12.5	43.7
Haverford	28.91	516	17.5	6703	12.4	52.2
Lansdowne	20.15	563	23.5	1512	12.0	38.3
Lower Chichester	17.39	432	30.6	652	14.6	35.0
Marcus Hook	52.72	513	7.2	575	17.4	18.4
Marple	17.07	474	24.4	3486	17.7	26.1
Media	39.33	528	24.3	830	14.6	20.9
Millbourne	84.16	718	.0	19	2.4	48.6
Morton	21.17	394	25.5	262	11.9	40.4
Nether Providence	20.28	491	26.8	2272	21.9	22.0
Newtown Twp.	16.41	508	25.4	1557	16.8	30.9
Norwood	20.79	420	37.8	951	14.1	35.7
Parkside	14.98	434	40.6	332	13.6	33.0
Prospect Park	21.39	456	34.6	978	14.8	28.2
Radnor	40.31	674	10.7	2679	12.3	25.2
Ridley Park	20.46	404	28.3	1002	13.6	42.1
Ridley Twp.	19.45	463	29.7	4659	13.0	43.8
Rose Valley	24.94	491	26.8	165	23.7	22.0
Rutledge	20.82	607	25.4	165	17.4	23.1
Sharon Hill	24.20	494	14.6	902	12.7	48.7
Springfield	28.75	504	22.8	4212	15.8	36.9
Swarthmore	27.46	607	25.4	1255	21.8	1.1
Tinicum	45.17	507	34.6	777	17.8	23.4
Trainer	27.98	381	9.2	405	17.2	20.7
Upland		349	57.6	797	18.4	17.5
Upper Chichester	11.00	424	57.7	1936	20.0	18.4
Upper Darby	29.48	540	16.5	9602	10.3	54.4

Table IV (cont'd)

Municipality	Municipal Operating Expenditures per Capita 1959[1]	School Revenue per Pupil 1959-1960[2]	Percent School Revenue from State Aid	Resident Public School Population[3]	Public School Population as a Percent of Total Population	Enrollment Intentions, Parochial as a Percent of Parochial and Public[4]
Upper Providence	13.18	486	35.7	1137	17.9	14.5
Yeadon	27.19	438	21.3	1285	11.1	46.4
Montgomery County						
Abington	25.09	578	20.6	9361	16.8	35.2
Ambler	25.40	477	26.5	934	13.8	36.1
Bridgeport	29.62	541	13.3	537	10.1	72.4
Bryn Athyn	39.29	918	6.1	9	.9	95.5
Cheltenham	30.30	590	17.5	6323	17.6	23.0
Collegeville	9.66	481	30.5	284	12.6	19.1
Conshohocken	25.31	489	17.9	804	7.8	62.8
East Norriton	6.89	506	23.7	1266	16.3	34.1
Hatboro	34.74	432	31.9	1506	20.6	21.5
Hatfield Boro.	15.30	505	39.6	384	19.8	10.5
Hatfield Twp.	7.97	444	36.8	1034	18.0	25.5
Horsham	16.17	562	32.8	1371	15.3	25.2
Jenkintown	45.09	650	8.0	633	12.6	33.0
Lansdale	46.71	460	36.0	1868	14.8	25.4
Lower Gwynedd	17.20	548	15.0	781	17.2	23.4
Lower Merion	45.24	644	6.8	8612	14.5	19.1
Lower Moreland	23.98	581	11.6	1161	20.2	25.5

Lower Providence	6.29	541	28.9	1559	15.9	23.8
Narberth	33.95	560	13.3	604	11.8	35.3
Norristown	28.22	458	29.4	3906	10.0	38.9
North Wales	20.30	373	47.2	734	20.0	18.1
Plymouth	20.22	555	8.2	1550	13.6	37.7
Rockledge	15.87	456	24.6	347	13.4	29.3
Springfield	21.33	524	24.7	3728	18.1	26.8
Trappe	12.42	469	29.4	224	17.7	16.5
Upper Dublin	22.57	566	27.9	2056	20.2	18.5
Upper Gwynedd	15	497	8.3	923	19.8	20.9
Upper Merion	27.72	606	20.0	2768	16.2	34.9
Upper Moreland	20.63	558	24.7	3109	14.8	28.8
West Conshocken	18.18	471	29.1	211	9.4	55.1
Whitemarsh	31.15	584	14.2	1892	15.4	36.4
Whitpain	14.15	561	19.3	1092	14.9	45.9

Townships

Bucks County

Bedminster	4.65	474	42.9	562	20.5	9.9
Bridgeton	7.38	479	45.4	179	18.9	9.9
Buckingham	14.15	562	30.2	729	18.1	9.5
Doylestown Twp.	8.96	537	29.2	655	17.3	9.5
Durham	12.97	485	46.5	177	24.1	9.5
East Rockhill	3.60	439	57.8	459	23.0	5.3
Haycock	8.42	489	54.5	281	22.0	7.4
Hilltown	5.83	464	48.7	1280	23.1	10.4

352   Suburban Differences and Metropolitan Policies

Table IV (cont'd)

Municipality	Municipal Operating Expenditures per Capita 1959[1]	School Revenue per Pupil 1959-1960[2]	Percent School Revenue from State Aid	Resident Public School Population[3]	Public School Population as a Percent of Total Population	Enrollment Intentions, Parochial as a Percent of Parochial and Public[4]
Lower Makefield	14.69	516	31.9	1900	22.1	16.1
Milford	5.59	500	47.3	702	19.9	6.7
New Britain Twp.	7.54	493	28.2	491	15.9	15.1
Newtown Twp.	15.73	564	19.5	284	19.3	18.5
Nockamixon	8.78	467	44.7	350	19.6	26.5
Northampton	14.38	498	30.2	1241	20.7	17.2
Plumstead	5.54	472	28.6	540	16.1	9.6
Richland	5.84	474	52.7	823	21.8	5.2
Solebury	19.33	543	15.4	600	20.1	3.0
Springfield	5.71	480	51.5	621	20.2	4.7
Tinicum	15.31	551	43.8	370	21.2	10.0
Upper Makefield	18.53	488	25.6	412	20.6	9.7
Warrington	10.10	458	37.8	860	20.6	24.6
Warwick	15.14	519	32.4	363	20.0	18.4
West Rockhill	11.17	441	48.7	405	16.3	12.3
Wrightstown	8.74	444	29.7	344	19.7	11.2
Chester County						
Birmingham	5.72	421	31.9	134	29.4	7.8
Charleston	4.45	602	18.6	199	10.3	17.1
East Bradford	6.50	579	24.1	309	18.0	10.8

East Brandywine	2.47	420	46.1	304	18.8	0
East Caln	2.31	497	27.2	138	18.2	2.7
East Coventry	7.54	429	49.7	431	19.8	8.9
East Fallowfield	5.97	440	52.4	655	23.8	2.0
East Goshen	3.56	546	22.2	282	16.6	10.3
East Marlborough	8.07	590	28.4	535	22.1	3.4
East Nantmeal	11.36	523	30.2	130	17.8	1.9
East Nottingham	11.61	388	66.3	541	23.5	.9
East Pikeland	5.87	594	34.3	537	19.1	15.4
East Whiteland	12.50	519	23.0	769	15.1	23.2
Elk	6.43	392	63.9	124	23.0	2.3
Elverson	7.23	476	49.5	96	20.3	8.7
Franklin	8.65	549	53.5	177	21.7	1.4
Highland	16.81	449	51.1	264	25.6	6.2
Honeybrook Twp.	14.33	452	48.8	374	23.4	12.1
Kennett	6.66	485	36.6	600	19.8	10.3
London Britain	7.31	553	54.0	171	24.9	3.9
London Grove	11.32	480	51.7	545	19.8	9.4
Londonderry	12.22	536	52.4	148	20.6	0
Lower Oxford	4.32	389	63.2	392	19.5	3.6
New Garden	13.56	384	49.9	858	23.1	15.6
New London	9.98	568	54.3	179	21.2	4.0
North Coventry	7.32	420	50.7	984	15.7	7.2
Penn	5.59	536	53.3	227	20.8	4.6
Pennsbury	14.02	635	16.9	172	18.4	12.0
Pocopson	10.24	478	34.3	209	15.9	9.2
Sadsbury	7.64	613	46.2	391	12.4	6.9

Table IV (cont'd)

Municipality	Municipal Operating Expenditures per Capita 1959	School Revenue per Pupil 1959-1960[a]	Percent School Revenue from State Aid	Resident Public School Population[a]	Public School Population as a Percent of Total Population	Enrollment Intentions, Parochial as a Percent of Parochial and Public[a]
Schuylkill	8.11	507	26.7	669	19.3	13.1
South Coventry	4.80	458	49.6	239	19.7	8.1
Upper Oxford	13.89	437	58.8	226	22.7	7.2
Upper Uwchlan	13.44	377	44.1	183	20.1	5.7
Uwchlan	10.86	497	37.0	145	14.5	1.6
Wallace	4.99	393	47.5	230	21.6	4.9
Warwick	7.03	435	53.6	302	21.0	3.3
West Bradford	6.77	417	44.0	400	21.1	9.5
West Brandywine	8.04	453	53.0	372	22.2	4.4
West Caln	14.56	470	57.5	466	21.8	2.9
West Fallowfield	16.22	462	51.2	300	21.1	17.2
West Marlborough	16.12	517	35.3	194	21.5	1.4
West Nantmeal	6.74	482	39.3	157	16.2	10.4
West Nottingham	10.43	368	71.2	301	26.5	.6
West Pikeland	9.90	579	34.2	119	15.2	5.2
West Sadsbury	6.23	512	53.3	192	17.4	23.6
West Vincent	13.50	456	39.7	313	21.9	2.1
West Whiteland	5.02	408	30.3	821	18.6	22.7
Westtown	4.16	523	30.8	393	20.2	19.0
Willistown	15.95	501	25.8	1280	19.7	16.2

Delaware County						
Bethel	8.77	358	41.3	367	20.0	14.5
Birmingham	7.22	587	31.2	181	16.6	12.0
Concord	5.76	476	38.1	517	16.4	9.4
Montgomery County						
Douglas	8.84	393	55.6	703	22.8	1.3
Franconia	9.04	417	43.2	787	20.2	13.4
Limerick	5.22	512	31.2	991	19.4	11.8
Lower Frederick	4.65	479	45.8	436	20.7	3.6
Lower Salford	9.17	420	42.4	725	21.4	14.7
Marlborough	8.53	447	56.5	392	20.9	2.7
Montgomery	15.83	503	25.2	666	24.7	27.0
New Hanover	5.39	276	51.2	603	18.7	8.7
Perkiomen	9.19	479	45.8	414	20.8	8.8
Salford	13.84	507	45.1	232	21.7	4.0
Towamencin	4.75	395	28.9	661	17.7	28.3
Upper Frederick	3.97	474	53.4	208	17.9	8.7
Upper Hanover	8.13	423	52.4	482	21.0	13.0
Upper Pottsgrove	4.70	421	49.4	470	23.7	5.9
Upper Providence	6.35	444	30.0	856	12.7	15.9
Upper Salford	10.13	414	52.2	277	21.8	6.4
Worcester	7.47	472	23.7	550	17.9	22.0
Towns						
Chalfont						
Bucks County	7.95	485	41.6	281	19.9	14.8

Table IV (cont'd)

Municipality	Municipal Operating Expenditures per Capita 1959¹	School Revenue per Pupil 1959-1960²	Percent School Revenue from State Aid	Resident Public School Population³	Public School Population as a Percent of Total Population	Enrollment Intentions, Parochial as a Percent of Parochial and Public⁴
Doylestown Boro.	41.45	554	35.3	953	16.1	19.1
Dublin	11.15	425	48.8	96	18.6	4.5
New Britain Boro.	9.05	561	32.4	180	16.3	10.9
New Hope	29.80	543	15.4	139	14.5	3.0
Newtown Boro.	20.05	446	28.5	389	16.7	20.4
Perkasie		400	48.6	1002	21.5	4.1
Quakertown	34.19	417	40.8	1147	18.2	10.7
Richlandtown	12.77	577	49.2	130	17.5	11.3
Riegelsville	13.25	399	52.4	190	19.9	4.0
Sellersville	39.33	493	35.2	447	17.9	13.6
Silverdale	9.40	411	52.8	114	23.3	2.8
Trumbauersville	9.08	480	50.0	166	21.2	4.2
Yardley	19.64	516	51.5	454	20.0	25.4
Chester County						
Atglen	12.62	442	51.3	155	21.5	1.5
Avondale	17.38	481	62.4	221	22.1	7.5
Coatesville	47.26	500	35.9	2316	17.8	12.2
Downingtown	32.94	497	31.6	973	17.4	48.8
Honeybrook Boro.	10.94	470	47.6	239	23.4	.4
Kennett Square	31.98	519	28.5	732	16.8	21.4

Modena	8.61	440	55.5	203	23.6	2.0
Oxford	22.16	451	49.2	572	16.9	5.0
Parkesburg	13.69	430	61.5	606	22.0	3.8
Phoenixville	27.63	478	28.1	1837	13.3	37.7
South Coatesville	28.06	438	48.8	542	26.7	9.1
Spring City	25.59	453	43.1	564	17.8	12.6
Valley	19.70	561	32.3	853	27.5	3.8
West Chester	31.69	500	31.7	2312	14.7	21.4
West Goshen	6.10	494	34.7	1431	12.1	20.7
West Grove	14.67	534	58.3	266	16.6	15.9
Montgomery County						
East Greenville	10.22	381	58.7	366	19.0	8.1
Green Lane	15.63	391	51.0	100	17.8	6.4
Lower Pottsgrove	10.35	484	26.7	840	22.0	6.9
Pennsburg	16.06	369	43.6	289	17.0	8.6
Pottstown	26.69	420	37.0	4787	18.3	16.1
Red Hill	10.34	460	49.8	216	19.9	4.5
Royersford	33.57	464	36.4	675	17.0	19.2
Schwenksville	11.24	479	45.8	118	19.0	3.4
Souderton	29.41	345	47.5	1102	20.5	8.8
Telford	19.36	435	39.4	484	17.5	7.1
West Pottsgrove	14.61	448	40.9	600	9.6	25.7

APPENDIX B

Municipalities with Over 10 per cent of 1950
Population in Institutions, for the Pennsylvania
Sector of the Philadelphia Metropolitan Area

	Institutional Population	Total Population	Per Cent Institutional
Bucks County			
Langhorne Manor	94	781	20
Chester County			
Caln	2113	5779	37
Easttown	423	3811	11
East Vincent	2787	4576	61
Newlin	326	957	34
Thornbury	44	297	15
Delaware County			
Chester Heights	65	474	14
Edgemont	249	1048	24
Middletown	1472	6038	24
Thornbury	700	2101	33
Montgomery County			
Skippack	1994	3843	52
West Norriton	1101	4879	22

APPENDIX C
List of Variables: Simple Correlation Matrix

Levels: 1959–60

1. Total Population
2. Population Density
3. Percentage Single-family Dwelling Units of Total Dwelling Units (1950)
4. Social Rank
5. Young Adult Ratio
6. Real Property, Total Market Value
7. Real Property, per Capita Market Value
8. Real Property, Percentage in Residential Use

9. Real Property, Percentage in Commercial and Industrial Use
10. Residential Property Value per Household
11. Area
12. Percent of Area in Industrial and Commercial Use
13. Percent of Area in Residential Use under ¼ Acre Lots
14. Total Municipal Revenue
15. Total Municipal Operating Expenditures
16. Per Capita Municipal Revenues
17. Per Capita Municipal Operating Expenditures, Total
18. Per Capita Municipal Operating Expenditures, General Government
19. Per Capita Municipal Operating Expenditures, Libraries
20. Per Capita Municipal Operating Expenditures, Parks and Recreation
21. Per Capita Municipal Operating Expenditures, Police
22. Per Capita Municipal Operating Expenditures, Fire
23. Per Capita Municipal Operating Expenditures, Planning
24. Per Capita Municipal Operating Expenditures, Sewage Disposal
25. Per Capita Municipal Operating Expenditures, Refuse Disposal
26. Per Capita Municipal Operating Expenditures, Streetlights
28. Percentage Highway Intergovernmental Revenue of Total Highway Expenditures
29. Percentage Public School Enrollment of Total Population
30. Percentage Parochial School Enrollment of Parochial plus Public
31. Resident Pupil Enrollment, Public
32. Total School Revenue
33. Total School Revenue, per Pupil
34. Total School Revenue, per Capita
35. Local School Revenue, Total
36. Local School Revenue, Per Pupil
37. School Revenue, Percentage from Intergovernmental Sources
38. Municipal plus School Revenue, per Capita
39. Municipal plus School Revue, Intergovernmental
40. Percentage School Revenue of Total School plus Municipal Revenue
41. Tax rate on Residential Property
42. Residential Tax Rate-Household Value Ratio

43. Total Taxes as Millage on Total Market Value
44. Percentage Property Tax or Total Tax
45. Percentage Republican Presidential Vote (1960)
46. Percentage Republican Gubernatorial Vote, (1958)
47. Percentage Republican Local Vote, (1959)
48. Voter Participation, Presidential Election (1960)
49. Voter Participation, Gubernatorial Election (1958)
50. Voter Participation, Local Election (1959)

Change: 1950–1960*

51. Population
52. Young Adult Ratio
53. Real Property, Total Market Value
54. Real Property, Total Market Value per Capita
55. Residential Market Value per Household
56. Total Municipal Revenue
57. Total Municipal Revenue, per Capita
58. Municipal Expenditures, Protection of Persons and Property
59. Municipal Expenditures, General Government
60. Municipal Expenditures, Recreation
61. Municipal Expenditures, Health
62. Municipal Expenditures, Highways
63. Total School Revenue
64. Total School Revenue, per Capita
65. Percentage School Revenue from Intergovernmental Sources
66. Total School plus Municipal Revenues per Capita
67. Percentage School Expenditures of School plus Municipal Expenditures
68. Percentage School and Municipal Revenues from Intergovernmental Sources
69. Percentage Republican Presidential Vote (1952–1960)
70. Percentage Republican Gubernatorial Vote (1950–1958)
71. Voter Participation, Presidential Election (1952–1960)
72. Voter Participation, Gubernatorial Election (1950–1958)

*Data sources dictated using some different variables for change than were used for levels.

Index

Andrews, Richard D., 33n

Banfield, Edward C., 300, 301, 312n
Bell, Wendell, 25-6, 30, 33n, 229
Beshers, James M., 34n, 210n
Blair, George S., 242
Bogue, Donald J., 23, 27
Bollens, John C., 90n, 162n
Bucks County, 35, 42, 186, 188-192, 197-8, 271-4, 276-87.
Burkhead, Jesse, 257

Carroll, J. Douglass, 33n
Chester County, 35, 42, 55
Cleveland, 148, 153, 257
Coke, James G., 33n, 208n
Cooperative arrangements:
  opinions about, 233
  legal provisions for, 240
  number of, 241-6
  partners in, 246-8
  for schools, 248-252
  for sewage disposal, 253-5
  for police radio, 255
  prospects for, 256-63
Coughlin, R. E., 33n

Delaware County, 35, 186, 188-197, 199, 213, 251-2

Draut, George, 266n
Duncan, Beverly, 33n, 34n, 210n
Duncan, Otis, 33n, 34n, 210n

Ecology, urban, 21-25, 296
Education:
  and social rank, 48-53
  responsibility for, 139
Efficiency, 76
Ethnicity, 26

Familism, 26
Fire protection, 26, 37, 120, 129
Firey, Walter, 33n, 208n
Force, Maryanne T., 33n, 229
Form, William H., 33n, 208n
Functional transfers:
  as a cooperative arrangement, 268-9
  and County Health Department movement, 270-271
  Bucks County health campaign, 271-4
  Montgomery County health campaign, 274-7

Goodman, Leo A., 34n
Greer, Scott, 33n, 34n
Grodzins, Morton, 300, 301, 312n

361

Gulick, Luther, 32n

Hawley, Amos A., 23, 34n
Health, 37, 131, 244, 270-287
Hellmuth, William F. Jr., 162n
Herbert, I. D., 33n

Jefferson, Thomas, 19
Jennings, Helen H., 238n

Kaufman, Walter, 34n
Kish, Leslie, 23

Land use:
  in study area, 66-7
  controls, 75, 187
  commercial and industrial, 94,
    98-9, 102-3, 107-113, 159-
    60, 189-93
  residential, 94, 103, 113-117,
    193-5
  and density, 97
  and functional expenditures,
    119-124, 128-130
  and tax effffort, 172-7
  and tax diversification, 182-3,
    185
  Delaware County policy, 195-6,
    198-205
  Montgomery county policy,
    196-7
  Bucks County policy, 197-8
Leadership:
  and suburban residents, 226-
    230
  opinions, 230-35
Libraries, 120, 129, 131, 244
Lindzey, Gardner, 238n

McKenzie, Roderick, 18, 22, 298
MacRae, Duncan, 34n
Madison, James, 19
Margolis, Julius, 186n

Mathews, Donald 228
Menzel, Herbert, 34n
Metropolitan areas:
  governing and governments,
    17, 29, 230, 297-9, 305-312
  political science analysis of,
    19-20
  sociological analysis of, 24-26
  economics analysis of, 26-27
  specialization and, 28-9, 35-6,
    69-73, 296-7
Montgomery County, 35, 55, 188-
  194, 196-7, 231, 269, 274-287
Municipal policies:
  Measures of, 79-80
Municipality, definition of, 37

New York, 44, 309

Occupation, 52-3

Party, 67-69, 280-3
Pennsylvania, 36, 144, 164, 270
Philadelphia, 35, 58-9, 139, 164,
  177-8, 269, 309
Planning, 37, 120, 131, 244
Police protection, 27, 37, 120,
  244, 254-5, 302
Population, as variable:
  size of municipality, 43-4,
    97-8, 120, 150-1, 244-5
  age distribution, 44-9, 97-9,
    112-3, 115-6, 294
  density, 93, 97-9, 107, 126,
    294
  percentage in public schools,
    151-2, 155, 158
Property value, 62-65, 94-5, 98-9,
  151-2, 158-9

Race, 59-62, 202, 220-6
Recreation, 120, 129, 131
Referendums:

in Bucks County, 272-4, 277-87
in Montgomery County, 275-87
Religion, 56-59, 158, 160-1
Riew, John, 257
Robinson, W. S., 31

Sacks, Seymour, 162n
St. Louis, 76, 148, 153, 287
San Francisco, 309
Schmandt, Henry J., 288n
Schnore, Leo F., 33n, 208n
Schools districts:
  policy measures, 81-3
  types of, 140-1
  state subsidies to, 145-6
  taxing powers of, 165-6
Scranton, Governor, 252
Sewage disposal:
  financial measure of, 80
  cooperative arrangements for,
    244-5, 253-5
  as a metropolitan problem, 304
  (see also waste disposal)
Shevky, Eshref, 25-6, 30, 33n
Social area analysis, 25-6, 30-2
Social rank:
  measure of, 48-52
  in study area, 52-3
  and municipal expenditures,
    94, 98-102, 115, 120, 131
  and school revenues, 151-2,
    155, 158-161
  and tax policy, 174-5, 178-9
  and land use, 189-203
  and housing choice, 203-5
  and opinions, 216-226
  and intermunicipal coopera-
    tion, 243-56, 260-1
Special districts, 306

Steinbicker, Paul G., 288n
Stevens, B. H., 33n
Stone, Gregory P., 33n
Street lights, 37, 120, 131
Suburbs, definition of, 38

Taxes:
  Pennsylvania Act 481, 164
  real property use, 166-70
  rates, 170-2
  resources, 258-61
Tax burden, 163, 179-81
Tax effort:
  measures of, 83-4
  and school policy, 158, 163
  in Suburbs, 172-7
  and school-municipal competi-
    tion, 177-9
Tiebout, Charles M., 138n, 238n
Towns, definition of, 39
Townships, definition of, 39
Transportation, 18, 26, 28, 37,
  243, 303, 311

Urban, definition of, 38

Washington, D.C., 309
Waste disposal, 28, 37, 129, 131,
  242, 244, 302
Water supply, 28, 80, 243, 304
Wealth:
  definition of, 55-6
  and municipal expenditures,
    96-7, 134-5
  and social rank, 115
Wendel, George P., 288n
Wilhelm, Sidney M., 208n
Wood, Robert, 20

Zoning, 24, 187-203, 222, 295